Eastern Arabic

The Richard Slade Harrell Arabic Series
General Editors: Richard S. Harrell† and Wallace M. Erwin

Eastern Arabic

Frank A. Rice
Majed F. Sa'id

Georgetown University Press, Washington, D.C. 20057

Library of Congress Cataloging in Publication Data

Rice, Frank A.
Eastern Arabic.

Originally published under title: Jerusalem Arabic.
1. Arabic language–Dialects–Syria. I. Sa'id, Majed F., 1927–1966 joint author. II. Title.
PJ6813.R5 1979 492'.7'83421 79-22782
ISBN 0-87840-021-4

Jerusalem Arabic appeared first in mimeographed form in 1953 under the auspices of the Georgetown University Institute of Languages and Linguistics. It was later revised and published as *Eastern Arabic* (1960).
This volume is a reprint of the 1960 edition.

Printed in the United States of America

ISBN 0-87840-021-4

Preface

This book is an introduction to the Arabic spoken by Palestinian, Syrian, and Lebanese Arabs.

The Arabic presented and described is the language of everyday conversation, and may be regarded as typical of the speech of the educated city dweller.

This book was first issued in 1953 in mimeographed form under the title « Jerusalem Arabic ». As a result of experience gained through extensive classroom use in the Institute of Languages and Linguistics of Georgetown University and in the Foreign Service Institute of the Department of State, the need for certain changes became apparent, and we have incorporated most of these in the book as it now appears.

The Arabic material represents primarily the speech of the second author, but also incorporates usages suggested by other native speakers of Arabic who have used the book in their classes. We are particularly grateful in this regard to Mr. Moukhtar Ani, Mr. Sirri Kaltakji, and Mr. Bourhan Chatti for their constructive criticism and comment.

Our greatest linguistic debt is to Dr. Charles A. Ferguson of Harvard University for his constant help and encouragement while the book was being written.

Finally, we wish to express our gratitude to Dr. Leon E. Dostert, Director of the Institute of Languages and Linguistics of Georgetown University, without whose whole-hearted cooperation the text could never have been produced.

Beirut, January 1958

Frank A. Rice

Majed F. Sa'id

Contents

Units

Grammar

For ease of reference, the *Grammar* sections are separately listed below. The first number refers to the Unit, the second number to the section.

Units

Units

Units

Units

Introduction

I. The Arabic language

The Arabic language is spoken today throughout an area that lies partly in southwest Asia and partly in Africa. The eastern boundary of this region is the Zagros Mountains, dividing Iraq from Iran ; the western boundary is the Atlantic ocean off the coast of Morocco. In the north the boundary is the Taurus range, dividing Turkey from the Fertile Crescent (Syria and Iraq), and in the south the Indian Ocean, the African jungle, and the Sahara Desert. Outside this region, the spread of Islam carried the language east into Central Asia and south into Africa ; and there are substantial groups of emigrants among whom Arabic is spoken in North and South America, especially in the United States, Brazil, and Argentina.

Though Arabic is the everyday speech of most of the inhabitants of the region described above, it would be a mistake to assume that they all speak the same kind of Arabic. Arabic has shared the fate of all languages that are spread out over a large area for a long period of time. It has developed a wide variety of dialects, some of them being so different from one another that they might almost be considered separate languages. The mutual intelligibility of different dialects depends, as in the case of other languages, upon the dialects themselves and upon the educational background and cultural bias of the speakers.

Apart from spoken Arabic, with its many dialects, there is the literary language, frequently called Classical Arabic. This is basically the language of the Koran and early literature.

Classical Arabic is the accepted standard for all written material, but is not used as a language of everyday conversation. As a spoken language it is confined to certain socially prescribed occasions, such as on the radio and in public addresses.

It is necessary to understand that no Arab grows up speaking Classical Arabic. Each Arab grows up speaking a modern dialect and learns the Classical — if he learns it at all — in school. Because of the general low level of education in the Arab world, a command of the Classical language is the possession of a limited number of people.

Classical Arabic enjoys the respect and veneration of all Arabs, in contrast to their attitude toward the modern dialects, which are usually regarded as corruptions of the literary language. Nonetheless, in an effort to salvage some prestige for modern Arabic, each Arab likes to believe that his own native dialect, with all its alleged corruptness, is closer to the Classical (and hence « purer ») than any dialect spoken elsewhere.

2. The transcription

Arabic is normally written and printed in a writing system called the Arabic alphabet. However, in this book all the Arabic material is presented in a special writing system called a **transcription**. *The transcription is better suited to represent the sounds and forms of modern spoken Arabic than is the traditional Arabic orthography, and is also a more efficient instrument for purposes of linguistic analysis and stating of grammatical facts.*

3. Arrangement of the book

This book is divided into thirty **Units**. *Practically all the Units have the following organization :*

Pattern Sentences

Structure Sentences

Grammar

Drills

(1) The **Pattern Sentences** *represent conversational material. Preceding most sentences are « breakdowns » giving the new words that occur in the sentence. The breakdowns are usually literal translations of the Arabic. The sentences are frequently a conversational English equivalent of the Arabic, not a word-for-word translation.*

(2) The **Structure Sentences** *do not represent conversational material. They are intended to introduce selected grammatical features in an inductive way. They form the basis both for formal grammatical statements and for grammatical drill.*

(3) The **Grammar** *is a formal statement of selected grammatical features of the language. This material is primarily for individual study.*

(4) The **Drills** *provide practice in using the vocabulary that has been introduced, and practice in making grammatical changes. The drill material is to be used after the Pattern Sentences and Structure Sentences have been thoroughly learned.*

Following the Pattern Sentences of some Units is a sub-section entitled « Additional Vocabulary » containing words closely related to the subject matter of the Unit. These words are of secondary importance, and are only occasionally used to illustrate grammatical points.

4. Suggestions for the use of the book

This book is designed to teach the spoken language, not the written, and is based on the principle that the only way to learn to understand a spoken language is to hear it spoken, and the only way to learn to speak it is to practice speaking.

The book is intended for use with an instructor who is a native speaker of Arabic ; he need not be a professional teacher. Less sa-

tisfactory, but still useful, are recordings made by a native speaker. It is preferable to choose as a native speaker someone whose speech corresponds pretty closely to the kind of Arabic presented in this book ; this will avoid the necessity for making numerous changes. But in all cases, if there is a disagreement between this book and the usage of the instructor, imitate the instructor.

The native speaker has three main functions : to serve as a model for imitation, to serve as the final judge of what is acceptable usage, and to serve as a conversational partner. The second point requires some comment. The usage of the instructor is always right. There is no standard spoken Arabic, and whatever he says is correct. This does not mean, however, that the instructor can necessarily explain the grammar of his language. This is because spoken Arabic is never taught in the schools ; it is studied only by a small number of specialists. For all grammatical explanation, rely on the statements in this book.

In what follows we offer a number of recommendations for procedures that have been found useful in teaching and learning a spoken language. We also offer words of caution against certain practices that have been found to interfere with successful language learning.

To the student

(1) *Mimic and imitate to the extent necessary to sound like a native speaker of Arabic.*

(2) *Review constantly, so that the speech habits of Arabic will become almost as familiar and well-established as the speech habits of English.*

(3) *Avoid the use of English in the classroom, except when necessary.*

(4) *Take advantage of every opportunity to use the language. This is the only way to build up real fluency and control.*

To the instructor

(1) Always speak at a normal conversational speed. Slow, deliberate, or syllabified speech is not frequent outside the classroom. If the student is taught to speak in a slow, hesitating way, he will not sound natural.

(2) Correct mistakes in pronunciation and grammar. If a student makes a mistake, stop him and have him repeat the word or sentence after you. Help him to form proper habits, and try to keep him from continuing wrong ones.

(3) Avoid the use of English in the classroom except for occasional brief explanations or instructions when necessary.

Teaching techniques

The following recommendations are intended primarily for the instructor. but the student should be familiar with them as well.

(1) Repetition. With new material the instructor says the sentence and the students repeat after him in chorus. Later, the instructor calls on each student to repeat individually.

(2) Timing. The words and sentences must be memorized for the most effective results. If the student repeats haltingly, or must refer to the book frequently, or makes numerous errors, he is not ready to proceed to a new lesson.

(3) Dialogue. When possible, practice the sentences as a dialogue. Sometimes the instructor takes one part and a student the other; sometimes students take both parts.

(4) Variation. The instructor should try to make variations in the sentences in the book to the extent possible at any given time.

(5) Review. About every five lessons, have a careful review of all preceding material.

5. Abbreviations and symbols

adj. *adjective*

f. feminine

lit. literally

m. masculine

pl. plural

/ Alternating with: w-/wi-means « w- alternating with wi -».

— The hyphen is used to indicate incompleteness: ma- means « the prefixed element ma- » ; -aat means « the suffixed element -aat ».

• Indicates a nonexistent or impossible form.

( ) Parentheses in the English text enclose explanatory material ; in the Arabic text material that is sometimes omitted.

The meaning of other special symbols is explained as they occur.

THE SOUNDS OF ARABIC

The variety of Arabic presented and described in this book has thirty-three *consonants* and five *vowels*, indicated by letter symbols. Both consonants and vowels occur short (indicated by a single symbol : r, a) and long (indicated by doubling the symbol : rr, aa). The distinction between short and long is very important, as it may distinguish otherwise identical words : mara *woman* beside marra *time*, safar *travel* beside saafar *he traveled*.

The consonants

Plain : b d f g ġ h ḥ j k l m n p q r s š t v w x y z ' 9

Velarized : ḍ ṣ ṭ ẓ *b l m r*

Most of the *plain* consonants have near equivalents in English or some of the more familiar languages of Europe.

b like the *b* in *bit* : baab *door*

d like the *d* in *dip* : dawa *medicine* .

f like the *f* in *fit* : fihim *he understood*.

g like the *g* in *get* : siigåara *cigarette*.

ġ like the *r* in Parisian French *mari* : ġaali *expensive.*

h like the *h* in *hot* : haada *this.*

j like the *s* in *measure* : jaab *he brought.*

k like the *k* in *kit* : katab *he wrote.*

l like the *l* in German *Lied* ; a « clear » *l*, not like the *l* in *deal* : laazim *necessary.*

m like the *m* in *met* : maktab *office.*

n like the *n* in *net* : naas *people.*

p like the *p* in *pet* : proova *fitting* ; this sound only occurs in borrowed words.

r like the *r* in Spanish *pero* when short : mara *woman*, like the *rr* in Spanish *perro* when long : marra *time.*

s like the *s* in *sit* : saadis *sixth.*

š like the *sh* in *ship* : šaaf *he saw.*

t like the *t* in *tip* : taamin *eighth.*

v like the *v* in *vat* : proova *fitting* ; this sound only occurs in borrowed words.

w like the *w* in *wet* : walad *child.*

x like the *ch* in German *ach* : xaamis *fifth.*

y like the *y* in *yet* : yoom *day.*

z like the *z* in *zinc* : zeet *oil.*

The following plain consonants have no equivalents as distinctive sounds in English or the more familiar languages of Europe.

' a quick catch in the throat before, between, or after vowels : 'aal *he said*, sa'al *he asked*, suu' *market* ; this sound is called « glottal stop.»

q a *k*-sound made at a point somewhat behind the *c* in English *cool* : qisim *part*, maqaale *article*, mulḥaq *attaché.*

ḥ a hissing *h*-sound made by lowering the back of the

tongue and tightening the muscles of the throat: ḥabb *he liked*, waaḥad *one*, raaḥ *he went*.

9 a somewhat strained vowel-like sound, produced like ḥ above, but with the vocal cords vibrating: 9arabi *Arabic*, na9am *yes*, baa9 *he sold*.

The *velarized* consonants (also called « emphatic » or « heavy » consonants) are basically like their plain counterparts, but have an accompanying secondary articulation: the back of the tongue is raised toward the soft palate, and the whole tongue is slightly retracted. This secondary articulation modifies the contact surfaces of the tongue in producing the consonants and alters the shape of the mouth cavity in producing the neighboring vowels. The effect on the vowels is the most striking acoustically (see below).

There are two series of velarized consonants: a major series and a minor series. The major series consists of ḍ ṣ ṭ ẓ. The following list shows words with plain consonants paired with otherwise identical words containing velarized consonants.

plain		velarized	
taab	*he repented*	ṭaab	*he recovered*
faadi	*savior*	faaḍi	*free*
saaḥib	*pulling*	ṣaaḥib	*friend*
zaahir	*shining*	ẓaahir	*appearing*
batt	*he decided*	baṭṭ	*ducks*

The minor series consists of *b l m r*, marked by italics to distinguish them from their plain counterparts. Following are some contrasts.

plain		velarized	
baabha	*her door*	*baaba*	*papa*
walla	*he appointed*	wa*ll*a	*by God*
mayy	*May (girl's name)*	*m*ayy	*water*
jaari	*flowing*	jaa*r*i	*my neighbor*

The velarized consonants of the major series play a very important role in the grammar, and are systematically marked in the transcription. The velarized consonants of the minor series have almost no grammatical importance. In the transcription we mark these only in words that contain no occurrences of ḍ, ṣ, ṭ, or ẓ, and then only in words that virtually all speakers agree on pronouncing with velarization. Since there is no general agreement about the presence or absence of velarized *r*, we have chosen not to mark it at all in the main text.

The vowels

long : ii uu ee oo aa

short : i u e o a

Most of the vowels have close equivalents in English, but the following descriptions are only approximate.

ii like the *ea* in *beat* : jiib *bring* !

uu like the *oo* in *boot* : šuuf *look* !

ee like the *ai* in *bait* : beet *house.*

oo like the *oa* in *boat* : yoom *day.*

aa like the *a* in *had* : kaan *he was.*

In the neighborhood of velarized consonants these vowels are considerably modified by the secondary articulation of tongue-raising and retraction : *ii* and *ee* are centered, *uu* and *oo* are retracted, *aa* resembles the *a* in *father*, with retraction.

ṭiin	*clay*	ṣuuf	*wool*
baṣiiṭ	*simple*	ṣooṭ	*voice*
ṣeef	*summer*	ṭoor	*ox*
ṭeer	*bird*	maṭaar	*airport*
ṭuul	*length*	ẓaabiṭ	*officer*

The short vowels show more variation than the long ones.

i at the end of a word, like Arabic *ii* above but shorter ; in the middle of a word, like the *i* in *bit* : nisi *he forgot.*

u at the end of a word, like Arabic *uu* above but shorter ; in the middle of a word, like the *u* in *put* : kuntu *you (pl) were.*

e like Arabic *ee* above but shorter : sitte *six.* In the middle of a word, this sound only occurs in borrowings.

o like Arabic *oo* above, but shorter : jibto *I brought it.* In the middle of a word, this sound only occurs in borrowings.

a at the end of a word, between the *a* in *father* and the *u* in *but* ; in the middle of a word, varying between the *e* in *get* and the *a* in *cat*, depending on the neighboring consonant : bada *he began*, ḥaka *he spoke.*

In the neighborhood of velarized consonants, *i* and *u* resemble the *e* in *wanted* (as pronounced by most speakers of English), with the lips rounded for *u* ; *a* is between the *a* in *father* and the *u* in *but*, with retraction ; *o* is lowered ; *e* does not occur.

ṭifil	*child*	ṭalab	*request*
ṣirt	*I became*	mwaẓẓaf	*official*
ṭuru'	*roads*	ḥaṭṭo	*he put it*
ẓulum	*injustice*	ḥafaẓo	*he kept it*

PRONUNCIATION PRACTICES

These *Practices* are not intended to cover all the relevant features of Arabic pronunciation, but rather concentrate on certain features that seem especially troublesome for speakers of English.

All the Practices work on the principle of contrast: items having different meanings and differing from one another only in certain features of pronunciation are grouped together in pairs, so that the differences will stand out when the items are pronounced in sequence.

1. Contrasts between t and ṭ

taab	*he repented*	ṭaab	*he recovered*
tiin	*figs*	ṭiin	*clay*
tuub	*repent!*	ṭuub	*bricks*
tall	*hill*	ṭall	*he looked*
batt	*he decided*	baṭṭ	*ducks*

2. Contrasts between d and ḍ

faadi	*savior*	faaḍi	*free*
bifiid	*it is useful*	bifiiḍ	*it overflows*
marduud	*rejected*	marḍuuḍ	*bruised*
dall	*he directed*	ḍall	*he stayed*
xadd	*cheek*	xaḍḍ	*he shook*
hadam	*he destroyed*	haḍam	*he digested*

3. Contrasts between s and ṣ

saaḥib	*pulling*	**ṣaaḥib**	*friend*
'asaas	*foundation*	**'aṣaaṣ**	*punishment*
nasiib	*relative*	**naṣiib**	*lot*
mansuub	*attributed to*	**manṣuub**	*suspended*
seef	*sword*	**ṣeef**	*summer*
sabb	*he cursed*	**ṣabb**	*he poured*

4. Contrasts between z and ẓ

zaahir	*shining*	**ẓaahir**	*appearing*
ḥaafiz	*stimulus*	**ḥaafiẓ**	*keeper*
9aziime	*banquet*	**9aẓiime**	*great (f)*
ḥazz	*he severed*	**ḥaẓẓ**	*luck*

5. Contrasts between h and ḥ

habb	*it blew*	**ḥabb**	*he liked*
hadd	*he demolished*	**ḥadd**	*boundary*
hayy	*here is*	**ḥayy**	*alive*
šabah	*resemblance*	**šabaḥ**	*phantom*

6. Contrasts between ' and 9

'aal	*he said*	**9aal**	*fine*
'aam	*he got up*	**9aam**	*year*
'iid	*hand*	**9iid**	*feast day*
'add	*as much as*	**9add**	*he counted*

'ala	*he fried*	9ala	*on*
xala'	*he created*	xala9	*he overthrew*
raafa'	*he accompanied*	raafa9	*he defended*
sa'al	*he asked*	sa9al	*he coughed*
su'aal	*question*	su9aal	*coughing*

7. Contrasts between final vowel, and final ' and 9

wara	*behind*	wara'	*paper*
mara	*woman*	mara'	*he passed*
fii	*in*	fii'	*wake up!*
lamma	*when*	lamma9	*he polished*
wadda	*he led*	wadda9	*he saw (someone) off*
bala	*without*	bala9	*he swallowed*

8. Contrasts between ḥ, k, and x

ḥaal	*condition*	xaal	*uncle*
ḥaṭṭ	*he put*	xaṭṭ	*line*
ḥeeṭ	*wall*	xeeṭ	*thread*
taḥt	*under*	taxt	*bed*
kaaf	*the Arabic letter kāf*	xaaf	*he was afraid*
kaan	*he was*	xaan	*he betrayed*
šakar	*he thanked*	šaxar	*he snored*
kabbar	*he enlarged*	xabbar	*he informed*

9. Contrasts between x and ġ

xaab	*he failed*	ġaab	*he was absent*
xaali	*my uncle*	ġaali	*expensive*
maxluuṭ	*mixed*	maġluuṭ	*wrong*
xeer	*goodness*	ġeer	*other*
xeeme	*tent*	ġeeme	*cloud*

10. Contrasts between short a and long aa

katab	*he wrote*	kaatab	*he corresponded*
jamal	*camel*	jaamal	*he was courteous*
nafas	*breath*	naafas	*he competed*
dawa	*medecine*	daawa	*he treated medically*
ḥaka	*he spoke*	ḥaaka	*he talked to*
9alam	*flag*	9aalam	*world*
xabar	*news*	xaabar	*he communicated with*
ġazal	*he spun*	ġaazal	*he flirted*
baṭaḥ	*he threw down*	baaṭaḥ	*he wrestled*
9araḍ	*he offered*	9aaraḍ	*he opposed*
ṣaḍar	*it came out*	ṣaaḍar	*he confiscated*
ḥafaẓ	*he kept*	ḥaafaẓ	*he maintained*

11. Contrasts between single and double consonants

sakan	*he dwelled*	sakkan	*he housed*
bana	*he built*	banna	*mason.*

jama9	*he added*	**jamma9**	*he collected*
šaraf	*honor*	**šarraf**	*he honored*
najaḥ	*he succeeded*	**najjaḥ**	*he made succeed*
ḥaram	*sanctuary*	**ḥarram**	*he forbad*
9alam	*flag*	**9allam**	*he taught*
xabar	*news*	**xabbar**	*he informed*
ġalab	*he overcame*	**ġallab**	*he bothered*
ṣaḍar	*it came out*	**ṣaḍḍar**	*he exported*
'aṭa9	*he cut*	**'aṭṭa9**	*he cut into pieces*

UNIT I • Greetings and Courtesy Expressions.

PATTERN SENTENCES

Hello.	marḥaba.
Hello (in reply).	marḥabteen.
how	kiif
your (m) condition	ḥaalak
How are you ?	kiif ḥaalak ?
well (m)	mabṣuuṭ
praise be to God	lḥamdilla
Well, praise God.	mabṣuuṭ, *i*lḥamdilla.
you (m)	'inte
How are *you* ?	kiif ḥaalak 'inte ?
I	'ana
too, also	kamaan
I'm well too, praise God.	'ana mabṣuuṭ kamaan, *i*lḥamdilla.
please (to a man, speaker offering something)	tfaḍḍal
rest (to a man)	striiḥ
Please sit down.	tfaḍḍal striiḥ.
Thank you.	šukran.
the family	l9eele
How's the family ?	kiif *i*l9eele ?
well (pl)	mabṣuuṭiin
Well, praise God.	mabṣuuṭiin, *i*lḥamdilla.
the children	liwlaad

How are the children ?	kiif liwlaad ?
let us thank God	nuškur 'a*ll*a
Well, thank God.	nuškur 'a*ll*a, mabṣuuṭiin.
By your (m) leave.	9an 'iznak.
Certainly (in reply).	tfaḍḍal.
you (m) permit me	btismaḥli
a little bit	šwayy
Will you excuse me?	btismaḥli šwayy ?
Certainly (in reply).	tfaḍḍal.
Good-by (to a man, said by person leaving).	xaaṭrak.
Good-by (said by person remaining).	ma9 *i*ssalaame.
May God keep you (m) (in reply to ma9 *i*ssalaame).	'a*ll*a ysallmak.

STRUCTURE SENTENCES

1. Feminine forms

your (f) condition	ḥaalik
How are you ?	kiif ḥaalik ?
By your (f) leave.	9an 'iznik.
Good-by (to a woman).	xaaṭrik.
May God keep you (f).	'a*ll*a ysallmik.
you (f)	'inti
How are *you* ?	kiif ḥaalik 'inti ?
please (to a woman; speaker offering something)	tfaḍḍali

rest (to a woman)	striiḥi
Please sit down.	tfaḍḍali striiḥi.
you (f) permit me	btismaḥiili
Will you excuse me?	btismaḥiili šwayy?
well (f)	mabṣuuṭa
I'm well, praise God.	'ana mabṣuuṭa, lḥamdilla.

2. Plural forms

your (pl) condition	ḥaalkum
How are you?	kiif ḥaalkum?
By your (pl) leave.	9an 'i*zi*nkum.
Good-by (to a group).	xaaṭirkum.
May God keep you (pl).	'a*ll*a ysallimkum.
you (pl)	'intu
How are *you*?	kiif ḥaalkum 'intu?
please (to a group, speaker offering something)	tfaḍḍalu
rest (to a group)	striiḥu
Please sit down.	tfaḍḍalu striiḥu.
you (pl) permit me	btismaḥuuli
Will you excuse me?	btismaḥuuli šwayy?
we	niḥna
We're well, praise God.	niḥna mabṣuuṭiin, *i*lḥamdilla.

3. Independent pronouns

I (m, f)	'ana
we	niḥna
you (m)	'inte

you (f)	'inti
you (pl)	'intu
he	huwwe
she	hiyye
they	humme
He's well.	huwwe mabṣuuṭ.
She's well.	hiyye mabṣuuṭa.
They're well.	humme mabṣuuṭiin.

GRAMMAR

1. General

Unless otherwise indicated, the term «Arabic» in the grammatical comments refers to the variety of Arabic presented and described in this book.

2. Word Stress

Every Arabic word of more than one syllable has one prominent syllable that stands out above the others when the word is pronounced in isolation. We call this prominence *stress*, and in the following examples will indicate its position by an accent mark (ʹ) over the vowel of the prominent syllable.

For the great majority of words the place of the stress is automatically determined by definite rules. If the word contains a «long» syllable (defined as a syllable that contains either a long vowel or a short vowel followed by two or more consonants), the stress falls on the long syllable that stands nearest the end of the word: ḥáalak *your condition*; mabṣúuṭ *well*; mabṣuuṭíin, *well* (*pl*); tfáḍḍal *please*; šúkran *thanks*. Otherwise the stress falls on the first syllable: 'ána *I*.

Since the position of the stress is almost completely automatic, we shall mark it in this text only for words that do not conform to the rules stated above.

3. Vowel prominence

In addition to word stress, Arabic also has another system of prominence that works independently of the stress. We call this *vowel prominence.* Like the stress, it too is automatic.

A long vowel has more sonority than a short vowel: compare the *aa* in kamaan with the *a* in 'ana; the *ii* in kiif with the *i* in 'inte; the *uu* in mabṣuuṭ with the *u* in šukran.

A short vowel immediately followed by a double consonant is more tense than a short vowel elsewhere: compare the first *a* in tfaḍḍal with the first *a* in marḥaba; also ysallimkum with kamaan. This tenseness is preserved even when the double consonant is not followed immediately by a vowel: compare the first *a* in ysallmak *may he keep you* with the first *a* in salma *Selma* (a girl's name).

As a result of the three features of word stress, sonority, and tenseness, the acoustic impression of Arabic is quite different from that of English.

4. Sentences without verbs

Arabic sentences of the following type do not have any element corresponding to English *is, am, are.*

kiif ḥaalak? *How is your condition?*

'ana mabṣuuṭ. *I am well.*

niḥna mabṣuuṭiin. *We are well.*

5. Independent pronouns

Arabic has the following set of independent pronouns.

'ana	*I (m, f)*	'intu	*you (pl)*
niḥna	*we*	huwwe	*he*
'inte	*you (m)*	hiyye	*she*
'inti	*you (f)*	humme	*they*

There is no pronoun corresponding to English *it.*

The independent pronouns are not used so much in Arabic

as are the corresponding forms in English. They are used mainly as subjects of sentences without verbs, to prevent possible ambiguities, and to add emphasis.

DRILLS

1. Give appropriate replies to the following sentences.

marḥaba.
kiif ḥaalak ?
tfaḍḍal striiḥ.
9an 'iznak.
btismaḥli šwayy ?
xaaṭrak.
ma9 *i*ssalaame.
kiif *i*l9eele ?
kiif liwlaad ?
kiif ḥaalik ?
kiif ḥaalkum ?

2. The following sentences are said to a man. How would you say them to a woman ? To a group ?

kiif ḥaalak ?
tfaḍḍal striiḥ.
9an 'iznak.
btismaḥli šwayy ?
xaaṭrak.
'a*ll*a ysallmak.

UNIT 2 • Directions. Numbers 1-10.

PATTERN SENTENCES

Good morning.	ṣabaaḥ *i*lxeer.
Good morning (in reply).	ṣabaaḥ *i*lxeer. *or* ṣabaaḥ *i*nnuur.
please (to a man, speaker requesting something)	min faḍlak
where	feen *or* ween
the American Embassy	ssafaara l'ameerk(aan)iyye
Please, where is the American Embassy ?	min faḍlak, feen *i*ssafaara l'ameerkaaniyye ?
to	9ala, 9a-
right	yamiin
To your (m) right.	9ala yamiinak.
the American Consulate	l'unṣliyye l'ameerkaaniyye
Please, where is the American Consulate ?	min faḍlak, ween *i*l'unṣliyye l'ameerkaaniyye?
left	šmaal
To your (m) left.	9ala šmaalak.
Where is the post office ?	feen *i*lboosṭa ?
walk (to a man)	'imši
straight ahead	duġri
later on	ba9deen
ask (to a man)	'is'al
Go straight ahead, then ask.	'imši duġri, ba9deen 'is'al.
Where is the market ?	ween *i*ssuu' ?
go (to a man)	ruuḥ

Go straight ahead.	ruuḥ duġri.
Where is the toilet?	feen beet *il*m*a*yy?
Here.	hoon.
Over there.	hunaak.
you (m) know	bti9raf
house	beet
Do you know where Yusif Haddad's house is?	bti9raf ween beet yuusif ḥaddaad?
sorry (m)	mit'assif
not	maa
I know	ba9raf
Sorry, I don't know.	mit'assif, maa ba9raf.
direct me (to a man)	dillni
hotel	'uteel
Please direct me to the Hotel Plaza.	min faḍlak, dillni '9a(la) 'uteel plaaza.
with me	ma9i
Please come along with me.	tfaḍḍal ma9i.
you (m) understood	fhimt
Did you understand?	fhimt?
yes	na9am
I (m, f) understood	fhimt
Yes, I understood.	na9am, fhimt.
no	la'
No, I didn't understand.	la', maa fhimt.

Additional expressions:

Good evening.	masa lxeer.
Good evening (in reply).	masa lxeer. *or* masa nnuur.

Welcome!	'ahlan wasahlan. *or* 'ahla wsahla.
Welcome (to a man, in reply)!	'ahla wsahla fiik.
Thank you.	šukran.
You're welcome (in reply).	9afwan.
The peace upon you.	'assalaamu 9alaykum.
And upon you the peace (in reply).	wa9alaykumu ssalaam.
Good night.	leele sa9iide.
Good night (in reply).	sa9iide mbaarake.
One	waaḥad (m), waḥde (f)
Two	tneen (m), tinteen (f)
Three	tlaate
Four	'arba9a
Five	xamse
Six	sitte
Seven	sab9a
Eight	tamaanye
Nine	tis9a
Ten	9ašra
Zero	sifir

STRUCTURE SENTENCES

I. Feminine forms

please (to a woman, speaker requesting something)	min faḍlik

Please, where is Yusif Haddad's house?	min faḍlik, ween beet yuusif ḥaddaad?
To your (f) right.	9ala yamiinik.
To your (f) left.	9ala šmaalik.
walk (to a woman)	'imši
ask (to a woman)	'is'ali
Go straight ahead, then ask.	'imši duġri, ba9deen 'is'ali.
go (to a woman)	ruuḥi
Go straight ahead.	ruuḥi duġri.
you (f) know	bti9rafi
Do you know where the American Embassy is?	bti9rafi ween *i*ssafaara l'ameerkaaniyye?
sorry (f)	mit'assfe
Sorry, I don't know.	mit'assfe, maa ba9raf.
direct me (to a woman)	dilliini
Please direct me to the market.	min faḍlik, dilliini 9assuu'.
Did you (f) understand?	fhimti?
Please come along with me.	tfaḍḍali ma9i.
Welcome(to a woman, in reply).	'ahla wsahla fiiki.

2. Plural forms

please (to a group, speaker requesting something)	min faḍ*i*lkum
Please, where is the Hotel Plaza?	min faḍ*i*lkum, ween 'uteel plaaza?
To your (pl) right.	9ala yamiinkum.
To your (pl) left.	9ala šmaalkum.

walk (to a group)	'imšu
ask (to a group)	'is'alu
Go straight ahead, then ask.	'imšu duġri, ba9deen 'is'alu.
go (to a group)	ruuḥu
Go straight ahead.	ruuḥu duġri.
you (pl) know	bti9rafu
Do you know where the American Consulate is?	bti9rafu ween *i*l'unṣliyye l'ameerkaaniyye?
sorry (pl)	mit'assfiin
we know	bni9raf
Sorry, we don't know.	mit'assfiin, maa bni9raf.
direct me (to a group)	dilluuni
Please direct me to the post office.	min faḍ*i*lkum, dilluuni 9alboosṭa.
direct us (to a group)	dilluuna
Please direct us to the market.	min faḍ*i*lkum, dilluuna 9assuu'.
Did you (pl) understand?	fhimtu?
Yes, we understood.	na9am, fhimna.
with us	ma9na
Please come along with us.	tfaḍḍalu ma9na.
Welcome (to a group, in reply).	'ahla wsahla fiikum.

GRAMMAR

1. The transition vowel

The transition vowel, indicated in the transcription by an italic *i* or *u*, is a weak vowel glide that serves to interrupt a sequence of consonants, both within words and across word boundaries. Within a word we find both *i* and *u*; across word boundaries only *i*.

The presence or absence of the transition vowel is almost completely predictable in terms of the consonant clusters involved.

(1) Within a word, a cluster of three consonants generally has a transition vowel between the first and second consonant: 9an 'iz*i*nkum *by your leave*, min faḍ*i*lkum, *please.* Such a cluster generally does not have a transition vowel if the second consonant is t, or if the first consonant is n, and never has one if the first two consonants of the cluster are identical: striiḥ *rest!*, 'unṣliyye *consulate*, dillni *direct me!*

(2) When two words coming together produce a cluster of three or more consonants, a transition vowel occurs at the point of word division if at least two of the consonants belong to the second word: ma9 *i*ssalaame *good-by*, feen *i*ssafaara? *where is the embassy?*

The transition vowel differs from the other vowels in four significant ways: it is never stressed; it is never tense, even before a double consonant; its occurrence and position are almost entirely automatic; it does not count as a vowel in determining the position of the main word stress. For example, 'iz*i*nkum *by your leave* is stressed on the *first* syllable, as though the word were 'iznkum.

Beginning with Unit 3 we shall not mark the transition vowel at word boundaries, where its presence is predictable.

2. Pronoun endings — I

In addition to the independent pronouns, Arabic has a set of pronoun forms that occur as suffixes. These are here called *pronoun endings.* Six of them have occured so far.

-i	*my, me, I*	wlaadi	*my children*
-na	*our, us, we*	wlaadna	*our children*
-ak	*your, you (m)*	wlaadak	*your (m) children*
-ik	*your, you (f)*	wlaadik	*your (f) children*

-kum	*your, you (pl)*	wlaadkum	*your (pl) children*
-ni	*me*	dillni	*direct me!*

The form -ni occurs only with verbs, where -i does not occur.

The translation of a pronoun ending depends upon the structure of English. For example -na is translated as «our» in wlaadna *our children*, but as «us» in dillna *direct us.*

DRILLS

1. Give appropriate replies to the following sentences.

ṣabaaḥ *i*lxeer.

masa lxeer.

leele sa9iide.

'assalaamu 9alaykum.

'ahla wsahla.

šukran.

fhimt?

2. The following sentences are said to a man. How would you say them to a woman? To a group?

min faḍlak.

9ala yamiinak.

9ala šmaalak.

'ahla wsahla fiik.

'imši duġri, ba9deen 'is'al.

ruuḥ duġri.

min faḍlak, dillni 9assuu'.

tfaḍḍal ma9i.

bti9raf ween beet yuusif?

fhimt?

3. Give appropriate replies to the following questions.

feen *i*ssafaara l'ameerkaaniyye?

ween *i*l'unṣliyye l'ameerkaaniyye?

ween *i*ssuu'?

feen beet *il*mayy ?

feen *il*boosṭa ?

feen beet yuusif ḥaddaad ?

ween 'uteel plaaza ?

UNIT 3 • Arrival. Numbers 11-20.

PATTERN SENTENCES

your presence (a term of address)	ḥaḍ*i*rtak
from	min, mni-
Where are you from?	ḥaḍ*i*rtak min feen ?
America	'ameerka
I'm from America.	'ana min 'ameerka.
how much, how long	'addeeš
it became for you	ṣarlak
How long have you been here?	'addeeš ṣarlak hoon ?
it became for me	ṣarli
day	yoom
two days	yoomeen
three days	tlat tiyyaam
I've been here two days.	ṣarli hoon yoomeen.
you (m) came	'ijiit
How did you come?	kiif 'ijiit ?
I came	'ijiit
in	fii, fi-
the boat	lbaaboor
the airplane	ṭṭayyaara
I came by plane.	'ijiit fiṭṭayyaara.
she was	kaanat
your trip	saf*i*rtak
if God wills	nšaa*ll*a

good (f)	mniiḥa
How was your trip? Good?	kiif kaanat saf*i*rtak? nšaa*ll*a mniiḥa?
It was good, praise God.	mniiḥa, lḥamdu lillaah.
staying (m)	naazil
Where are you staying?	feen naazil?
I'm staying at the Hotel Plaza.	'ana naazil fii 'uteel plaaza.
this (m)	haada
place	maḥall
good (m)	mniiḥ
Oh, that's a good place.	'oo, haada maḥall mniiḥ.
thing, something	šii
fine (invariable adj.)	9aal
That's fine.	šii 9aal.
there is, there are	fii
restaurant	maṭ9am
Where's there a good restaurant?	ween fii maṭ9am mniiḥ?
the Salam Restaurant	maṭ9am ssalaam
not	miš
not bad	miš baṭṭaal
The Salam Restaurant isn't bad.	maṭ9am ssalaam, miš baṭṭaal.
inexpensive (m)	rxiiṣ
It's also inexpensive.	kamaan rxiiṣ.
other than it	ġeero
Is there any other?	fii ġeero?
Italian (m)	tilyaani
next to	jamb *or* janb
There's an Italian restaurant next to the hotel.	fii maṭ9am tilyaani jamb l'uteel.

but	bass
expensive (m)	ġaali
But it's a little expensive.	bass, ġaali šwayy.
Eleven	ḥda9š
Twelve	ṭna9š
Thirteen	tlat ṭa9š
Fourteen	'arba9 ṭa9š
Fifteen	xams ṭa9š
Sixteen	sitt ṭa9š
Seventeen	saba9 ṭa9š
Eighteen	taman ṭa9š
Nineteen	tisi9 ṭa9š
Twenty	9išriin

STRUCTURE SENTENCES

1. Feminine forms

(said to a woman)

your presence	ḥaḍ*i*rtik
Where are you from?	ḥaḍ*i*rtik min feen?
it became for you	ṣarlik
How long have you been here?	'addeeš ṣarlik hoon?
your trip	saf*i*rtik
How was your trip?	kiif kaanat saf*i*rtik?
you (f) came	'ijiiti
How did you come?	kiif 'ijiiti?
staying (f)	naazle

Where are you staying?	feen naazle?

2. Plural forms

(said to a group)

your presences	ḥaḍraatkum
Where are you from?	ḥaḍraatkum min feen?
it became for you	ṣarlkum
How long have you been here?	'addeeš ṣarlkum hoon?
your trip	safritkum
How was your trip?	kiif kaanat safritkum?
you (pl) came	'ijiitu
How did you come?	kiif 'ijiitu?
staying (pl)	naazliin
Where are you staying?	feen naazliin?

3. Plural forms

(said by or for a group)

Damascus	ššaam
We're from Damascus.	niḥna mniššaam.
it became for us	ṣarlna
week	'usbuu9 *or* jum9a
two weeks	'usbuu9een *or* jum*i*9teen
three weeks	tlat 'asabii9 *or* tlat juma9
We've been here two weeks.	ṣarlna hoon 'usbuu9een.
we came	'ijiina
the car	ssayyaara
We came by car.	'ijiina fissayyaara.

We're staying at the Hotel Plaza.	niḥna naazliin fii 'uteel plaaza.

4. Masculine forms
(said about a man)

his presence	ḥaḍ*i*rto
Where's he from?	ḥaḍ*i*rto min feen?
Lebanon	lubnaan
He's from Lebanon.	huwwe min lubnaan.
it became for him	ṣarlo
How long has he been here?	'addeeš ṣarlo hoon?
month	šahir
two months	šahreen
three months	tlat tušhur
He's been here two months.	ṣarlo hoon šahreen.
his trip	saf*i*rto
How was his trip?	kiif kaanat saf*i*rto?
he came	'aja
How did he come?	kiif 'aja?
He came by plane.	'aja fiṭṭayyaara.

5. Feminine forms
(said about a woman)

her presence	ḥaḍritha
Where's she from?	ḥaḍritha min feen?
She's from America.	hiyye min 'ameerka.
it became for her	ṣarlha

How long has she been here?	'addeeš ṣarlha hoon?
She's been here three days.	ṣarlha hoon tlat tiyyaam.
her trip	safritha
How was her trip?	kiif kaanat safritha?
she came	'ajat
How did she come?	kiif 'ajat?
She came by boat.	'ajat filbaaboor.

6. Plural forms
(said about a group)

their presences	ḥaḍraathum
Where are they from?	ḥaḍraathum min feen?
Syria	suuriyya
They're from Syria.	humme min suuriyya.
it became for them	ṣarlhum
How long have they been here?	'addeeš ṣarlhum hoon?
They've been here three months.	ṣarlhum hoon tlat tušhur.
their trip	safrithum
How was their trip?	kiif kaanat safrithum?
they came	'aju
or	willa
Did they come by plane or by ship?	'aju fiṭṭayyaara, willa filbaaboor?
They came by plane.	'aju fiṭṭayyaara.

GRAMMAR

1. Intonation

The accentual features of the sentence in Arabic have never been fully described, and only the chief types of intonation can be indicated here.

There appear to be four main sentence-final intonations :

(1) *Statement.* The voice begins on a mid pitch, rises slightly on the last stressed syllable, and drops to a low pitch at the end.

'ana min 'ameerka. *I'm from America.*

haada maḥall mniiḥ. *That's a good place.*

'ijiit fiṭṭayyaara. *I came by plane.*

(2) *Yes-or-No Question.* The intonation is like that for the statement, but with a distinct rise on the last stressed syllable and no drop at the end.

btismaḥli šwayy ? *Will you excuse me ?*

'ijiit fiṭṭayyaara ? *Did you come by plane?*

fhimt ? *Did you understand?*

(3) *Specific Question* (a question containing a special interrogative word). The voice is high on the stressed syllable of the interrogative word, and falls quickly to mid pitch for the rest of the sentence.

kiif ḥaalak ? *How are you?*

'addeeš ṣarlak hoon ?. *How long have you been here ?*

ḥaḍirtak min feen ? *Where are you from?*

(4) *Alternative Question* (a question containing a word for « or »). The voice is above mid pitch on the word for « or » and falls to below mid pitch for the rest of the sentence.

'ijiit fiṭṭayyara, willa filbaaboor ? *Did you come by plane or by boat ?*

There are also two non-final intonations.

(1) *Continuing.* The voice rises and dips slightly, with an optional pause.

min faḍlak, dillni 9assuu'. *Please direct me to the market.*

maṭ9am ssalaam, miš baṭṭaal. *The Salam Restaurant isn't bad.*

(2) *Suspensive.* The voice is level, with no rise or fall.

'oo, haada maḥall mniiḥ. *Oh, that's a good place.*

An accurate control of intonation is just as important for intelligibility as is an accurate control of the vowels and consonants. Most speakers of a second language fail to master the intonation system, and this failure is one of the principal features of what is called a «foreign accent».

2. Pronoun endings — II

In Unit 2 we listed six of the pronoun endings. The remaining three are given below.

-o	*his, him, he*	wlaado	*his children*
-ha	*her, she*	wlaadha	*her children*
-hum	*their, them, they*	wlaadhum	*their children*

3. Negation

The word maa *not* is used with verbs (and a few other verb-like words).

maa fhimt. *I didn't understand.*

maa ba9raf. *I don't know.*

maa fii maṭ9am hoon. *There isn't any restaurant here.*

The word miš *not* is used only with adjectives and adverbs.

huwwe miš mabṣuuṭ. *He's not well.*

huwwe miš hoon. *He's not here.*

Both these words frequently have a louder stress than the words that they negate.

4. The word nšaa*ll*a

The word nšaa*ll*a (lit. *if God wills*) indicates that the speaker hopes that something has turned out favorably, or will turn out favorably. When used in a question, the sentence frequently has the intonation of the specific question, with the voice high on the word nšaa*ll*a.

DRILLS

1. Give appropriate replies to the following sentences.

ḥaḍ*i*rtak min feen ?	fii ġeero ?
'addeeš ṣarlak hoon ?	fii maṭ9am fil'uteel ?
kiif 'ijiit ?	fii maṭ9am tilyaani hoon ?
kiif kaanat saf*i*rtak ?	feen 'uteel plaaza ?
feen naazil ?	feen beet l*m*ayy ?
ween fii maṭ9am mniiḥ ?	'ijiit fiṭṭayyaara ?
kiif maṭ9am ssalaam ?	'ijiit filbaaboor ?
feen maṭ9am ssalaam ?	'ijiit fissayyaara ?

2. The following sentences are said to a man. How would you say them to a woman? To a group ?

min feen ḥaḍ*i*rtak ?	kiif kaanat saf*i*rtak ?
'addeeš ṣarlak hoon ?	feen naazil ?
kiif 'ijiit ?	

3. The following sentences are said about a man. How would you say them about a woman ? About a group ?

min feen ḥaḍirto ?

min feen huwwe ?

'addeeš ṣarlo hoon ?

kiif 'aja ?

feen naazil ?

4. In each of the following sentences replace the word yoomeen by a different time expression.

ṣarlo hoon yoomeen.

ṣarlha yoomeen fii 'uteel plaaza.

ṣarlna fiššaam yoomeen.

UNIT 4 • Getting around. Numbers 20 - 100 by tens.

PATTERN SENTENCES

take me (to a man)	xudni
the town	lbalad
Please take me to the town.	min faḍlak, xudni 9albalad.
With pleasure.	tikram. *or* 9ala 9eeni. *or* 9ala raasi.
ready, present (m)	ḥaaḍir.
I'm ready.	ḥaaḍir.
going (m)	raayiḥ
Where are you going?	ween raayiḥ?
you want	biddak
you (m) go	truuḥ
Where do you want to go?	ween biddak truuḥ?
I want	biddi
I go	'aruuḥ
the movies	ssinama
I want to go to the movies.	biddi 'aruuḥ 9assinama.
How much do you want?	'addeeš biddak?
it is enough	bikaffi
one pound (currency)	liira
two pounds	liirteen
three pounds	tlat liiraat
Two pounds is enough.	bikaffi liirteen.
much, a lot, too much	ktiir
That's too much.	haada ktiir.

I give you	ba9ṭiik
half	nuṣṣ
and	w-/wi-
I'll give you a pound and a half.	ba9ṭiik liira wnuṣṣ.
good, all right	ṭayyib
it doesn't matter	ma9aleeš
All right. Get in.	ṭayyib, ma9aleeš. tfaḍḍal.
Slow down.	9a(la) mahlak.
stop for me	wa''ifli
Stop here.	wa''ifli hoon.
Good-by.	ma9 ssalaame.
Good-by (in reply).	'a*ll*a ysallmak.
Twenty	9išriin
Thirty	tlaatiin
Forty	'arb9iin
Fifty	xamsiin
Sixty	sittiin
Seventy	sab9iin
Eighty	tamaniin
Ninety	tis9iin
One hundred	miyye

STRUCTURE SENTENCES

1. Feminine forms

(said to a woman)

going (f)	raayḥa

Where are you going?	ween raayḥa?
you want	biddik
you (f) go	truuḥi
Where do you want to go?	ween biddik truuḥi?
How much do you want?	'addeeš biddik?
I give you	ba9ṭiiki
I'll give you three pounds.	ba9ṭiiki tlat liiraat.

2. Plural forms

(said to a group)

going (pl)	raayḥiin
Where are you going?	ween raayḥiin?
you want	bidkum
you (pl) go	truuḥu
Where do you want to go?	ween bidkum truuḥu?
How much do you want?	'addeeš bidkum?
I give you	ba9ṭiikum
I'll give you four pounds.	ba9ṭiikum 'arba9 liiraat.

3. Plural forms

(said by or for a group)

take us	xudna
the airport	lmaṭaar
Please take us to the airport.	min faḍlak, xudna 9almaṭaar.
we want	bidna
we go	nruuḥ
We want to go to the town.	bidna nruuḥ 9albalad.

stop for us	wa''ifilna
Stop here.	wa''ifilna hoon.

4. **Masculine forms**
(said about a man)

take him	xudo
Take him to the airport.	xudo 9almaṭaar.
he wants	biddo
he goes	yruuḥ
Where does he want to go?	ween biddo yruuḥ ?
How much does he want?	'addeeš biddo ?
I give him	ba9ṭii(h)
I'll give him five pounds.	ba9ṭii xamis liiraat.

5. **Feminine forms**
(said about a woman)

take her	xudha
Take her to the Embassy.	xudha 9assafaara.
she wants	bidha
she goes	truuḥ
Where does she want to go?	ween bidha truuḥ ?
How much does she want?	'addeeš bidha?
I give her	ba9ṭiiha
I'll give her six pounds.	ba9ṭiiha sitt liiraat.

6. **Plural forms**
(said about a group)

take them	xudhum

Take them to the hotel.	xudhum 9al'uteel.
they want	bidhum
they go	yruuḥu
Where do they want to go?	ween bidhum yruuḥu?
How much do they want?	'addeeš bidhum?
I give them	ba9ṭiihum
I'll give them seven pounds.	ba9ṭiihum sabi9 liiraat.

GRAMMAR

1. Variants of the pronoun endings

After stems ending in a vowel, four of the pronoun endings have a variant form.

-y	*my, me, I*	waraay	*behind me*
-k	*your, you (m)*	ba9ṭiik	*I give you (m)*
-ki	*your, you (f)*	ba9ṭiiki	*I give you (f)*
-(h)	*his, him, he*	ba9ṭii(h)	*I give him*

The ending -(h) *his, him, he* often drops in the middle of a sentence, but the preceding vowel remains long.

2. Summary of the pronoun endings

The following summarizes the pronoun endings. For a stem ending in a consonant we use beet *house*; for a stem ending in a vowel, bya9ṭi *he gives.*

beeti	*my house*	bya9ṭiini	*he gives me*
beetna	*our house*	bya9ṭiina	*he gives us*
beetak	*your (m) house*	bya9ṭiik	*he gives you (m)*

beetik	*your (f) house*	bya9ṭiiki	*he gives you (f)*
beetkum	*your (pl) house*	bya9ṭiikum	*he gives you (pl)*
beeto	*his house*	bya9ṭii(h)	*he gives him*
beetha	*her house*	bya9ṭiiha	*he gives her*
beethum	*their house*	bya9ṭiihum	*he gives them*

3. The word bidd-

The word bidd- *want* combines with pronoun endings to produce the following forms.

biddi	*I want*
bidna	*we want*
biddak	*you (m) want*
biddik	*you (f) want*
bidkum	*you (pl) want*
biddo	*he wants*
bidha	*she wants*
bidhum	*they want*

This word, in spite of its verbal meaning, is not a verb in terms of Arabic grammar. Its negative is maa : maa biddi *I don't want*, maa bidna *we don't want*, etc.

4. The word fii

The word fii *there is, there are* is not a verb in terms of Arabic grammar, in spite of its meaning. Its negative is maa : maa fii *there isn't, there aren't.*

DRILLS

1. Give appropriate replies to the following sentences.

   ween raayiḥ ?

   'addeeš biddak ?

   raayiḥ 9assinama ?

   feen biddak truuḥ ?

   'inte ḥaadir ?

2. The following sentences are said to a man. How would you say them to a woman ? To a group ?

   min faḍlak, xudni 9albalad.

   ween raayiḥ ?

   ween biddak truuḥ ?

   'addeeš biddak?

   ba9ṭiik xamis liiraat.

   ḥaaḍir ?

   9a(la) mahlak.

3. The following sentences are said about a man. How would you say them about a woman ? About a group ?

   ween biddo yruuḥ?

   huwwe ḥaaḍir.

   xudo 9almaṭaar.

   'addeeš biddo ?

   ba9ṭii tlat liiraat.

4. In each of the following sentences replace the word 9albalad by a different place expression.

   min faḍlak, xudni 9albalad.

   biddi 'aruuḥ 9albalad.

   huwwe raayiḥ 9albalad.

   maa biddo yruuḥ 9albalad.

5. Answer each of the following questions twice, once affirmatively and once negatively, as illustrated in the first one.

   fii maṭ9am hoon ? Replies : na9am, fii.
   la', maa fii.

   fii hoon beet *m*ayy ?

   fii sinama hoon ?

   fii maṭ9am fil'uteel ?

   fii maṭ9am rxiiṣ hoon?

   fii 'uteel mniiḥ hoon ?

Unit 5 • Requests and Information. Numbers 21-29.

PATTERN SENTENCES

heat	šoob
today	lyoom
It's very warm today.	šoob ktiir lyoom.
open (to a man)	'iftaḥ
the window	ššubbaak
Please open the window.	min faḍlak, 'iftaḥ ššubbaak.
coldness	bard
It's very cold today.	bard ktiir lyoom.
close (to a man)	sakkir
the door	lbaab
Please close the door.	min faḍlak, sakkir lbaab.
what	šuu , 'eeš
in	bi-/b-
in Arabic	bil9arabi
What's this in Arabic ?	šuu haada bil9arabi ?
book	ktaab
This is a book.	haada ktaab.
And what's this ?	wšuu haada ?
this (f)	haadi
map	xaarṭa, xariiṭa
This is a map.	haadi xaarṭa.
cigarette	siigaara
Do you want a cigarette ?	biddak siigaara ?
Please.	min faḍlak.

No, thanks.	la', šukran.
with you	ma9ak
box of matches	kibriite
lighter	'addaaḥa
Have you a match?	ma9ak kibriite?
with me	ma9i
Yes, I have. Here (offering it).	na9am, ma9i. tfaḍḍal.
Sorry, I haven't.	mit'assif, maa fii ma9i.

Additional vocabulary

1. Masculine nouns

	sing.	*plural*
book	ktaab	kutub
window	šubbaak	šababiik
door	baab	bwaab
office	maktab	makaatib
chair	kursi	karaasi
pencil, pen	'alam	'laam
fountain pen	'alam ḥibir	'laam ḥibir
notebook	daftar	dafaatir

2. Feminine nouns

map	xaarṭa, xariiṭa	xaraayiṭ
cigarette	siigaara	siigaaraat, sagaayir
lighter	'addaaḥa	'addaaḥaat
table	ṭaawle	ṭaawlaat
room	'uuḍa	'uwaḍ
sheet of paper	war'a	war'aat, wraa'
newspaper	jariide	jaraayid

magazine	majalle	majallaat
Twenty-one	waaḥad w9išriin	
Twenty-two	tneen w9išriin	
Twenty-three	tlaate w9išriin	
Twenty-four	'arba9a w9išriin	
Twenty-five	xamse w9išriin	
Twenty-six	sitte w9išriin	
Twenty-seven	sab9a w9išriin	
Twenty-eight	tamaanye w9išriin	
Twenty-nine	tis9a w9išriin	

STRUCTURE SENTENCES

I. The prefix for « the »

the cup	lfinjaan
the door	lbaab
the office	lmaktab
the sheet of paper	lwar'a
the chair	lkursi
the customs	lgumruk
the day, today	lyoom
the map	lxariiṭa
the midday meal	lġada
the Koran	lqur'aan
the bath (room)	lḥammaam
the evening meal	l9aša
the identity card	lhawiyye
the pencil	l'alam

the doors	libwaab
the children	liwlaad
the book	liktaab
the pencils	li'laam
the history, the date	ttaariix
the airplane	ṭṭayyaara
the notebook	ddaftar
the noon	ḍḍuhur
the car	ssayyaara
the soap	ṣṣaabuun
the oil	zzeet
the officer	ẓẓaabiṭ
the window	ššubbaak
the people	nnaas
the night, tonight	lleele
the head man	rra'iis
the newspaper	ljariide *or* jjariide

2. Commands

(said to a man)

Please sit down.	tfaḍḍal striiḥ.
Bring the chair.	jiib lkursi.
Go straight ahead.	ruuḥ duġri.
Ask at the hotel.	'is'al fil'uteel.
Direct me to the movie.	dillni 9assinama.
Close the door.	sakkir lbaab.
Go straight ahead.	'imši duġri.
Give me a pencil.	'a9ṭiini 'alam.
Take this.	xood haada.

Take the newspaper with you.	xud ljariide ma9ak.

3. Commands

(said to a woman)

Please sit down.	tfaḍḍali striiḥi.
Bring the newspaper.	jiibi ljariide.
Go straight ahead.	ruuḥi duġri.
Ask at the airport.	'is'ali filmaṭaar.
Direct me to the office.	dilliini 9almaktab.
Close the window.	sakkri ššubbaak.
Go straight ahead.	'imši duġri.
Give me a match.	'a9ṭiini kibriite.
Take the children with you.	xudi liwlaad ma9ik.

4. Commands

(said to a group)

Please sit down.	tfaḍḍalu striiḥu.
Bring the children with you.	jiibu liwlaad ma9kum.
Go straight ahead.	ruuḥu duġri.
Ask at the office.	'is'alu filmaktab.
Direct us to the post office.	dilluuna 9alboosṭa.
Close the doors.	sakkru libwaab.
Go straight ahead.	'imšu duġri.
Give me the magazines.	'a9ṭuuni lmajallaat.
Take the identity cards with you.	xudu lhawiyyaat ma9kum.

5. Adjectives

(masculine forms)

Where is there a good restaurant?	ween fii maṭ9am mniiḥ?
new	jdiid
This is a new restaurant.	haada maṭ9am jdiid.
The new restaurant is next to the Hotel Plaza.	lmaṭ9am jjdiid, jamb 'uteel plaaza.
He's not well.	huwwe miš mabṣuuṭ.
I'm sorry (man speaking).	'ana mit'assif.

6. Adjectives

(feminine forms)

He has a new car.	9indo sayyaara jdiide.
He came in his new car.	'aja fii sayyaarto jjdiide.
She's not well.	hiyye miš mabṣuuṭa.
I'm sorry (woman speaking).	'ana mit'assfe.
There are three new hotels here.	fii hoon tlat 'uteelaat jdiide.

7. Adjectives

(Plural forms)

Their children aren't well.	wlaadhum miš mabṣuuṭiin.
We're sorry.	niḥna mit'assfiin.

GRAMMAR

1. The prefix for « the »

The Arabic equivalent of the English definite article *the* is a prefix. This prefix has the form l- if the first consonant of the word to which it is attached is one of the following : f b m w k g y x ġ q ḥ 9 h '. It is li- if the word begins with a consonant cluster whose first member is one of the preceding series.

The l- is completely assimilated, resulting in a double consonant, if the first consonant is one of the following : t ṭ d ḍ s ṣ z ẓ š n l r. The l- may or may not be assimilated if the first consonant is j.

After silence or a pause, this prefix may be preceded by a short 'i-, as 'ilbaab *the door*, 'issayyara *the car*, 'iliktaab *the book*.

2. Command forms of verbs

The command form of the Arabic verb indicates whether the command is said to a man, to a woman, or to a group. The masculine form has no ending ; the feminine form ends in -i ; the plural form ends in -u. There is often some change in the underlying form before the endings -i and -u. Following are some examples taken from the Structure Sentences:

masculine	*feminine*	*plural*	
jiib	jiibi	jiibu	*bring !*
dill	dilli	dillu	*direct !*
'is'al	'is'ali	'is'alu	*ask !*
sakkir	sakkri	sakkru	*close !*
'imši	'imši	'imšu	*walk !*
xood, xud	xudi	xudu	*take !*

The formation of the command stem will be discussed in Unit 8.

3. Nouns

Nouns in Arabic show two grammatical genders, traditionally labelled masculine and feminine. These terms are merely labels, and do not necessarily correspond to natural gender, though nouns denoting male beings are usually masculine, and nouns denoting female beings are usually feminine.

Most feminine nouns end in -e or -a; most masculine nouns end in a consonant. The exceptions are few.

Most nouns have three grammatical numbers: singular, denoting one individual of the kind; dual, denoting two individuals and plural, denoting more than two individuals.

4. Definite and indefinite nouns

A noun in Arabic is said to be grammatically definite if it has the prefix for « the » or a pronoun ending. A small class of nouns, chiefly proper names, is also definite, though lacking these elements. All other nouns are grammatically indefinite.

5. Adjectives

Adjectives in Arabic typically have three forms: masculine, feminine, and plural. The feminine is formed from the masculine by adding -e/ -a, frequently with some change in the underlying form. The plural of some adjectives is formed from the feminine by adding –iin; with others the plural shows a different internal arrangement of the vowels in respect to the consonants. Following are some typical adjectives.

masculine	*feminine*	*plural*	
mabṣuuṭ	mabṣuuṭa	mabṣuuṭiin	*well*
ḥaaḍir	ḥaaḍra	ḥaaḍriin	*ready*
mit'assif	mit'assfe	mit'assfiin	*sorry*
mniiḥ	mniiḥa	mnaaḥ	*good*

rxiiṣ	rxiiṣa	rxaaṣ	*cheap*
ġaali	ġaalye	ġaalyiin	*expensive*

The dividing line between an adjective and a noun in Arabic is not sharply drawn.

6. Noun-adjective agreement

Adjectives are tied to the nouns they modify by a system of agreement. With masculine nouns the adjective is masculine; with feminine nouns it is feminine. With personal plurals (i.e., plurals denoting human beings) the adjective is plural. With non-personal plurals the adjective is usually feminine singular, occasionally plural. With dual nouns the adjective is plural.

In a noun-adjective construction the adjective follows the noun. If the noun is definite the adjective has the prefix for « the ».

7. The feminine ending -e/-a

The typical marker of the feminine noun or adjective is the ending -e/-a. The choice of -e or -a is almost completely determined by the nature of the consonant that immediately precedes the ending. If it is a throat consonant (x ġ q ḥ 9 h ') or a velarized consonant (ṭ ḍ ṣ ẓ) the ending is -a. After r it is usually -a, occasionally -e. After all the other consonants it is -e. There are a few exceptions.

DRILLS

1. Answer each of the following questions twice, once affirmatively and once negatively, as illustrated in the first two.

(1) biddak siigaara? — na9am. biddi.
la'. maa biddi.

(2) ma9ak jariide?	na9am. ma9i.
	la'. maa fii ma9i.
biddak 'alam ?	ma9o hawiyye ?
ma9ak majalle ?	ma9ak daftar ?
biddo xaarṭa ?	ma9ak kibriite ?
biddak war'a ?	

2. Each of the following sentences contains a noun without the prefix for « the ». For each make up a matching sentence containing the same noun with the prefix for « the », as illustrated in the first two.

(1) ween fii maṭ9am ?	ween lmaṭ9am ?
(2) min faḍlak, 'a9ṭiini war'a.	min faḍlak, 'a9ṭiini lwar'a.
ma9ak jariide ?	ween fii xaarṭa ?
ween fii 'uteel ?	ween fii ṭaawle ?
'a9ṭiini war'a.	ween fii jariide ?
biddak xaarṭa ?	min faḍlak, xood 'alam ma9ak.
ween fii 'alam ?	'a9ṭiini ktaab.
xood war'a.	jiib kursi ma9ak.
jiib kursi.	

3. In the following sentence replace siigaara by as many different nouns as possible.

btismaḥli bsiigaara ? *May I take a cigarette ?*

4. In the following sentence replace ljariide by as many different nouns as possible.

btismaḥli biljariide ? *May I take the newspaper ?*

5. Each of the following command sentences is said to a man. Match each with two sentences, one a command sentence as

said to a woman, the other as said to a group, changing anything in the rest of the sentence that has to be changed. The first two are completed.

1) 'iftaḥ ššababiik.	'iftaḥi ššababiik.
	'iftaḥu ššababiik.
2) min faḍlak, jiib ljariide ma9ak.	min faḍlik, jiibi ljariide ma9ik.
	min faḍilkum, jiibu ljariide ma9kum.
'is'al yuusif.	tfaḍḍal ma9i.
xudhum ba9deen 9al'uteel.	min faḍlak, sakkir ššababiik.
xud lwar'a.	'imši 9alyamiin.
min faḍlak, 'iftaḥ lmaktab.	ba9deen 'is'al.
tfaḍḍal striiḥ.	min faḍlak, 'a9ṭiini lmajalle.
ba9deen, xudni 9almaṭaar.	'imši duġri, wba9deen 'is'al.

UNIT 6 • Where is it? Numbers 100 - 1,000 by hundreds.

PATTERN SENTENCES

today's newspaper	jariitt lyoom
Do you have today's newspaper ?	ma9ak jariitt lyoom?
Yes. Here it is.	na9am. tfaḍḍal.
key	muftaaḥ
the door key	muftaaḥ lbaab
Where is the door key ?	ween muftaaḥ lbaab ?
you (m) put it	ḥaṭṭeeto
I don't know where you put it.	maa ba9raf ween ḥaṭṭeeto.
that, which, who	('i)lli
I brought it	jibto
Where's the book that I brought with me ?	ween liktaab lli jibto ma9i ?
I put it	ḥaṭṭeeto
suit case, brief case	šanta
I put it in the brief case.	ḥaṭṭeeto fiššanta.
you know for me	bti9rafli
bookstore, library	maktabe
Do you know where there's a good bookstore here ?	bti9rafli ween fii maktabe mniiḥa hoon ?
I find	'alaa'i
to, for	la-
the Middle East	ššarq l'awṣaṭ
the Near East	ššarq l'adna

I want to get a good map of the Middle East.	biddi 'alaa'i xaarṭa mniiḥa laššarq l'awṣaṭ.
the Arab Library	lmaktabe l9arabiyye
in it	fiiha
The Arab Library has good maps.	lmaktabe l9arabiyye, fiiha xaraayiṭ mniiḥa.
Where is this bookstore?	ween haadi lmaktabe?
between	been
the hospital	lmustašfa
Between the post office and the hospital.	been lboosṭa wilmustašfa.
you (m) would like	bitḥibb
you (m) come	tiiji
Would you like to come with me?	bitḥibb tiiji ma9i?
why	leeš
Why not?	leeš la'?
One hundred	miyye
Two hundred	miteen
Three hundred	tlat miyye
Four hundred	'arba9 miyye
Five hundred	xamis miyye
Six hundred	sitt miyye
Seven hundred	sabi9 miyye
Eight hundred	taman miyye
Nine hundred	tisi9 miyye
One thousand	'alf

STRUCTURE SENTENCES

1. Prepositions

in front of	'uddaam
The car is in front of the house.	ssayyaara 'uddaam lbeet.
Walk in front of me.	'imši 'uddaami.
behind	wara
The chair is behind the door.	lkursi wara lbaab.
Walk behind me.	'imši waraay.
The restaurant is behind you.	lmaṭ9am waraak.

2. Prefix tense verbs : simple prefix

necessary	laazim
tomorrow	bukra
I have to go tomorrow.	laazim 'aruuḥ bukra.
I want to close the office.	biddi 'asakkir lmaktab.
I want to open the door.	biddi 'aftaḥ lbaab.
We have to go tomorrow.	laazim nruuḥ bukra.
We want to close the office.	bidna nsakkir lmaktab.
We want to open the door.	bidna niftaḥ lbaab.
You (m) will have to go tomorrow.	laazim truuḥ bukra.
Do you (m) want to close the office ?	biddak tsakkir lmaktab ?
Do you (m) want to open the door ?	biddak tiftaḥ lbaab ?
You (f) will have to go tomorrow.	laazim truuḥi bukra.

Do you (f) want to close the office?	biddik tsakkri lmaktab?
Do you (f) want to open the door?	biddik tiftaḥi lbaab?
You (pl) will have to go tomorrow.	laazim truuḥu bukra.
Do you (pl) want to close the office?	bidkum tsakkru lmaktab?
Do you (pl) want to open the door?	bidkum tiftaḥu lbaab?

3. Prefix tense verbs : B-prefix

I'll go tomorrow.	baruuḥ bukra.
I'll close the office.	basakkir lmaktab.
I'll open the door.	baftaḥ lbaab.
We'll go tomorrow.	binruuḥ bukra.
We'll close the office.	binsakkir lmaktab.
We'll open the door.	bniftaḥ lbaab.
You (m) will go tomorrow.	bitruuḥ bukra.
You (m) will close the office.	bitsakkir lmaktab.
You (m) will open the door.	btiftah lbaab.
You (f) will go tomorrow.	bitruuḥi bukra.
You`(f) will close the office.	bitsakkri lmaktab.
You (f) will open the door.	btiftaḥi lbaab.
You (pl) will go tomorrow.	bitruuḥu bukra.
You (pl) will close the office.	bitsakkru lmaktab.
You (pl) will open the door.	btiftaḥu lbaab.

GRAMMAR

1. Verbs

The verb in Arabic consists of a *stem* and a *subject marker*. The stem indicates the meaning of the verb. The subject marker indicates the doer of the action. For example, the verb truuḥ *you (m) go* consists of the stem -ruuḥ *go*, and the prefixed subject marker t- *you (m)*. Similarly, kaanat *she was* consists of the stem kaan- *was*, and the suffixed subject marker -at *she*.

The Arabic verb has two tenses: a *prefix tense*, having subject markers in the form of prefixes, and a *suffix tense*, having subject markers in the form of suffixes. The prefix tense usually indicates present or future time, the suffix tense past time.

In addition to the two tenses, most verbs have a command form.

2. The prefix tense — I

The prefix tense has two forms: *simple prefix* and *B-prefix*. The following shows the forms that have occurred so far.

Most of the prefixes have variants, depending upon whether the underlying stem begins with one consonant or with a consonant cluster. Note that some of the subject markers are a combination of a prefix (for person) and a suffix (for gender or number).

(1) Stem beginning with a single consonant

		simple	*B-prefix*	
'a-/ba-	*I*	'aruuḥ	baruuḥ	*I go*
n-/bin-	*we*	nruuḥ	binruuḥ	*we go*
t-/bit-	*you (m)*	truuḥ	bitruuḥ	*you (m) go*
t-/bit-...-i	*you (f)*	truuḥi	bitruuḥi	*you (f) go*
t-/bit-...-u	*you (pl)*	truuḥu	bitruuḥu	*you (pl) go*

(2) Stem beginning with a consonant cluster

'a-/ba-	*I*	'aftaḥ	baftaḥ	*I open*

ni-/bni-	*we*	niftaḥ	bniftaḥ	*we open*
ti-/bti-	*you (m)*	tiftaḥ	btiftaḥ	*you (m) open*
ti-/bti-...-i	*you (f)*	tiftaḥi	btiftaḥi	*you (f) open*
ti-/bti-...-u	*you (pl)*	tiftaḥu	btiftaḥu	*you (pl) open*

The simple prefix is a dependent form; it occurs when the verb is closely tied in meaning to a preceding word (such as bidd- *want*, laazim *have to*, or another verb). The B-prefix is independent.

One special use of the simple prefix form is to express wish : 'alla ysallmak *May God keep you*, nuškur 'alla *Let us thank God.*

3. Demonstratives

The principal demonstratives are: haada *this, that* (*m*); haadi *this, that* (*f*); hadool *these, those* (*pl*). When they form a unitary construction with a following noun that has the prefix for « the », they may be reduced to unstressed ha-. For example :

haada ktaab. *This is a book.*

haadi xaarṭa. *This is a map.*

hadool wlaadi. *These are my children.*

xood haliktaab. *Take this book.*

xood halxaarṭa. *Take this map.*

min ween haliwlaad? *Where are these children from?*

DRILLS

1. Give appropriate replies to the following sentences.

feen ḥaṭṭeet ššanta?

feen jariitt lyoom?

feen ljariide lli kaanat 9aṭṭaawle?

biddak jariide?

feen lmaktabe l9arabiyye?

feen balaa'i xaarṭa laššarq l'adna?

ma9ak muftaaḥ lbaab ?	ma9ak xaarṭa laššarq l'awṣaṭ ?

2. In the following sentences replace ljariide by as many nouns as possible.

feen ḥaṭṭeet ljariide ?	feen ljariide?
ḥaṭṭeet ljariide 9aṭṭaawle.	ljariide miš hoon.

3. In the following sentences replace the various forms of 'uddaam by the appropriate forms of wara.

lboosṭa 'uddaam l'uteel.	lmaṭ9am 'uddaamak.
lmaktabe l9arabiyye 'uddaam lmaṭ9am.	ššanta 'uddaami.
	šuu haada lli 'uddaamha ?
lkursi 'uddaam lbaab.	lboosṭa 'uddaamkum.

4. Each of the following sentences contains a prefix tense verb in the « I » form. Go through the sentences, replacing the «I» forms by « we » forms, and changing anything in the rest of the sentence that needs to be changed. The first two are completed.

(1) biddi 'aruuḥ 9albalad.	bidna nruuḥ 9albalad.
(2) maa ba9raf.	maa bni9raf.
laazim 'aruuḥ bukra 9albalad.	biddi 'asakkir lmaktab.
	laazim 'alaa'i lmuftaaḥ.
bukra baruuḥ ma9ak.	maa biddi 'as'al yuusif.
laazim 'ajiib ššanta ma9i.	bas'al yuusif.
bajiib ššanta ma9i.	maa ba9raf ween ḥaṭṭeeto.
biddi 'aftaḥ lmaktab.	biddi 'a9raf ween ḥaṭṭeeto.
ba9deen baruuḥ 9almaṭaar.	biddi 'adillo 9almaṭaar.

5. Each of the following sentences contains a verb in the « you (m) » form. Go through the sentences, replacing the « you (m) » forms by « you (pl) » forms, and changing anything in the rest of the sentence that needs to be changed. The first two are completed.

(1) biddak truuḥ bukra 9assuu'?

bidkum truuḥu bukra 9assuu'?

(2) bitruuḥ ma9hum?

bitruuḥu ma9hum?

laazim truuḥ ma9i.

bti9raf ween ḥaṭṭeet lmuftaaḥ?

maa biddak truuḥ ma9na?

laazim ti9raf.

laazim tis'al yuusif.

biddak tiftaḥ lmaktab?

laazim tsakkir baab lmaktab.

UNIT 7 • Introductions.

PATTERN SENTENCES

I would like	baḥibb
I introduce you	'a9arrfak
Mr.	sayyid
Mr. West, I'd like to introduce you to Mr. Ahmad.	mistir west, baḥibb 'a9arrfak 9assayyid 'aḥmad.
How do you do? (Lit. We are honored.)	tšarrafna.
journalist	ṣuḥufi
Mr. West is a journalist.	mistir west ṣuḥufi.
before, ago	'abil
He came from America a week ago.	'aja min 'ameerka 'abil 'usbuu9.
he visits	yzuur
our country	blaadna
He wants to visit our country.	biddo yzuur blaadna.
in this country	bhaliblaad
Do you like it in this country?	nšaa*ll*a mabṣuuṭ bhaliblaad ?
I like it very much, thank you.	mabṣuuṭ ktiir, lḥamdilla.
you (m) visited	zurt
places	maḥallaat
Have you visited many places?	zurt maḥallaat ktiire?
up to now	lissa *or* ba9d
Up to now I haven't visited many places.	lissa, maa zurt maḥallaat ktiire.

because	li'anno *or* leeš
I was	kunt
busy	mašġuul
Because I've been very busy.	li'anno kunt mašġuul ktiir.
going to...	raḥ-, raayiḥ
you stay	tib'a
particle of address	yaa
How long are you going to stay here, Mr. West?	'addeeš raḥtib'a hoon, yaa mistir west?
I return	'arja9
after	ba9id
I have to return after six months.	laazim 'arja9 ba9id sitt tušhur.
knowing	ma9rife
in knowing you	bma9riftak, mma9riftak
I'm honored to have met you, Mr. Ahmad.	tšarrafna mma9riftak, yaa sayyid 'aḥmad.
to, for	'il-
honor	šaraf
The honor's mine, Mr. West.	w'ilna ššaraf, yaa mistir west.

Additional vocabulary

consul	'unṣul
vice consul	naayib 'unṣul, naa'ib 'unṣul
counselor	mustašaar
ambassador	safiir
attaché	mulḥaq
army attaché	mulḥaq 9askari

naval attaché	mulḥaq baḥri
air attaché	mulḥaq jawwi
commercial attaché	mulḥaq tijaari
agricultural attaché	mulḥaq ziraa9i
press attaché	mulḥaq ṣaḥaafi
air force officer	ẓaabiṭ ṭayaraan
government official	mwaẓẓaf ḥukuume
mayor	ra'iis baladiyye
director, manager	mudiir
bank director	mudiir bank

STRUCTURE SENTENCES

1. Prefix tense verbs : simple prefix

He has to go tomorrow.	laazim yruuḥ bukra.
He wants to close the office.	biddo ysakkir lmaktab.
He wants to open the door.	biddo yiftaḥ lbaab.
She has to go tomorrow.	laazim truuḥ bukra.
She wants to close the office.	bidha tsakkir lmaktab.
She wants to open the door.	bidha tiftaḥ lbaab.
They have to go tomorrow.	laazim yruuḥu bukra.
They want to close the office.	bidhum ysakkru lmaktab.
They want to open the door.	bidhum yiftaḥu lbaab.

2. Prefix tense verbs : B-prefix

He'll go tomorrow.	biruuḥ bukra.

He'll close the office.	bisakkir lmaktab.
He'll open the door.	biftaḥ lbaab.
She'll go tomorrow.	bitruuḥ bukra.
She'll close the office.	bitsakkir lmaktab.
She'll open the door.	btiftaḥ lbaab.
They'll go tomorrow.	biruuḥu bukra.
They'll close the office.	bisakkru lmaktab.
They'll open the door.	biftaḥu lbaab.

3. Prefix tense stems ending in a vowel

How long are you (m) going to stay here ?	'addeeš raḥtib'a hoon ?
How long are you (f) going to stay here ?	'addeeš raḥtib'i hoon ?
How long are you (pl) going to stay here ?	'addeeš raḥtib'u hoon ?
Go straight ahead (to a man).	'imši duġri.
Go straight ahead (to a woman).	'imši duġri.
Go straight ahead (to a group).	'imšu duġri.

4. Counting : 1-10

One month	šahir
Two months	šahreen
Three months	tlat tušhur
Four months	'arba9 tušhur
Five months	xamis tušhur
Six months	sitt tušhur

Seven months	sabi9 tušhur
Eight months	taman tušhur
Nine months	tisi9 tušhur
Ten months	9ašar tušhur
One year	sane
Two years	santeen
Three years	tlaat sniin
Four years	'arba9 sniin
Five years	xams sniin
Six years	sitt sniin
Seven years	sab9 sniin
Eight years	tamn sniin
Nine years	tis9 sniin
Ten years	9ašr sniin

5. Suffix tense verbs

I haven't visited many places.	maa zurt maḥallaat ktiire.
I've been very busy.	kunt mašġuul ktiir.
We haven't visited many places.	maa zurna maḥallaat ktiire.
We've been very busy.	kunna mašġuuliin ktiir.
Have you (m) visited many places?	zurt maḥallaat ktiire?
Have you (m) been very busy?	kunt mašġuul ktiir?
Have you (f) visited many places?	zurti maḥallaat ktiire?
Have you (f) been very busy?	kunti mašġuule ktiir?

Have you (pl) visited many places ?	zurtu maḥallaat ktiire ?
Have you (pl) been very busy?	kuntu mašġuuliin ktiir ?
He hasn't visited many places.	maa zaar maḥallaat ktiire.
He's been very busy.	kaan mašġuul ktiir.
She hasn't visited many places.	maa zaarat maḥallaat ktiire.
She's been very busy.	kaanat mašġuule ktiir.
They haven't visited many places.	maa zaaru maḥallaat ktiire.
They've been very busy.	kaanu mašġuuliin ktiir.

GRAMMAR

1. The prefix tense — II

In Unit 6 we listed five of the prefix tense subject markers. The remaining three are given below.

(1) Stem beginning with a single consonant

		simple	*B-prefix*	
y-/bi-	*he*	yruuḥ	biruuḥ	*he goes*
t-/bit-	*she*	truuḥ	bitruuḥ	*she goes*
y-/bi-...-u	*they*	yruuḥu	biruuḥu	*they go*

(2) Stem beginning with a consonant cluster

yi-/bi-	*he*	yiftaḥ	biftaḥ	*he opens*
ti-/bti-	*she*	tiftaḥ	btiftaḥ	*she opens*
yi-/bi-...-u	*they*	yiftaḥu	biftaḥu	*they open*

Note that the subject marker for « she » is the same as for « you (m). »

2. Prefix tense stems ending in a vowel

Prefix tense verb stems in which the « he » form ends in a vowel drop this vowel when the endings -i *feminine* and -u *plural* are added. The following two verbs illustrate this.

bib'a	*he stays*	bilaa'i	*he finds*
btib'a	*she stays*	bitlaa'i	*she finds*
bib'u	*they stay*	bilaa'u	*they find*
btib'a	*you (m) stay*	bitlaa'i	*you (m) find*
btib'i	*you (f) stay*	bitlaa'i	*you (f) find*
btib'u	*you (pl) stay*	bitlaa'u	*you (pl) find*
bnib'a	*we stay*	binlaa'i	*we find*
bab'a	*I stay*	balaa'i	*I find*

Any verb form ending in a vowel lengthens the vowel before a pronoun ending.

bilaa'iini *he meets me*

balaa'iik *I meet you (m)*

bilaa'uuh *they meet him*

3. Stem vowels

The vowel that appears before the last consonant of the stem of a word is called the *stem vowel.* When this vowel is *i* or *u* it is almost invariably dropped before an ending beginning with a vowel :

naazle *staying* (*f*), for *naazil-e

ḥaaḍra *ready* (*f*), for *ḥaaḍir-a

naazliin *staying* (*pl*), for *naazil-iin

ḥaaḍriin *ready* (*pl*), for *ḥaaḍir-iin

bisakkru *they close,* for *bisakkir-u

bisakkro *he closes it,* for *bisakkir-o

baaxdo *I take him*, for *baaxud-o

The stem vowel *a* does not drop :

bis'alu *they ask*

bis'alo *he asks him*

bis'alak *he asks you (m)*

maktabe *bookstore*

šarafi *my honor*

4. The suffix tense

The following shows the complete suffix tense forms of two typical verbs.

subject markers

—	*he*	kaan	*he was*	fihim	*he understood*
-at	*she*	kaanat	*she was*	fihmat	*she understood*
-u	*they*	kaanu	*they were*	fihmu	*they understood*
-t	*you (m)*	kunt	*you (m) were*	fhimt	*you (m) understood*
-ti	*you (f)*	kunti	*you (f) were*	fhimti	*you (f) understood*
-tu	*you (pl)*	kuntu	*you (pl) were*	fhimtu	*you (pl) understood*
-t	*I*	kunt	*I was*	fhimt	*I understood*
-na	*we*	kunna	*we were*	fhimna	*we understood*

In discussing the suffix tense, we regard the « he » form as basic; it has no subject marker, and thus shows the bare stem.

Most suffix tense verbs have two variants of the stem: one occurs in the third person forms; the other in the first and second person forms. For example: kaan-/kun-; fih(i)m-/fhim-.

Note that the « I » and « you (m) » forms are identical.

5. The verb prefix raḥ-

The prefix rah- is used before a simple prefix tense verb to indicate the future: *will, shall, going to*: 'addeeš raḥtib'a hoon? *How long are you (m) going to stay here?*

Occasionally the participle raayiḥ *going* (and its feminine and plural forms raayḥa and raayḥiin) are used in place of raḥ-: 'addeeš raayḥiin tib'u hoon? *How long are you (pl) going to stay here?*

6. The verb 'aja

A verb that may be considered irregular is 'aja *he came*. Following is a complete listing of the forms.

'aja	*he came*	biiji	*he comes*
'ajat	*she came*	btiiji	*she comes*
'aju	*they came*	biiju	*they come*
'ijiit	*you (m) came*	btiiji	*you (m) come*
'ijiiti	*you (f) came*	btiiji	*you (f) come*
'ijiitu	*you (pl) came*	btiiju	*you (pl) come*
'ijiit	*I came*	baaji	*I come*
'ijiina	*we came*	bniiji	*we come*

DRILLS

1. Give appropriate replies to the following questions.

mistir west ẓaabiṭ ṭayaraan?	zaar maḥallaat ktiire?
min feen huwwe?	'addeeš raḥyib'a hoon?
'addeeš ṣarlo hoon?	leeš maa zaar maḥallaat ktiire?
'aja yzuur liblaad?	huwwe mabṣuuṭ bhaliblaad?

2. In the following sentences, replace the expression in pa-

rentheses by a different expression denoting an occupation or profession.

mistir west (ṣuḥufi).

(l'unṣul) raḥyib'a hoon 'usbuu9een.

(ssafiir) laazim yirja9 ba9id šahreen.

(lmulḥaq ljawwi) mašġuul ktiir.

(mudiir lbank) kaan ma9 'aḥmad.

bti9raf (ra'iis lbaladiyye)?

'aḥmad (mwaẓẓaf ḥukuume).

mistir west biddo yzuur (lmulḥaq l9askari).

3. In each of the following sentences replace the word yoomeen by a different time expression.

'aja min beeruut 'abil yoomeen.

raayiḥ 'ab'a hoon yoomeen.

lmudiir kaan hoon 'abil yoomeen.

bidna nzuur blaadkum ba9id yoomeen.

ra'iis lbaladiyye biiji ba9id yoomeen.

laazim 'arja9 ba9id yoomeen.

4. Go through the following sentences, replacing the « he » form of the verb by the « they » form, and changing anything in the rest of the sentence that needs changing. The first two are completed.

(1) biddo yruuḥ 9albalad.	bidhum yruuḥu 9albalad.
(2) bya9ṭiik lmajalle.	bya9ṭuuk lmajalle.
laazim yruuḥ bukra.	biddo yiftaḥ lmaktab.
raayiḥ yjiib ššanta ma9o.	maa bi9raf feen ḥaṭṭeetha.
biddo yzuur ssafaara.	biddo ysakkir lmaktab.
maa biddo yruuḥ. biddo yib'a.	biddo ydill 'aḥmad 9al'uteel.
biruuḥ bukra fissayyaara.	feen bilaa'i xaarṭa mniiḥa?
bizuur blaadna ba9id šahir.	biddo ya9ṭiik ljariide.

birja9 ma9hum.

maa biddo yis'al lmudiir.

bis'al l'unṣul.

biddo yib'a filbeet ?

laazim yirja9 la'ameerka.

5. Go through the sentences of Drill 4, replacing the « he » forms of the verbs by « I » forms.

6. Match each of the following sentences with a sentence containing the appropriate form of kaan. The first two are completed.

(1) 'inte feen naazil ?	'inte feen kunt naazil ?
(2) niḥna mašġuuliin ktiir.	kunna mašġuuliin ktiir.
'aḥmad hoon.	hiyye mašġuule ktiir.
lmudiir fiššaam.	feen lmajalle ?
'aḥmad miš mašġuul.	'ana w'aḥmad mašġuuliin ktiir.
mistir west fii ameerka.	'ana naazil fii 'uteel plaaza.
liktaab 9aṭṭaawle.	humme fii 'uteel plaaza.
kiif safirtak ?	humme mašġuuliin ktiir.
'inte mašġuul ?	feen lxaarṭa ?
ššanta 9aṭṭaawle.	

Unit 8 • Family and children.

PATTERN SENTENCES

How long are you going to stay here, Mr. West?	'addeeš raḥtib'a hoon, yaa mistir west?
I have to return in a couple of months.	laazim 'arja9 ba9id šahreen.
you have	9indak
Do you have a family in America?	fii 9indak 9eele fii 'ameerka?
my wife	marti
Yes, my wife and children.	na9am. marti wiwlaadi.
how many	kam
child, boy	walad
How many children do you have, Mr. West?	kam walad 9indak, yaa mistir west?
I have	9indi
boy	ṣabi
two boys	ṣabiyyeen
girl	bint
I have two boys and a girl.	9indi ṣabiyyeen wbint.
may he leave for you	yxalliilak
May God leave them for you.	'*all*a yxalliilak yyaahum.
May God keep you (in reply).	'*all*a yiḥfaẓak.
big, old (pl)	kbaar

small, young (pl)	ẓġaar
Are they big or small ?	kbaar, willa ẓġaar ?
big, old (m)	kbiir
age, life	9umur
sixteen years	sitt ṭa9šar sane
The older boy is sixteen years old.	lwalad likbiir, 9umro sitt ṭa9šar sane.
small, young (m)	ẓġiir
And the younger one is ten years old.	wiẓẓġiir, 9ašr sniin.
And what's the girl's age ?	wšuu 9umr lbint ?
eleven years	ḥda9šar sane
The girl is eleven years old.	lbint, 9umurha ḥda9šar sane.
visit !	zuur
Please visit us at our home.	tfaḍḍal zuurna filbeet.
Thank you.	šukran.

Alternate expressions

How many children do you have ?	kam walad 9indak ?
I have one boy.	9indi ṣabi waaḥad.
May God leave him for you.	'a*ll*a yxalliilak yyaa(h).
May God keep you.	'a*ll*a yiḥfaẓak.
I have one girl.	9indi bint waḥde.
May God leave her for you.	'a*ll*a yxalliilak yyaaha.
May God keep you.	'a*ll*a yiḥfaẓak.
I have two boys.	9indi ṣabiyyeen.
I have two girls.	9indi binteen.

I have three boys.	9indi tlat ṣubyaan.
I have three girls.	9indi tlat banaat.
May God leave them for you.	'a*ll*a yxalliilak yyaahum.
May God keep you.	'a*ll*a yiḥfaẓak.
I haven't any children.	maa (fii) 9indi wlaad.
married	mijjawwiz
I'm not married.	›ana miš mijjawwiz.
bachelor	'a9zab
I'm a bachelor.	ana 'a9zab.

STRUCTURE SENTENCES

1. Counting: 11-20

eleven years	ḥda9šar sane
twelve years	ṭna9šar sane
thirteen years	tlat ṭa9šar sane
fourteen years	'arba9 ṭa9šar sane
fifteen years	xamis ṭa9šar sane
sixteen years	sitt ṭa9šar sane
seventeen years	saba9 ṭa9šar sane
eighteen years	taman ṭa9šar sane
nineteen years	tisi9 ṭa9šar sane
twenty years	9išriin sane

2. Singular and dual of nouns

day	yoom
two days	yoomeen
week	'usbuu9

two weeks	'usbuu9een
girl	bint
two girls	binteen
child, boy	walad
two children, two boys	waladeen
piastre	'irš
two piastres	'iršeen
month	šahir
two months	šahreen
boy	ṣabi
two boys	ṣabiyyeen
hospital	mustašfa
two hospitals	mustašfayeen
pound	liira
two pounds	liirteen
year	sane
two years	santeen
week	jum9a
two weeks	jum*i*9teen
suitcase	šanta
two suitcases	šan*i*tteen
newspaper	jariide
two newspapers	jariitteen
room	'uuḍa
two rooms	'uuṭṭeen

GRAMMAR

1. Counting

The numbers from 3-19 have one form when they are used independently and a variant form when they immediately precede a counted noun: 3-10 lose the ending -e/-a; 11-19 add -ar: sitte *six,* sitt wlaad *six children*; sitt ṭa9š *sixteen,* sitt ṭa9šar sane *sixteen years.*

The Arabic counting system differs from English in the following ways.

(1) The noun by itself means « one », though it may be followed by waaḥad *one* (*m*), waḥde *one* (*f*), according to its gender.

(2) The noun plus the ending -een means « two ».

(3) Immediately following the numbers 3-10 the noun is in the plural.

(4) Immediately following any of the other numbers the noun is in the singular.

2. The word kam

The word kam *how many* is always followed by an indefinite noun in the singular: kam walad 9indak? *How many children do you have?*

3. The dual

The dual ending -een added to a noun is the usual way of indicating two individuals of a kind. Occasionally the number forms tneen *two* (*m*) and tinteen *two* (*f*) are used in special expressions.

Nouns ending in -e/-a *feminine* replace the -e/-a by -t before -een *two*. For example: sane *a year,* santeen *two years*; sayyaara *a car,* sayyaarteen *two cars.*

Masculine nouns ending in -i or -a modify the stem before the dual ending. For example: ṣabi *a boy*, ṣabiyyeen *two boys*; mustašfa *a hospital*, mustašfayeen *two hospitals*.

4. Formation of commands

The command form of the verb is based on the prefix tense «you» form. How it is made depends upon whether the stem is stressed or unstressed. In what follows we give the «you» form of the verb for comparison.

(1) If the stem is stressed, the command is the same as the stem.

«you» form	*command*	
bitrúuḥ	rúuḥ	*go !*
bitjíib	jíib	*bring !*
btistríiḥ	stríiḥ	*rest !*
bitdíll	díll	*direct !*
btitfáḍḍal	tfáḍḍal	*please !*
bitsákkir	sákkir	*close !*
bitxálli	xálli	*keep !, allow !*

(2) If the stem is unstressed, the command has a prefixed 'i- or 'u-, depending on the vowel that follows the subject marker.

btíftaḥ	'íftaḥ	*open !*
btís'al	'ís'al	*ask !*
btímši	'ímši	*walk !*
btíb'a	'íb'a	*remain !*

If the stress shifts as a result of added suffix material, the 'i- (or 'u-) is frequently dropped. For example.

btis'álni	s'álni	*ask me !*
btis'alúuni	s'alúuni	*ask (pl) me !*

The verb btá9ṭi *you give* has the command form 'á9ṭi, as in 'a9ṭiini *give me!*

The verb btáaxud *you take* has the command forms xóod, xúd (m), xúdi (f), xúdu (pl) *take!*

The verb btiiji *you come* has for its command a suppletion form (i.e. having a different root): ta9aal (m), ta9aali (f), ta9aalu (pl) *come!*

DRILLS

1. Give appropriate replies to the following sentences.

'addeeš raḥtib'a hoon?	ḥaḍ*i*rtak mijjawwiz?
fii 9indak 9eele?	'addeeš 9umrak?
'addeeš 9umr lwalad?	tfaḍḍal zuurna filbeet.
'addeeš 9umr lbint?	9indak wlaad?
'a*ll*a yxalliilak yyaahum.	'addeeš ṣarlak mijjawwiz?

2. In the following sentences replace the singular nouns by the corresponding duals. The first two are completed.

(1) ba9ṭiik 'irš.	ba9ṭiik 'iršeen.
(2) fii 9indo 'uuḍa.	fii 9indo 'uuṭṭeen.
kaan hoon 'abil šahir.	biddo majalle.
9indo bint.	laazim 'arja9 ba9id 'usbuu9.
min faḍlak, 'a9ṭiini liira.	kaan fii 'ameerka 'abil sane.

3. Give the Arabic equivalents of the following.

three years	two rooms
two houses	two cigarettes
seven maps	four places

three days	seven years
twenty officers	twenty years
three weeks	two tables
ten days	eighteen officers
six months	fourteen chairs
one year	nineteen cars
eight piastres	four doors
five windows	

4. Go through the following sentences, replacing the singular verbs by the corresponding plurals, and changing anything in the rest of the sentence that needs to be changed. The first two are completed.

(1) biddo yzuur blaadna.	bidhum yzuuru blaadna.
(2) maa biddi 'azuuro.	maa bidna nzuuro.
laazim 'arja9 ba9id šahreen.	biddo yzuurna filbeet.
leeš bidha tirja9 ?	biddak dzuurna ?
biddo yirja9 9albeet.	bitḥibb blaadna ?
maa bi9raf 'aḥmad.	'addeeš raḥtib'a hoon ?
biddak tirja9 ma9hum ?	raḥyib'a hoon santeen.
hiyye bidzuurna bukra.	

5. Go through the following sentences, replacing the «we» forms of the verbs by «I» forms, and changing anything in the rest of the sentence that needs to be changed. The first two are completed.

(1) laazim nis'al 'aḥmad.	laazim 'as'al 'aḥmad.
(2) laazim njiib 'aḥmad ma9na.	laazim 'ajiib 'aḥmad ma9i.

bniiji ma9ak.	raayḥiin nis'al lmudiir.
ba9deen binruuḥ 9almaṭaar.	laazim nirja9 ba9id yoomeen.
bidna nzuur ššaam.	bnib'a hoon šahreen.
bidna nruuḥ ma9ak.	feen binlaa'iik?
maa bni9raf.	bna9ṭiik ššanta.

UNIT 9 • Where have you been?

PATTERN SENTENCES

Good evening.	masa lxeer.
Good evening (in reply).	masa nnuur.
for the safety	9assalaame
Welcome back (an expression said to a person who has just returned from a trip, a hospital, etc.).	lḥamdilla 9assalaame.
May God keep you (in reply).	'a*ll*a ysallmak.
absence	ġeebe
Where have you been?	ween halġeebe ?
I was in Damascus.	kunt fiššaam.
longing for you	mištaa'lak
I've missed you very much.	'ana mištaa'lak ktiir.
more, most	'aktar
And I even more.	w'ana bil'aktar.
when	'eemta(n)
you honored	šarraft
When did you get back?	'eemta šarraft ?
yesterday	mbaariḥ
I got back yesterday.	tšarrafna mbaariḥ.
now	halla
free, empty	faaḍi

Are you busy now or are you free ?	mašġuul halla, willa faaḍi ?
possible	mumkin
we drink	nišrab
coffee, coffee shop	'ahwe
Could you come with me and drink a cup of coffee ?	mumkin tiiji ma9i nišrab finjaan 'ahwe ?
Why not ?	leeš la' ?

Alternate expressions

I do, I make	'a9mal
I'm free. I haven't a thing to do.	'ana faaḍi. maa fii 9indi šii 'a9mal(o).
believe	saddi'
Believe me, I'm rather busy.	saddi'ni mašġuul šwayy.
we have	9inna
visitors	zuwwaar
We have visitors at home.	fii 9inna zuwwaar filbeet.

Additional vocabulary

Egypt	maṣir
Iraq	l9iraaq
Jordan	l'urdun
Saudi Arabia	ssu9uudiyye
Turkey	turkiyya
Aleppo	ḥalab
Amman	9ammaan

Baghdad	bağdaad
Beirut	beeruut
Cairo	lqaahira
Dhahran	ḍḍahraan
Jerusalem	l'uds
Tripoli	ṭaraablus̩

STRUCTURE SENTENCES

I. Feminine T-nouns: free forms and combining forms

How was the trip?	kiif kaanat ssafra?
How was Ahmad's trip?	kiif kaanat safrit 'aḥmad?
His trip was good.	saf*i*rto kaanat mniiḥa.
And how was your trip?	wkiif kaanat safritkum?
This room isn't free.	haadi l'uuḍa miš faaḍye.
who, whom	miin
Whose room is this?	'uuḍit miin haadi?
This is our room.	haadi 'uuḍitna.
His room is over there.	'uuṭṭo hunaak.
Where is the newspaper?	feen ljariide?
Where's today's newspaper?	feen jariitt lyoom?
Whose newspaper is this?	jariidit miin haadi?
Where's *Al-Ahram* (a newspaper)?	feen jariitt l'ahraam?
His wife is in Beirut.	marto fii beeruut.

2. The word 9ind

How many children do you have?	kam walad 9indak?
I have a girl and a boy.	9indi bint wṣabi.
I don't have any children.	maa (fii) 9indi wlaad.
Could you come to my place?	mumkin tiiji la9indi?
The children aren't at Yusif's.	liwlaad miš 9ind yuusif.
They're at Ahmad's.	humme 9ind 'aḥmad.

GRAMMAR

1. Feminine T-nouns

Nouns ending in -e/-a *feminine* in their free form have a *combining form* in which the -e/-a is replaced by -(i)t. This combining form is used before the dual ending -een, a pronoun ending, or a following noun in a unitary construction. Nouns that behave this way will be called *feminine T-nouns.* For example: sayyaara *a car*, sayyaarteen *two cars*, sayyaarto *his car*, sayyaaritna *our car*, sayyaart ssafaara *the Embassy's car.*

2. The word 9ind

The word 9ind *in the possession of*, in the sense of English *have*, combines with pronoun endings to produce the following forms.

9indi	*in my possession, I have*
9inna	*in our possession, we have*
9indak	*in your (m) possession, you (m) have*
9indik	*in your (f) possession, you (f) have*

9indkum *in your (pl) possession, you (pl) have*

9indo *in his possession, he has*

9indha *in her possession, she has*

9indhum *in their possession, they have*

The negative is maa or maa fii, as in maa (fii) 9indi wlaad. *I haven't any children.*

This word also may mean «at the house of», as in mumkin tiiji la9indi ? *Could you come to my place ?* The negative, with this meaning, is miš, as in liwlaad miš 9ind yuusif *the children aren't at Yusif's.*

3. Assimilation

Certain consonant clusters that result from the processes of the grammar are affected by *assimilation* : the shift of a sound to match its neighbor. The commoner case is a change in the pronunciation of the first member of the cluster.

Within words

(1) d becomes t before t : jariitti *my newspaper* (for jariidti).

(2) t becomes d before d, z, and j : biddill *you direct* (for bitdill), bidzuur *you visit* (for bitzuur), bidjiib *you bring* (for bitjiib). Occasionally t becomes j before j : mijjawwiz *married* (for mitjawwiz).

(3) n may become m before b : jamb *next to* (for janb).

(4) b may become m before m : mma9riftak *in knowing you* (for bma9riftak).

(5) If one of the consonants is velarized, the velarization extends over the whole cluster: xaariṭṭeen *two maps* (for xaariṭteen), 'uuṭṭi *my room* (for 'uuṭti from 'uuḍti).

These particular assimilations occur within words, and are

consistently marked in the transcription. Other assimilations occur across word boundaries. Following are some examples.

Across word boundaries

(1) t becomes d before j: tlad juma9 *three weeks* (for tlat juma9); occasionally j: tlaj juma9.

(2) š becomes s before ṣ: 'addees ṣarlak hoon? *how long have you been here?* (for 'addeeš ṣarlak hoon?).

(3) ḥ drops before 9: ruu 9ašmaalak *go to your left* (for ruuḥ 9ašmaalak).

Assimilations like the above are not uniformly handled by all speakers and are not indicated in the transcription.

It is worth noting that velarization very rarely carries across a word boundary.

DRILLS

I. Give appropriate replies to the following sentences.

ṣabaaḥ lxeer.
masa lxeer.
lḥamdilla 9assalaame.
ween halġeebe?
'ana mištaa'lak ktiir.
'eemta(n) šarraft?
ween kunt?
kiif 'ijiit? fiṭṭayyaara, willa filbaaboor?
kiif kaanat safirtak?

zurt maḥallaat ktiire?
mašġuul halla, willa faaḍi?
mumkin tiiji ma9i nišrab finjaan 'ahwe?
ween kuntu?
'ana mištaa'ilkum ktiir.
'eemta(n) šarraftu?
kiif 'ijiitu? fissayyaara, willa fiṭṭayyaara?

2. Match each of the following sentences with a command sentence. The first two are completed.

(1) mumkin tis'al mistir west?	'is'al mistir west.
(2) mumkin taaxudni 9assafaara?	xudni 9assafaara.
mumkin tiftaḥ lbaab?	mumkin tsakkir ššubbaak?
mumkin tis'al lmudiir?	mumkin dzuurna filbeet?
mumkin ddillni 9almaṭaar?	mumkin djiib 'aḥmad ma9ak?
mumkin ddillna 9alboosṭa?	mumkin ta9ṭiini kibriite?

3. Go through Drill 2, replacing the masculine verbs by feminine verbs and then matching each with a command sentence.

4. Go through Drill 2, replacing the masculine verbs by plural verbs and then matching each with a command sentence.

5. Give the Arabic equivalents of the following.

Ahmad's trip	our room	Ahmad's wife
his trip	their room	his wife
my trip	two rooms	my wife
your (m) trip	whose room?	two newspapers
your (pl) trip	today's newspaper	two cigarettes
their trip	his newspaper	two days
Ahmad's room	our newspaper	two offices
his room	her newspaper	two houses
my room	your (m) newspaper	two tables

6. In the following sentences replace the singular verbs by the corresponding plurals, changing anything in the rest of the sentence that needs changing. The first two are completed.

(1) bitḥibb ti9mal haada? bitḥibbu ti9malu haada?

(2) 'aja yzuurna mbaariḥ.	'aju yzuuruuna mbaariḥ.
biddi 'ašrab 'ahwe.	'aja min beeruut mbaariḥ.
šuu biddak tišrab ?	'ijiit lahoon min baġdaad.
šuu biddo yi9mal ?	'ajat min ḥalab.
maa biddo yišrab 'ahwe.	kaan fii 9ammaan.
whalla, šuu ba9mal ?	kunt fiḍḍahraan.
miin bitḥibb 'aktar? ššaam willa beeruut ?	feen kunt ?

7. In the following sentences replace 9indi, 9indak, 9indo, and 9indha by the corresponding plurals, changing anything in the rest of the sentence that needs changing. The first two are completed.

(1) šuu fii 9indo ?	šuu fii 9indhum ?
(2) fii 9indha 9eele fii 'ameerka.	fii 9indhum 9eele fii 'ameerka.
'ana faaḍi. ma fii 9indi šii 'a9mal.	fii 9indo 'uuḍa mniiḥa.
šuu fii 9indak šii jdiid ?	šuu fii 9indak?
fii 9indi zuwwaar filbeet.	fii 9indo sayyaara jdiide.
	maa fii 9indi šii jdiid.
	9indak sayyaara ?

UNIT 10 • In a coffee shop.

PATTERN SENTENCES

you order, command	btu'*u*mru
What will you order?	šuu btu'*u*mru ?
Two coffees.	tneen 'ahwe.
How would you like the coffee?	kiif bitḥibbu l'ahwe ?
sweet (f)	ḥilwe
plain (invariable adj.)	saada
With sugar or black?	ḥilwe, willa saada ?
One with sugar and one black.	waaḥad ḥilwe, wwaaḥad saada.
Yes, indeed (lit. your command).	'amrak.
beer	biira
Do you have beer?	fii 9indkum biira ?
I'm sorry. We don't have beer.	mit'assif. maa fii 9inna biira.
no need	balaaš
That's all right. No need for beer.	ma9aleeš. balaaš biira.
bring to us	jib*i*lna.
water	*m*ayy
Please bring us some water.	min faḍlak, jib*i*lna *m*ayy.
With pleasure.	tikram.
May it do you good (said to someone who has just drunk some water).	hanii'an.

May God give you joy (in reply).	'a*ll*a yhanniik.

Alternate expressions

you order	btu'mur
What will you order ?	šuu btu'mur ?
tea	šaay
One tea.	waaḥad šaay.
How would you like the tea ?	kiif bitḥibb ššaay ?
light.	xafiif
heavy	t'iil
Weak or strong ?	xafiif, willa t'iil ?
Weak, please.	xafiif, min faḍlak.
he will be	ykuun
sweet	ḥilu
But don't make it too sweet.	bass, balaaš ykuun ḥilu ktiir.

Additional vocabulary

cola	koola
hot chocolate	kakaaw
ice cream	buuẓa
milk	ḥaliib
sugar	sukkar

STRUCTURE SENTENCES

1. Ordering things

One order of coffee.	waaḥad 'ahwe.
Two orders of coffee.	tneen 'ahwe.
Three orders of coffee.	tlaate 'ahwe.
Four orders of tea.	'arba9a šaay.
Two orders of hot chocolate.	tneen kakaaw.
Three orders of cola.	tlaate koola.
Five orders of ice cream.	xamse buuẓa.

2. The preposition fii

We came by plane.	'ijiina fiṭṭayyaara.
They came by boat.	'aju filbaaboor.
Please visit us at home.	tfaḍḍal zuurna filbeet.
His wife is in Damascus.	marto fiššaam.
The Arab Library has good maps.	lmaktabe l9arabiyye, fiiha xaraayiṭ mniiḥa.
tourism	siyaaḥa
The Office of Tourism has lots of newspapers.	maktab ssiyaaḥa, fii jaraayid ktiire.
They're staying at the Hotel Plaza.	humme naazliin fii 'uteel plaaza.
My wife is in America.	marti fii 'ameerka.
I'm staying in Beirut.	'ana naazil fii beeruut.

GRAMMAR

1. Ordering things

In ordering things, Arabic uses the independent form of the number followed by a singular noun, e.g. tneen 'ahwe *two coffees*. Note that the dual in -een is not used here.

2. The preposition fii

The preposition fii *in* is shortened to fi- before a noun having the prefix for «the», e.g. filbalad *in the town*. Before a pronoun ending it is fii-, e.g. fiihum *in them*.

3. Roots and patterns

So far in our analysis of Arabic words we have concentrated on prefix and suffix elements. For example: l- *the* in lbeet *the house*; -ak *your* (*m*) in wlaadak *your children*; -at *she* in kaanat *she was*. It is usually possible to carry the analysis to the *stems* to which these affixes are attached.

Most stems consist of a nucleus of consonants which occur together with various vowel combinations, including sometimes an added extra consonant. For example, ktaab *book* consists of the consonant nucleus ktb plus long *aa* between the second and third consonants; naazil *staying* consists of the consonant nucleus nzl plus long *aa* between the first and second consonants and short *i* between the second and third.

This consonant nucleus is called a *root* (*R*:), and what is left over is called a *pattern* (*P*:). Expressed symbolically, the word naazil consists of *R*: nzl + *P*: -aa-i-. The hyphens in the pattern indicate the position of the root consonants relative to the rest of the material.

A root frequently has a general *lexical* meaning that is reflected in all words containing that root. For example, the root ktb has the general meaning of «writing», and this meaning appears in the following words : katab *he wrote*, kaatib *writer*, ktaab *book*, maktuub *letter*, maktab *writing place* (*i.e. office*).

A pattern frequently has a *grammatical* meaning. For example, the pattern --ii- (occasionally -a-ii-) has the meaning «simple adjective» as in rxiiṣ *cheap*, t'iil *heavy*, jdiid *new*, xafiif *light*.

4. Vowel harmony

Prefix tense verb forms with the stem vowel *u* show a kind of vowel harmony: the vowel of the subject marker is *u*, and when a transition vowel occurs, it is *u* also. The verb bu'mur *he orders* illustrates this.

	simple prefix	*B-prefix*
he	yu'mur	bu'mur
she	tu'mur	btu'mur
they	yu'*u*mru	bu'*u*mru
you (m)	tu'mur	btu'mur
you (f)	tu'*u*mri	btu'*u*mri
you (pl)	tu'*u*mru	btu'*u*mru
I	'a'mur	ba'mur
we	nu'mur	bnu'mur

	command
(m)	'u'mur
(f)	'u'*u*mri
(pl)	'u'*u*mru

This harmony is regressive, i.e. the following stem vowel *u* affects preceding vowels. The reverse is not usually true: jum*i*9teen *two weeks* (and not *jum*u*9teen) from jum9a *week*.

DRILLS

1. Give appropriate replies to the following sentences.

mumkin tiiji ma9i nišrab finjaan 'ahwe?

šuu btu'*u*mru?

kiif bitḥibb l'ahwe?

bitḥibb 'ahwe, willa šaay?

min faḍlak, jib*i*lna *m*ayy.

šuu bitḥibb? 'ahwe, willa šaay?

bitḥibb l'ahwe ḥilwe, willa saada?

hanii'an.

2. In each of the following sentences replace the word 'ahwe by a different noun indicating a food or a drink.

kiif bitḥibb l'ahwe?

fii 9indkum 'ahwe?

mit'assif. maa fii 9inna 'ahwe.

min faḍlak, jib*i*lna tneen 'ahwe.

ma baḥibb l'ahwe ktiir.

bitḥibb l'ahwe?

marti maa bitḥibb l'ahwe.

min faḍlak, jibli waaḥad 'ahwe.

3. Give the Arabic for the following orders.

two coffees

three colas

four ice creams

one hot chocolate

three coffees

one tea

three beers

one coffee and one tea

two coffees and one tea

five beers and two coffees and one cola

two colas and a beer

4. In each of the following sentences replace the form of the verb kaan *was* by the appropriate form of bikuun *will be*. The first two are completed.

(1) 'aḥmad kaan mašġuul. — 'aḥmad bikuun mašġuul.

(2) 'ana kunt mašġuul ktiir. — bakuun mašġuul ktiir.

nšaa*ll*a ssafra kaanat mniiḥa?

'ana w'aḥmad, kunna mašġuuliin ktiir.

'aḥmad wyuusif, kaanu ma9 lmudiir.

'aḥmad, kaan lyoom filbeet.

5. In each of the following sentences replace the singular verb by the corresponding plural, changing anything in the rest of the sentence that needs to be changed. The first two are completed.

(1) 'eemta bitkuun faaḍi ? — 'eemta bitkuunu faaḍyiin ?

(2) 'eemta bitkuun ḥaaḍir? — 'eemta bitkuunu ḥaaḍriin ?

raayiḥ 'akuun mašġuul ktiir.

bikuun faaḍi bukra ?

bitkuun ḥaaḍir ba9d šwayy?

nšaa*ll*a bakuun faaḍi ba9id yoomeen.

UNIT 11 • Telling time.

PATTERN SENTENCES

hour, watch	saa9a
Please, what time is it ?	min faḍlak, 'addeeš ssaa9a ?
It's six thirty.	ssaa9a sitte wnuṣṣ.
early	bakkiir
That's all right. It's still early.	ma9aleeš. lissa bakkiir.
work	šuġul
Do you have some work ?	fii 9aleek šuġul ?
eight o'clock	ssaa9a tamaanye
No, but I have to return home before eight o'clock.	la'. bass laazim 'arja9 9albeet, 'abl ssaa9a tamaanye.
out of order (f)	xarbaane
My watch is out of order.	saa9ti xarbaane.
repairing	taṣliiḥ
It needs repairing.	bidha taṣliiḥ.
cleaning	tanḍiif
It needs cleaning, too.	bidha tanḍiif, kamaan.
watchmaker	saa9aati
Where is there a good watchmaker ?	ween fii saa9aati mniiḥ ?
look, see	šuuf
across from	'baal
Look, there's a good watchmaker across from the Post Office.	šuuf. fii saa9aati mniiḥ, 'baal lbooṣṭa.

prices	'as9aar
But how are his prices ?	bass, kiif 'as9aaro ?
reasonable (f)	ma9'uule
His prices are reasonable.	'as9aaro ma9'uule.

Alternate expressions

she delays	bit'axxir
My watch is losing time.	saa9ti bit'axxir.
she advances	bit'addim
My watch is gaining time.	saa9ti bit'addim.
stopped (f)	waa'fe
My watch has stopped.	saa9ti waa'fe.

Additional vocabulary

alarm clock	saa9a mnabbih
hand	'iid
wrist watch	saa9it 'iid
pocket	jeeb
pocket watch	saa9it jeeb

STRUCTURE SENTENCES

I. Time expressions

It's one o'clock.	ssaa9a waḥde.
It's two o'clock.	ssaa9a tinteen.
It's three o'clock.	ssaa9a tlaate.

It's six thirty.	ssaa9a sitte wnuṣṣ.
quarter	rubu9
It's six fifteen.	ssaa9a sitte wrubu9.
third	tult
It's six twenty.	ssaa9a sitte wtult.
except, minus	('i)lla
It's a quarter to six.	ssaa9a sitte ('i)lla rubu9.
It's twenty minutes to six.	ssaa9a sitte ('i)lla tult.
It's five minutes past six.	ssaa9a sitte wxamse.
It's six thirty-five.	ssaa9a sitte wnuṣṣ wxamse.
It's five minutes to six.	ssaa9a sitte ('i)lla xamse.
It's six twenty-five.	ssaa9a sitte wnuṣṣ ('i)lla xamse.
come (m)	ta9aal
minute	d'ii'a
Come after one minute.	ta9aal ba9d d'ii'a.
come (f)	ta9aali
time	wa't
Come on time.	ta9aali 9alwa't.
come (pl)	ta9aalu
minutes	da'aayi'
Come after five minutes.	ta9aalu ba9id xamis da'aayi'.

2. The preposition 9ala

We want to go to the market.	bidna nruuḥ 9assuu'.
He wants to go home.	biddo yruuḥ 9albeet.
We're going to the coffee shop.	niḥna raayḥiin 9al'ahwe.
I didn't understand you.	maa fhimt 9aleek.
I didn't understand him.	maa fhimt 9alee(h).

Have you some work ?	fii 9aleekum šuġul ?
Has he some work ?	fii 9alee šuġul ?
I have a lot of work.	fii 9alayy šuġul ktiir.
The hotel is on your right.	l'uteel 9ala 'iidak lyamiin.
When are you going to Beirut ?	'eemta raayiḥ 9a(la) beeruut ?
With pleasure (lit. on my eye).	9ala 9eeni.
With pleasure (lit. on my head).	9a(la) raasi.

GRAMMAR

1. The preposition 9ala

The preposition 9ala has two principal meanings : «to,» indicating direction, and «on,» indicating position. It may also have the meaning of «incumbent upon» in certain expressions. The word has four variants.

(1) 9ala, when followed by a word without the prefix for «the» : 9ala yamiinak *to your right.*

(2) 9a-, when followed by a word with the prefix for «the» : 9alyamiin *to the right* ; also, optionally, in the cases of (1) above : 9abeeruut *to Beirut.*

(3) 9alee-, when followed by pronoun endings, (except -y *me*): 9aleek *on you.*

(4) 9alay-, when followed by -y *me* : 9alayy *on me.*

2. Types of roots

The typical root consists of three consonants in a fixed order.

Changing the order results in a non-existent root or a root with a different meaning. There are four main types of roots :

(1) *Regular.* All the consonants of the root appear in all words containing the root, e.g. *R* : ftḥ *opening* in :

fataḥ *he opened*

faatiḥ *open*

maftuuḥ *opened*

muftaaḥ *key*

(2) *Doubled.* Essentially like regular roots, but with the last two consonants identical, e.g. *R* : ḥbb *loving* in :

ḥabb *he loved, liked*

ḥabiib *loved one*

maḥbuub *loved*

ḥubb *love*

(3) *Hollow.* The second consonant is w or y, but this consonant is unstable, alternating between w, y, long vowel, glottal stop ('), and nothing, e.g. *R* : zwr *visiting* in :

zaar *he visited*

bizuur *he visits*

zaayir *visiting*

zuwwaar *visitors*

ziyaara *visit*

zurt *I visited*

(4) *Weak.* The last consonant is w or y, and behaves much as in a hollow root, e.g. *R* : b'y *remaining* in :

bi'i *he remained*

bi'yat *she remained*

bib'a *he remains*

baa'i *remaining* (*m*)

baa'ye *remaining* (*f*)

Roots that begin with w- and some that begin with glottal stop (') show alternations somewhat like the hollow and weak roots. For example :

R : wld *begetting* in :

walad *boy, child*

waalid *begetter (i.e. father)*

miilaad *birth*

R : 'xd *taking* in :

'axad *he took*

byaaxud *he takes*

xood *take !*

3. Noun and adjective plurals

Arabic noun and adjective plurals differ from the corresponding English forms in two principal ways : the plural usually sounds quite different from the singular, and the form of the plural is usually not predictable.

It is traditional to divide Arabic plurals into two classes : *sound* and *broken*. There are two varieties of sound plurals : those ending in -aat and those ending in -iin. The broken plurals show more variety ; some grammars list about two dozen kinds, but many of these are quite rare. Some nouns have more than one plural.

Sound plurals in -aat

These frequently correlate with an underlying feminine T-noun in the singular, and for this reason are often called sound feminine plurals. This plural rarely occurs with adjectives.

singular	*plural*	
'unşliyye	'unşliyyaat	*consulate*
sayyaara	sayyaaraat	*car*

saa9a	saa9aat	*hour, watch*
war'a	war'aat	*piece of paper*
bint	banaat	*girl*
mustašfa	mustašfayaat	*hospital*
maḥall	maḥallaat	*place*
maṭaar	maṭaaraat	*airport*
'uteel	'uteelaat	*hotel*

Sound plurals in -iin

These frequently correlate with singulars that may refer to masculine human beings, and for this reason are often called sound masculine plurals.

mwaẓẓaf	mwaẓẓafiin	*official*
mulḥaq	mulḥaqiin	*attaché*
mustašaar	mustašaariin	*counselor*
ṣuḥufi	ṣuḥufiyyiin	*journalist*
sane	sniin	*year*
ḥaaḍir	ḥaaḍriin	*ready*
naazil	naazliin	*staying*
faaḍi	faaḍyiin	*free*
ṭayyib	ṭayybiin	*good*
mabṣuuṭ	mabṣuuṭiin	*well*
mašġuul	mašġuuliin	*busy*
mit'assif	mit'assfiin	*sorry*

Broken plurals

These plurals have the same root as the singular, but a different pattern. They are more common than the sound plural.

kbiir	kbaar	*big, old*
żġiir	żġaar	*small, young*
rxiiṣ	rxaaṣ	*inexpensive*
mniiḥ	mnaaḥ	*good*
suu'	swaa'	*market*
baab	bwaab	*door*
walad	wlaad	*boy, child*
'alam	'laam	*pencil*
war'a	wraa'	*piece of paper*
yoom	'ayyaam	*day*
żaabiṭ	żubbaaṭ	*officer*
naayib	nuwwaab	*deputy*
mudiir	mudara(a')	*director*
ra'iis	ru'asa(a')	*head man*
'irš	'ruuš	*piastre*
beet	byuut	*house*
muftaaḥ	mafatiiḥ	*key*
'usbuu9	'asabii9	*week*
šubbaak	šababiik	*window*
maṭ9am	maṭaa9im	*restaurant*
maktab	makaatib	*office*
xaarṭa, xariiṭa	xaraayiṭ	*map*
jariide	jaraayid	*newspaper*
kursi	karaasi	*chair*
'ahwe	'ahaawi	*coffee house*
šahir	'ašhur	*month*
9eele	9iyal	*family*
jum9a	juma9	*week*

'uuḍa	'uwaḍ	*room*
ktaab	kutub	*book*

Occasionally the plural is a suppletion form (i.e. has a different root).

mara	niswaan	*woman, wife*

Some nouns have a special *counting plural*, used after the numbers 3-10.

šahir	tušhur (in tlat tušhur)	*month*
yoom	tiyyaam (in tlat tiyyaam)	*day*

The examples above are for illustration; for complete listings see the vocabulary at the end of the book.

4. Velarization by assimilation

If the root of a word has one or more velarized consonants, the velarization generally carries over to other consonants in the word. We call this *velarization by assimilation.* In the transcription we mark it only under two conditions: when velarization by assimilation affects t, d, s, and only when these form a cluster with a velarized root consonant. The following examples will illustrate this.

root	*transcribed*	*pronounced*	
9ṭy	bta9ṭiini	bṭa9ṭiini	*you give me*
ṭyr	maṭaaraat	maṭaaraaṭ	*airports*
ḥṭṭ	ḥaṭṭeet	ḥaṭṭeeṭ	*I put*
'wḍ	'uuḍitna	'uuḍiṭna	*our room*
'wḍ	'uuṭṭi	'uuṭṭi	*my room*
ṣlḥ	taṣliiḥ	ṭaṣliiḥ	*repairing*

nḍf	tanḍiif	ṭanḍiif	*cleaning*
bṣṭ	mabṣuuṭ	*mab*ṣuuṭ	*well*
fḍl	tfaḍḍal	ṭfaḍḍal	*please*

DRILLS

1. Give appropriate replies to the following sentences.

min faḍlak, 'addeeš ssaa9a ?
'eemta laazim tirja9 9albeet ?
fii 9aleek šuġul ?
fii saa9aati mniiḥ hoon ?
kiif 'as9aaro ?

2. In each of the following sentences replace the expression ssaa9a xamse by a different time expression.

laazim 'arja9 9albeet 'abl ssaa9a xamse.
ta9aal ba9d ssaa9a xamse.
'aḥmad kaan hoon ssaa9a xamse.
ta9aalu lahoon ssaa9a xamse.
nšaa*ll*a bašuufkum ssaa9a xamse.
bakuun hunaak ssaa9a xamse.

3. Go through the following sentences replacing the noun in parentheses by the appropriate pronoun ending. The first three are completed.

(1) feen ḥaṭṭeet (ššanta) ? — feen ḥaṭṭeetha ?
(2) feen ḥaṭṭeetu (ššanta) ? — feen ḥaṭṭeetuuha ?
(3) ḥaṭṭeena (ššanta) hoon. — ḥaṭṭeenaaha hoon.
bi9raf ('aḥmad) ?
bašuuf (lmudiir) ba9d šwayy.
ḥaṭṭeet (lmuftaaḥ) 9aṭṭaawle.
'išrab (l'ahwe).
'išrab (ššaay).
'is'al ('aḥmad).

mumkin nšuuf (lmudiir)?	bukra bazuur (9eelto).
mumkin 'ašuuf (l'uuḍa)?	bitlaa'i (lxaarṭa) filmaktab.
leeš maa zurt ('aḥmad) fii beeruut?	bidjiib ('aḥmad) ma9ak?
min faḍlak, dill ('aḥmad) 9al'uteel.	feen ('aḥmad)?
	'eemta biddak tšuuf ('aḥmad)?

4. Go through the sentences of Drill 3 changing all the singular verbs to plural and replacing the noun in parentheses by the appropriate pronoun ending.

5. Give the following times in Arabic.

1:00	1:05	12:20	2:40
2:15	10:00	11:00	11:15
3:20	12:30	3:15	4:55
6:00	4:00	7:45	10:56
3:40	4:10	12:00	6:20
2:00	3:00	3:02	5:15
9:45	9:30	7:05	6:45
9:00	5:00	8:50	1:12
5:35	7:25	8:35	6:25

Unit 12 • Eating out.

PATTERN SENTENCES

opinion	ra'i
we eat	naakul
What do you say we go eat?	šuu ra'yak nruuḥ naakul?
idea	fikra
That's a good idea.	fikra mniiḥa.
you prefer	bitfaḍḍil
Where do you prefer we go?	ween bitfaḍḍil nruuḥ?
she makes a difference	btifri'
It makes no difference to me.	maa btifri' ma9i.
important	muhimm
clean	nḍiif
food	'akil
The important thing is to find a clean place and good food.	lmuhimm nlaa'i maḥall nḍiif, w'akil ṭayyib.
All right, then.	ṭayyib, 'izan.
let us	xalliina
the National Restaurant	lmaṭ9am lwaṭani
Let's go to the National Restaurant.	xalliina nruuḥ 9almaṭ9am lwaṭani.

(In the restaurant)

Welcome! What will you order?	'ahla wsahla. šuu btu'*u*mru?
chicken	jaaj

roasted	mḥammar
plate	ṣaḥin
salad	ṣalaṭa
Please bring me roast chicken and a salad.	min faḍlak, jibli jaaj mḥammar, wṣaḥin ṣalaṭa.
soup	šooraba
Please bring me a bowl of soup.	min faḍlak, jibli ṣaḥin šooraba.
squash	kuusa
stuffed	maḥši
vine leaves	wara' 9inab
And stuffed squash with vine leaves.	wkuusa maḥši, ma9 wara' 9inab.
second, other	taani
Do you want anything else ?	btu'*u*mru šii taani ?
No, thanks.	la'. salaamtak.
Would you like anything to drink ?	bitḥibbu tišrabu šii ?
arak (an alcoholic beverage)	9ara'
Please bring us two araks.	min faḍlak, jib*i*lna tneen 9ara'.
you want	bitriidu
Do you want anything sweet ?	bitriidu šii ḥilu ?
What do you have ?	šuu fii 9indkum ?
baklava	ba'laawe
kenafeh	knaafe
maamul	ma9muul
There is baklava and kenafeh and maamul.	fii ba'laawe, wiknaafe, wma9muul.

fruits	fawaakih
Don't you have any fruit ?	maa fii 9indkum fawaakih ?
of course	ma9luum
Of course we have.	ma9luum, 9inna.
bananas	mooz
apples	tuffaaḥ
grapes	9inab
figs	tiin
There are bananas and apples and grapes and figs.	fii mooz, wtuffaaḥ, w9inab, wtiin.
Bring me some grapes, please.	jibli 9inab, min faḍlak.
Bring *me* some apples.	jibli 'ana tuffaaḥ.
bill, account	ḥsaab
Please give us the bill.	min faḍlak, 'a9ṭiina liḥsaab.

Additional vocabulary

boiled	masluu'
bottle	'anniine
bread	xubz
breakfast	fṭuur
broiled	mašwi
butter	zibde
cheese	jibne
eggs	beeḍ
evening meal	9aša
fish	samak
fork	šooke
fried	ma'li

glass	kaas
hors d'œuvres (with drinks)	maaza
ice	talj
juice	9aṣiir
knife	sikkiin
meat	laḥme
menu	liista
midday meal	ġada
napkin	fuuṭa
pepper	filfil
rice	ruzz
salt	miliḥ
spoon	ma9la'a
vegetables	xuḍra
wine	nbiid

STRUCTURE SENTENCES

1. Verb phrases

Would you like to go with me?	bitḥibb truuḥ ma9i?
What do you say we go eat?	šuu ra'yak nruuḥ naakul?
What do you want to drink?	šuu bitriid tišrab?
Would you like anything to drink?	bitḥibbu tišrabu šii?
Where do you prefer we go?	ween bitfaḍḍil nruuḥ?
He prefers to stay at home.	bifaḍḍil yib'a filbeet.
I'll go to see him tomorrow.	baruuḥ 'ašuufo bukra.

GRAMMAR

1. Verb phrases

Most English verbs have a general form that can be preceded by *to*, as in *to see*, *to go*, *to stay*. This general form does not specify any particular doer of the action, and is often called the infinitive. The infinitive often appears in phrases together with another verb, as in *I'd like to go to see him*.

The Arabic verb, in contrast to English, has no infinitive ; all verbs indicate the doer of the action. When Arabic verbs occur together in phrases, each verb has its own subject marker. Thus the phrase šuu bitḥibb taakul ? *what would you like to eat ?* is literally « what would you like you eat ? »

The first verb in the phrase may or may not have the B-prefix, depending on what precedes. The second and subsequent verbs have (almost invariably) the simple prefix.

2. Types of patterns

In the Grammar of Unit 10 it was shown that it is usually possible to analyze the stem of an Arabic word as consisting of two elements: a root and a pattern. The root consists of consonants, typically three in number and in a fixed order, having a general lexical meaning. The pattern consists typically of vowels staggered in respect to the consonants of the root. Patterns frequently have a grammatical meaning. Note that neither the root nor the pattern ever occurs alone (compare the *re-* and *-ceive* of English *receive*).

In its simplest form, the pattern consists of one or more vowels and no other material. This will be called the *simple* pattern. For example :

root	*pattern*	*stem*	
ktb	--aa-	ktaab	*book*

9rf	- -a-	(bi)9raf	*he knows*
w'f	-aa-i-	waa'if	*stopped*
šrf	-a-a-	šaraf	*honor*

In some cases, a given pattern is associated with one or more specific added features in such a way that it is best to regard the combination as a unit, often with a meaning of its own. Such a combination will be called a *pattern complex*. Among the more common added features are prefixed m-, t-, consonant doubling, and vowel length, including also combinations of these. The following examples illustrate some of the possibilities.

root	*pattern complex*	*stem*	
ktb	ma- -a-	maktab	*office*
šġl	ma- -uu-	mašġuul	*busy*
w'f	-a- -i-	wa''if	*stop !*
wẓf	m-a- -a-	mwaẓẓaf	*official*
ẓbṭ	-u- -aa-	ẓubbaaṭ	*officers*
s9d	-aa-a-	saa9ad	*he helped*
s9d	m-aa-i-	msaa9id	*assistant*
šrf	-a- -a-	šarraf	*he honored*
šrf	t-a- -a-	tšarraf	*he was honored*
nḍf	ta- -ii-	tanḍiif	*cleaning*
'sf	mit-a- -i-	mit'assif	*sorry*

DRILLS

1. Give appropriate replies to the following sentences.

'ahlan wasahlan.	šuu btu'*u*mru ?
kiif ḥaalak ?	šuu fii 9indkum ?
šuu ra'yak nruuḥ naakul ?	šuu bitḥibbu tišrabu ?

feen bitfaḍḍil nruuḥ ?
šuu ra'yak nruuḥ 9almaṭ9am lwaṭani ?
kiif lmaṭ9am lwaṭani ? nḍiif ?
kiif l'akil hunaak ?
feen haada lmaṭ9am ?
maa fii 9indkum biira ?
bitḥibbu tišrabu šii ma9 l'akil ?
bitḥibbu kaas 9ara', 'abl l'akil?
bitriidu šii ḥilu ?

2. In each of the following sentences replace the words in parentheses by a different expression denoting something to eat or drink.

min faḍlək jibli ('anniint nbiid).
min faḍlak jib*i*lna (tneen 9ara').
fii 9indkum (kuusa maḥši) ?
maa baḥibb (lbeeḍ).
biddak (samak), willa (laḥme)?
jibli (tuffaaḥ).
(rruzz) mniiḥ ktiir.

3. Match each of the following sentences with a sentence beginning with xalliina *let us.* The first two are completed.

(1) binruuḥ 9almaṭ9am.	xalliina nruuḥ 9almaṭ9am.
(2) bnis'al 'aḥmad.	xalliina nis'al 'aḥmad.

bnišrab 'ahwe.
binlaa'i maḥall nḍiif.
binruuḥ naakul.
binjiib 'aḥmad ma9na.
bniftaḥ ššababiik.
bnib'a hoon.
binšuufo bukra.
binruuḥ ma9 'aḥmad.

4. In each of the following sentences replace the singular verb by the corresponding plural. The first two are completed.

(1) šuu bitḥibb tišrab ?	šuu bitḥibbu tišrabu ?
(2) 'aja yšuufni.	'aju yšuufuuni.

bitḥibb truuḥ ma9i ?
huwwe biḥibb yšuufak.
nšaa*ll*a bitruuḥ dzuuro bukra.
ba9deen barja9 'aakul.

feen bitfaḍḍil nruuḥ ?

baḥibb 'alaa'i maṭ9am mniiḥ.

barja9 'ašuufkum ba9d šwayy.

baḥibb 'aaji ma9ak.

hiyye bitḥibb tšuuf šuu bi9malu.

baḥibb 'a9arrfak 9assayyid 'aḥmad.

ṭayyib, 'izan. baruuḥ 'as'alo.

bifaḍḍil yib'a filbeet.

laazim tirja9 tšuufni.

bafaḍḍil 'ab'a hoon.

'eemta bitfaḍḍil 'aaji ?

'eemta biiji yšuufna ?

tfaḍḍal zuurna filbeet.

baḥibb 'arja9 'ašuufo.

ta9aal bukra.

'ijiit 'ašuuf lmudiir.

tfaḍḍal striiḥ.

UNIT 13 • Buying some cloth.

PATTERN SENTENCES

Persons: W: Mr. West; A: Ahmad; C: Cloth merchant.

you help	tsaa9id
I buy	'aštri
suit	badle
W: Ahmad, could you help me buy a suit?	mumkin tsaa9idni, yaa 'aḥmad, 'aštri badle?
all, every	kull
pleasure	suruur
A: With pleasure.	bikull suruur.
you want her	biddak yyaaha
What kind of suit do you want?	šuu lbadle lli biddak yyaaha?
I buy for myself	'aštriili
summer (adj.)	ṣeefi, f. ṣeefiyye
winter (adj.)	šatawi, f. šatawiyye
W: I want to buy myself a summer suit.	biddi 'aštriili badle ṣeefiyye.
cloth	'maaš
Do you know where I can find some good cloth?	bti9raf ween balaa'i 'maaš mniiḥ?
wait	stanna
A: Please wait a moment. I'll go right along with you.	min faḍlak, stanna šwayy. halla baruuḥ ma9ak.

I put on	'albas
jacket	jakeet
I just want to put on my jacket.	bass biddi 'albas ljakeet.

(In the shop)

kind, sort	jins
you want him	biddah yyaa(h)
C: What kind of cloth do you want?	šuu jins li'maaš lli biddak yyaa?
W: I want something for summer.	biddi šii ṣeefi.
choose	na''i
C: Here you are. Choose what you want.	tfaḍḍal na''i lli biddak yyaa.
here is	hayy
everything	kullši
Here's everything right in front of you.	hayy kullši 'uddaamak.
price	si9ir, ḥa''
meter	mitir
A: What's the price per meter?	šuu si9r lmitir?
word	kilme
C: Do you want the bottom price?	biddak kilme waḥde?
A: Of course.	ma9luum.
I sold it	bi9to
dinar	diinaar
two dinars	diinaareen

three dinars	tlat dananiir
C: A little while ago I sold it for two dinars.	'abl šwayy, bi9to bdiinaareen.
for your sake	min šaan xaaṭrak
I give it to you	ba9ṭiik yyaa(h)
But for your sake I'll give it to you for a dinar and a half.	bass min šaan xaaṭrak, ba9ṭiik yyaa bdiinaar wnuṣṣ.
usually	9aadatan
he is necessary for you	bilzamak
How many meters do you usually need?	kam mitir 9aadatan bilzamak?
cut for me	'i'ṭa9li
W: Please cut me three meters.	min faḍlak, 'i'ṭa9li tlaat mtaar.
C: Blessed (an expression said to someone who has just purchased a new article).	mabruuk.
W: May God bless you (in reply).	'a*ll*a ybaarik fiik.

Additional vocabulary

I. Articles of clothing

	sing.	*plural*
blouse	bluuze	-aat
dress	fuṣṭaan	faṣaṭiin.
hat	burneeṭa	baraniiṭ
handkerchief	maḥrame	maḥaarim
necktie	gravaat	gravattaat
shirt	'amiiṣ	'umṣaan
pair of shoes	kundara	kanaadir

skirt	tannuura	tananiir
socks (pl)		kalsaat
undershirt	'amiiṣ	'umṣaan
	taḥtaani	taḥtaaniyye
undershorts	kalsoon	-aat

2. Kinds of cloth

cotton	'uṭun
linen	kittaan
silk	ḥariir
wool	ṣuuf

3. Measures

dra' (an arm's length)	draa9
two dra's	draa9een
three dra's	tlat tudru9
yard	yard, pl. -aat
length	ṭuul
width	9arḍ

4. Seasons

the spring	rrabii9
the summer	ṣṣeef
the fall	lxariif
the winter	ššita
the summertime	ṣṣeefiyye
the wintertime	ššatawiyye

STRUCTURE SENTENCES

1. The suffix -l-

he became	ṣaar
he became for me	ṣarli
I've been here a month and a half.	ṣarli hoon šahr wnuṣṣ.
bring	jiib
bring to me	jibli
Bring me one beer.	jibli waaḥad biira.
I buy	'aštri
I buy for myself	'aštriili
I want to buy myself a new hat.	biddi 'aštriili burneeṭa jdiide.
you give permission	btismaḥ
you give permission to me	btismaḥli
Will you excuse me ?	btismaḥli šwayy ?
stop	wa''if
stop for me	wa''ifli
Stop here for me.	wa''ifli hoon.
I brought	jibt
I brought for you	jibtillak
I brought you the book.	jibtillak liktaab.
you know	bti9raf
you know for me	bti9rafli
Do you know where there's a good bookstore here ?	bti9rafli ween fii maktabe mniiḥa hoon ?

2. The particle yyaa-

you want him	biddak yyaa(h)
What kind of cloth do you want?	šuu jins li'maaš lli biddak yyaa?
you want her	biddak yyaaha
What kind of suit do you want?	šuu lbadle lli biddak yyaaha?
Choose what you want.	na''i lli biddak yyaa.
I give you it	ba9ṭiik yyaa(h)
I'll give it to you for three dinars.	ba9ṭiik yyaa bitlat dananiir.
put them for me	ḥuṭṭilli yyaahum
Put them on the table for me.	ḥuṭṭilli yyaahum 9aṭṭaawle.

GRAMMAR

1. The suffix -l-

The suffix -l- *to, for, on behalf of* is added to verb forms and some other words. The pronoun endings (-i, -ak, -na, etc.) are then added to the -l-, as in jibli *bring to me!* and jibilna *bring to us!* Note that the pronoun ending for «me» is -i (and not -ni).

Most words having a long vowel before the final consonant shorten this vowel when the suffix -l- is added. For example, jiib plus -li becomes jibli.

When the underlying word ends in two consonants, or (optionally) with the subject marker -t *you (m), I*, the -l- has the variant -ill-, as in jibtillak *I brought for you*, ḥaṭṭeetillak (or ḥaṭṭeetlak) *I put for you*.

This suffix has two main uses. One is to indicate the second or indirect object of a verb (i.e. the person or thing indirectly affected by the action) as in jibli waaḥad 'ahwe *bring me a coffee.* The other use is to indicate the person in regard to whom the statement is being made, as in bti9rafli ween fii saa9aati mniiḥ hoon ? *do you know for me where there's a good watchmaker here?* In this second use it is frequently not translated in the English equivalent.

2. The particle yyaa-

This particle cannot be translated ; it is, so to speak, an «empty» word that serves as a support for a pronoun ending. The forms are as follows :

yyaa(h) *him*

yyaaha *her*

yyaahum *them*

yyaak *you (m)*

yyaaki *you (f)*

yyaakum *you (pl)*

yyaani *me*

yyaana *us*

Note that the pronoun ending for «me» is -ni (and not -y).

The particle yyaa- plus a pronoun ending is used in expressions involving two pronoun endings that go with a single verb or verb-like word. Arabic cannot have two pronoun endings attached to one word, and if the expression requires two, then one goes with the verb or verb-like word, and the other goes with yyaa-.

3. Suffix tense verb classes — I

There are four main classes of suffix tense verbs, some with subdivisions : Regular, Doubled, Hollow, and Weak. In what follows we discuss the Regular class. The remainder will be discussed in the Grammar of Unit 14.

(1) *Regular.* The examples are : 'addam *he advanced*, saa9ad *he helped*, sa'al *he asked*, fihim *he understood*.

he	'addam	saa9ad	sa'al	fihim
she	'addamat	saa9adat	sa'lat	fihmat
they	'addamu	saa9adu	sa'alu	fihmu
you (m)	'addamt	saa9att	sa'alt	fhimt
you (f)	'addamti	saa9atti	sa'alti	fhimti
you (pl)	'addamtu	saa9attu	sa'altu	fhimtu
I	'addamt	saa9att	sa'alt	fhimt
we	'addamna	saa9adna	sa'alna	fhimna

The verbs of this class have in the «he» form a stem that ends in a single consonant preceded by a short vowel, either *a* or *i* (*u* does not occur).

The short *a* drops before the subject marker -at *she* (e.g. sa'lat), unless it is «protected.» It may be protected in two different ways : by an immediately preceding consonant cluster (e.g. 'addamat) or by a preceding long vowel (e.g. saa9adat).

In the fihim type, the second short *i* drops before subject markers beginning with a vowel (e.g. fihmat, fihmu), and the first short *i* drops before subject markers beginning with a consonant (e.g. fhimt, fhimna).

Most of the verbs of this class have regular roots, though doubled and hollow roots occur.

Like 'addam (bi'addim) *advance*:

'axxar	(bi'axxir)	*delay*
faḍḍal	(bifaḍḍil)	*prefer*
sadda'	(bisaddi')	*believe*
sakkar	(bisakkir)	*close*
sallam	(bisallim)	*keep safe, greet*

šarraf	(bišarrif)	*honor*
wa''af	(biwa''if)	*stop*
9arraf	(bi9arrif)	*introduce*
tfaḍḍal	(bitfaḍḍal)	*be kind enough to*
tšarraf	(bitšarraf)	*be honored*

Like saa9ad (bisaa9id) *help* :

baarak	(bibaarik)	*bless*

Like sa'al (bis'al) *ask* :

'aṭa9	(bi'ṭa9)	*cut*
'akal	(byaakul)	*eat*
'amar	(bu'mur)	*order*
'axad	(byaaxud)	*take*
fara'	(bifri')	*make a difference*
fataḥ	(biftaḥ)	*open*
ḥafaẓ	(biḥfaẓ)	*keep*
samaḥ	(bismaḥ)	*permit*
šakar	(buškur)	*thank*

Like fihim (bifham) *understand* :

libis	(bilbas)	*dress*
lizim	(bilzam)	*be necessary*
riji9	(birja9)	*return*
širib	(bišrab)	*drink*
9imil	(bi9mal)	*do*
9irif	(bi9raf)	*know*

The preceding includes all Regular verbs that have occurred in Units 1-13, with the exception of tikram *with pleasure*. This verb has only three forms : tikram, tikrami, tikramu.

DRILLS

1. Give appropriate replies to the following sentences.

mumkin tsaa9idni 'aštri badle ?	šuu jins li'maaš lli biddak yyaa(h) ?
šuu lbadle lli biddak yyaaha?	'addeeš ḥa" ddraa9 ?
biddak badle ṣeefiyye, willa šatawiyye ?	kam yard 9aadatan bilzamak ?
bti9raf ween balaa'i 'maaš mniiḥ ?	mabruuk.

2. In each of the following sentences replace the word in parentheses by an expression denoting a different article of clothing.

biddi 'aštriili (badle).	mumkin tsaa9idni 'aštri (jakeet) ?
šuu si9r (l'amiiṣ) ?	
fii 9indkum (baraniiṭ) ?	fii 9indkum ('umṣaan) ?

3. In each of the following sentences replace -lak *for you* (*m*) by -lkum *for you* (*pl*). The first two are completed.

(1) bajiblak lbadle bukra.	bajib*i*lkum lbadle bukra.
(2) ba'ṭa9lak tlaat mtaar.	ba'ṭa9*i*lkum tlaat mtaar.
biddak 'aštriilak šii mnilbalad ?	bana"iilak šii mniiḥ.
	bašuflak lbeet.
ba9raflak saa9aati mniiḥ.	bas'allak yuusif.

4. Go through the sentences of Drill 3 replacing -lak *for you* (*m*) by -lo *for him*.

5. Go through the following sentences adding the following to the verb forms :

-li *for me*

-lna *for us*

The first two are completed for -li *for me.*

(1) jiib tneen 'ahwe.	jibli tneen 'ahwe.
(2) 'ištri badle.	'ištriili badle.
'i'ṭa9 mitir wnuṣṣ.	bukra bijiibu lbadle.
'iftaḥ lbaab.	na''i badle mniiḥa.
xud lbadle.	'eemta bitšuuf lbeet ?
šuuf 'addeeš ssaa9a.	bti9raf saa9aati mniiḥ ?
bištri sagaayir.	wa''if hoon.

6. Match each of the following sentences with a sentence beginning with the appropriate form from the following list. The first two are completed.

xalliini *let me*	xallii(h) *let him*
xalliina *let us*	xalliiha *let her*
	xalliihum *let them*

(1) bas'alhum.	xalliini 'as'alhum.
(2) bnišrab 'ahwe.	xalliina nišrab 'ahwe.
basakkir lbaab.	baštri badle.
binruuḥ 9almaṭ9am lwaṭani.	bnib'a hoon.
bajiibo ma9i.	bnistanna 'aḥmad.
biftaḥ ššanta.	biruuḥu ma9 'aḥmad.
bnistriiḥ halla.	biiju bukra.
bidill 'aḥmad 9al'uteel.	bisaa9du 'aḥmad.
bana''i lli biddi yyaa(h).	btis'alo.
bib'u hoon.	btis'alni.

7. In each of the following sentences replace the word in parentheses by the appropriate form of yyaa- plus pronoun ending. The first two are completed.

(1) ba9ṭiik (ljariide).	ba9ṭiik yyaaha.
(2) bašuflak ('aḥmad).	bašuflak yyaa(h).
bajiblak (lbadle) bukra.	ḥuṭṭilli (ssagaayir) 9aṭṭaawle.
bas'allak (yuusif).	'a*ll*a yxalliilak (wlaadak).
štriili (ljakeet).	'a9ṭiini (lmuftaaḥ).
ftaḥli (lbaab).	jibli (l'umṣaan).

UNIT 14 • At the tailor's.

PATTERN SENTENCES

Persons: W: Mr. West; A: Ahmad; R: Rashed.

tailor	xayyaaṭ
W: Now, Ahmad, I want you to find me a good tailor.	halla, yaa 'aḥmad, biddi yyaak tlaa'iili xayyaaṭ mniiḥ.
close to	'ariib min
far from	b9iid min
station	mḥaṭṭa
A: I know a good tailor near the station.	ba9raflak xayyaaṭ mniiḥ, 'ariib min limḥaṭṭa.
W: Are you free to go now?	faaḍi nruuḥ halla?
A: Certainly. Certainly.	ma9luum. ma9luum.

(At the tailor's)

A: Hello, *S*ayyid Rashed.	marḥaba, yaa sayyid raašid.
R: Hello, Sayyid Ahmad. Welcome. You honor us.	marḥabteen, sayyid 'aḥmad. 'ahlan wasahlan. šarraftuuna.
A: We are honored (in reply). How are you these days?	tšarrafna. kiif ḥaalak haliyyaam?
R: Let us thank God. Not bad.	nuškur '*all*a. miš baṭṭaal.
A: I'd like to introduce you to Mr. West.	baḥibb 'a9arrfak 9ala mistir west.
Mr. West is a journalist from America.	mistir west ṣuḥufi min 'ameerka.

R: I'm honored. You're very welcome.	tšarrafna. 'ahlan wasahlan.
prosperous, successful	mwaffa'
A: How's business? Prosperous?	kiif šuġlak? nšaal*l*a mwaffa'?
R: Well, it's not very good.	saddi', miš ktiir mniiḥ.
business	'ašġaal
people	naas
money	maṣaari
Business is at a standstill, and people haven't any money.	l'ašġaal waa'fe, winnaas maa fii ma9ha maṣaari.
service	xidme
Now, can I do anything for you?	halla, btu'*u*mru šii xidme?
piece	ša'fe
A: Why, yes. We have a piece of cloth with us.	saddi'. fii ma9na ša'fit 'maaš.
cut out a garment	faṣṣal bifaṣṣil
And Mr. West wants you to cut a suit out of it for him.	wmistir west, biddo tfaṣṣillo yyaaha badle
R: Welcome. With pleasure.	'ahlan wasahlan. bikull suruur.
color	loon
It's a very nice color.	loonha ktiir ḥilu.
I take	'aaxud
measurement	'yaas
If you please, I'll take your measurement, Mr. West.	tfaḍḍal 'aaxud 'yaasak, yaa mistir west.

A: How much are you going to charge for it?	'addeeš raḥtaaxud 9aleeha?
as much as, whatever	'add maa
R: Whatever you want.	'add maa bitriid.
it means, that is, well...	ya9ni
A: Well, how much?	ya9ni, 'addeeš?
as much as, as	mitil maa
R: As much as I charged you last month.	mitil maa 'axatt minnak 'abil šahir.
A: All right.	ṭayyib mniiḥ.
to my place	la9indi
Monday	yoom ttineen
fitting	proova
R: (To Mr. West) Could you come here Monday to have a fitting?	mumkin tiiji la9indi yoom ttineen, taaxud proova?
what, which, any	'ayy
be convenient, be suitable	naasab binaasib
W: What time is convenient for you?	'ayy wa't binaasbak?
R: Any time after five o'clock. (To one of his boys) Zaki, go get us three coffees.	'ayy wa't ba9d ssaa9a xamse. yaa zaki, ruuḥ jib*i*lna tlaate 'ahwe.
necessary	ḍaruuri
bother	ġallab biġallib
yourself	ḥaalak
effendi (a term of address)	'afandi

A: It's not necessary to bother yourself, Rashed Effendi.	miš ḍaruuri tġallib ḥaalak, yaa raašid (')afandi.
trouble, bother	ġalabe
at all (with negative)	wala
R: It's no trouble at all. You're very welcome.	maa fii wala ġalabe. 'ahlan wasahlan fiikum.
A: & W: Always. (Expression said after drinking coffee and returning the cup.)	daayme.
R: Two healths (in reply).	ṣaḥḥteen.

(N. B. The expression daayme is not used if there is misfortune in the family of the host.)

Additional vocabulary

1. Days of the week

Sunday	(yoom) l'aḥad
Monday	(yoom) ttineen
Tuesday	(yoom) ttalaata
Wednesday	(yoom) l'arba9a
Thursday	(yoom) lxamiis
Friday	(yoom) ljum9a
Saturday	(yoom) ssabt

2. Color adjectives

	masc.	*fem.*	*plural*
black	'aswad	sooda	suud
blue	'azra'	zar'a	zuru'
green	'axḍar	xaḍra	xuḍur
red	'aḥmar	ḥamra	ḥumur
white	'abyaḍ	beeḍa	biiḍ
yellow	'aṣfar	ṣafra	ṣufur
brown	binni	binniyye	binniyyiin
gray	ramaadi	ramaadiyye	ramaadiyyiin

3. Sewing needs

	sing.	*plural*
button	zirr	zraar
needle	'ibre	'ubar
pin	dabbuus	dababiis
scissors	m'aṣṣ	m'aṣṣaat
thimble	kuštbaan	kašaatbiin
thread	xeeṭ	xiiṭaan

STRUCTURE SENTENCES

1. Noun annexion

the newspaper of today	jariitt lyoom
Who took today's newspaper?	miin 'axad jariitt lyoom?

don't forget	laa tinsa
the key of the door	muftaaḥ lbaab
Don't forget to bring the door key with you.	laa tinsa djiib ma9ak muftaaḥ lbaab.
the office of tourism	maktab ssiyaaḥa
Go to the Office of Tourism.	ruuḥ 9amaktab ssiyaaḥa.
the head man of the municipality	ra'iis lbaladiyye
Do you know the new mayor?	bti9raf ra'iis lbaladiyye jjdiid?
the age of your daughter	9umur bintak
How old is your small daughter?	šuu 9umur bintak ẓẓġiire?
the kind of cloth	jins li'maaš
What kind of cloth do you want?	šuu jins li'maaš lli biddak yyaa(h)?
the car of whom	sayyaarit miin
Whose car is this?	sayyaarit miin haadi?
an official of a government	mwaẓẓaf ḥukuume
Mr. Haddad is a government official.	ssayyid ḥaddaad mwaẓẓaf ḥukuume.
a piece of cloth	ša'fit 'maaš
We have a piece of cloth with us.	fii ma9na ša'fit 'maaš.
an officer of aviation	ẓaabiṭ ṭayaraan
Mr. West was an air force officer.	mistir west kaan ẓaabiṭ ṭayaraan.

the head man of the office of tourism	ra'iis maktab ssiyaaḥa
Do you know the head of the Office of Tourism ?	bti9raf ra'iis maktab ssiyaaḥa?

GRAMMAR

I. Noun annexion

A frequent construction in Arabic is one consisting of two or more nouns in a closely-knit arrangement called *annexion.* This is a translation of the Arabic grammatical term *'iḍaafe.* An example of annexion is the noun mwaẓẓaf *official* and the noun ḥukuume *government* in the phrase mwaẓẓaf ḥukuume *a government official.*

The annexion construction has the following special characteristics :

(1) The prefix for «the,» or a pronoun ending, may occur only once in the construction, and then only with the last noun. For example, with maktab *office* and mudiir *director* in that order we have the following possibilities : maktab mudiir *a director's office* ; maktab lmudiir *the director's office* ; with a pronoun ending, maktab mudiirna *our director's office.*

(2) Each noun «governs» the immediately following noun, which is «dependent.» All feminine T-nouns in a governing position have the combining form in -(i)t. For example, maktabe *library* and mudiir *director* combine as maktabt lmudiir *the director's library.*

(3) If the last noun is definite (i.e. has the prefix for «the,» or a pronoun ending, or belongs to the class called proper nouns), the construction as a whole is grammatically definite ; otherwise it is grammatically indefinite. For example, 9umur bintak *the age*

of your daughter and sayyaarit 'aḥmad *Ahmad's car*, are definite ; ša'fit 'maaš *a piece of cloth* is indefinite.

(4) An accompanying adjective follows the construction and modifies only one of the nouns. For example, 9umur bintak ẓẓġiire *the age of your small daughter*, sayyaarit 'aḥmad jjdiide *Ahmad's new car*, and ša'fit 'maaš ḥilwe *a nice piece of cloth*.

In meaning, the Arabic annexion phrase is the equivalent of various constructions in English: constructions with the possessive, as in *the girl's age* ; constructions with «of,» expressing a similar relation, as in *the age of the girl* ; noun phrases, as in *the door-key* (= *the key of the door*).

2. Suffix tense verb classes — II

In the Grammar of Unit 13 we discussed the Regular class. In what follows we discuss the remaining three classes : Doubled, Hollow, and Weak.

(1) *Doubled.* The example is dall *he directed.*

he	dall
she	dallat
they	dallu
you (m)	dalleet
you (f)	dalleeti
you (pl)	dalleetu
I	dalleet
we	dalleena

The verbs of this class have in the «he» form a stem that ends in a double consonant preceded by short *a*.

Before subject markers beginning with a consonant this stem is «extended» by -ee- (e.g. dalleet, dalleena).

Most of these verbs have doubled roots.

Like dall (bidill) *direct* :

ḥabb	(biḥibb)	*like, love*
ḥaṭṭ	(biḥuṭṭ)	*put*

(2) *Hollow.* The examples are : šaaf *he saw*, jaab *he brought*, staraaḥ *he rested.*

he	šaaf	jaab	staraaḥ
she	šaafat	jaabat	staraaḥat
they	šaafu	jaabu	staraaḥu
you (m)	šuft	jibt	staraḥt
you (f)	šufti	jibti	staraḥti
you (pl)	šuftu	jibtu	staraḥtu
I	šuft	jibt	staraḥt
we	šufna	jibna	staraḥna

The verbs of this class have in the «he» form a stem that ends in a single consonant preceded by long *aa*.

Before subject markers beginning with a consonant this long *aa* is replaced by a short vowel (e.g. šuft, šufna).

The replacement short vowel is *u* if the corresponding prefix tense has long *uu* (e.g. šaaf bišuuf) ; it is *i* if the corresponding prefix tense has the simple pattern -ii- (e.g. jaab bijiib) ; it is *a* if the corresponding prefix tense has a pattern complex (e.g. staraaḥ bistriiḥ).

All these verbs have hollow roots.

Like šaaf (bišuuf) *see* :

kaan	(bikuun)	*be*
raaḥ	(biruuḥ)	*go*
zaar	(bizuur)	*visit*

Like jaab (bijiib) *bring* :

baa9	(bibii9)	*sell*
ṣaar	(biṣiir)	*become*

Note : Omitted is the suffix tense of biriid *want* ; its occurrence is rare.

(3) *Weak.* The examples are: maša *he walked*, bi'i *he stayed*:

he	maša	bi'i
she	mašat	bi'yat
they	mašu	bi'yu
you (m)	mašeet	b'iit
you (f)	mašeeti	b'iiti
you (pl)	mašeetu	b'iitu
I	mašeet	b'iit
we	mašeena	b'iina

The verbs of this class have in the «he» form a stem that ends in a vowel, -a or -i.

The -a drops before subject markers beginning with a vowel (e.g. mašat, mašu), and is replaced by -ee- before subject markers beginning with a consonant (e.g. mašeet, mašeena).

The -i becomes y before subject markers beginning with a vowel (e.g. bi'yat, bi'yu) and -ii- (with loss of the first *i*) before subject markers beginning with a consonant (e.g. b'iit, b'iina).

All these verbs have weak roots.

Like maša (bimši) *walk*:

'a9ṭa	(bya9ṭi)	*give*
hanna	(bihanni)	*give joy*
kaffa	(bikaffi)	*be enough*
laa'a	(bilaa'i)	*find, meet*
na''a	(bina''i)	*choose*
stanna	(bistanna)	*wait*

štara	(bištri)	*buy*
xalla	(bixalli)	*keep, allow*

Omitted is the suffix tense of the verb 'aja biiji *come*. This verb is somewhat irregular; the forms are given in the Grammar of Unit 7.

3. Prefix tense of 'axad and 'akal.

The prefix tense forms of 'axad *take* and 'akal *eat* lose the glottal stop (') and have a stem beginning with long *aa*.

he	byaaxud	yaaxud
she	btaaxud	taaxud
they	byaaxdu	yaaxdu
you (m)	btaaxud	taaxud
you (f)	btaaxdi	taaxdi
you (pl)	btaaxdu	taaxdu
I	baaxud	'aaxud
we	bnaaxud	naaxud

The command is xood, xud (m), xudi (f), xudu (pl). The shorter form xud is used when a transition vowel is present. For example, xood haada *take this!* as against xud iljariide *take the newspaper!*

The verb 'akal *eat* behaves the same way: byaakul, btaakul, yaakul, taakul, etc. The command is kool, kul, kuli, kulu.

Other verbs that have a glottal stop as the first consonant of the root do not behave this way. For example, ba'mur *I order*, ba'ṭa9 *I cut*.

DRILLS

1. Give appropriate replies to the following sentences.

bti9rafli ween fii xayyaaṭ lxayyaaṭ ?

kiif šuġlak ?

min ween štareet hali'maaš ?

b'addeeš baa9ak lmitir ?

mumkin 'aaxud 'yaasak ?

mumkin tiiji la9indi yoom ssabt taaxud proova ?

'ayy wa't binaasbak ?

miš ḍaruuri tġallib ḥaalak.

mniiḥ ?

kiif 'as9aaro ?

faaḍi nruuḥ halla 9ind lxayyaaṭ ?

2. In the following sentences replace yoom ssabt by different days of the week.

mumkin tiiji la9indi yoom ssabt ?

raašid kaan hoon yoom ssabt.

raayiḥ yzuurna yoom ssabt.

šufto fii beeruut yoom ssabt.

šuu ra'yak nruuḥ 9al'uds yoom ssabt ?

3. In each of the following sentences replace the suffix tense «I» form of the verb by the suffix tense «we» form. The first two are completed.

(1) 'axatt lbadle min 9ind lxayyaaṭ.	'axadna lbadle min 9ind lxayyaaṭ.
(2) štareet lbadle min beeruut.	štareena lbadle min beeruut.

'akalt hoon mbaariḥ.

fataḥt ššababiik.

maa 'axatt l'umṣaan.

'axatt lbadle.

lissa ma bi9t lbeet.

jibt kullši ma9i.

ḥaṭṭeet ljaraayid hoon.

maa xalleeto yruuḥ 9al9iraaq.

rji9t min beeruut yoom ttalaata.

fhimt kullši.

sakkart lmaktabe.

saa9att 'aḥmad.

ruḥt 9abeeruut yoom ljum9a.

zurt fiiha maḥallaat ktiire.

kunt fiššaam kamaan.

'aḥmad šufto fii ḥalab.

laa'eet beet mniiḥ.

štareet lbadle min 9ind raašid.

nsiit 'as'alak 9anno.

nsiit 'asakkir lmaktab.

'ijiit ma9 raašid.

'ijiit fii sayyaarto.

kunt 9indak yoom l'arba9a.

ṣarli yoomeen maa šuftak.

4. In each of the following sentences replace the suffix tense «he» form of the verb by the suffix tense «she» form. The first two are completed.

(1) maa sa'al 'aḥmad. — maa sa'lat 'aḥmad.

(2) fihim kullši. — fihmat kullši.

leeš fataḥ lbaab ?

'axad ssayyaara.

'akal ktiir.

riji9 yoom ljum9a.

sakkar libwaab ?

saa9ad 'aḥmad.

raaḥ 9alimḥaṭṭa.

zaar l'uds.

kaan fii 'ameerka 'abil santeen.

maa baa9 lbeet.

feen ḥaṭṭ lburneeṭa ?

laa'a beet mniiḥ ?

maa xallaa yruuḥ 9al9iraaq.

štara badle jdiide.

nisi yis'alni.

nisi ysakkir ššubbaak.

kiif 'aja ?

'aja ma9ak ?

'aja zaarni filqaahira.

'eemtan šaaf raašid ?

jaab kullši ma9o.

5. Go through the sentences of Drill 4 replacing the suffix tense «he» forms of the verbs by «they» forms. For example :

(1) maa sa'al 'aḥmad.	maa sa'alu 'aḥmad.
(2) fihim kullši.	fihmu kullši.

6. In each of the following sentences replace the prefix tense verb forms by the corresponding suffix tense forms. The first two are completed.

(1) leeš maa btis'al yuusif ?	leeš maa sa'alt yuusif ?
(2) raayiḥ dzuur raašid?	zurt raašid ?

bisaa9idni bkullši.

fii 'ayy maṭ9am raḥtaakul ?

raḥyaaxud minni tlat dananiir.

'ayy saa9a raayḥiin tirja9u 9al'uteel ?

basaa9id raašid.

baruuḥ ma9hum yoom ttineen.

hiyye bitkuun filbeet ssaa9a sitte.

raayḥiin nzuur 'aḥmad.

miin bijiib raašid hoon ?

binxalli ssayyaara ma9 'aḥmad.

bištriili badle jdiide.

nšaa*ll*a bilaa'i šuġul.

7. Give the English equivalents of the following Arabic noun annexions.

jariitt lyoom	mustašaar ssafaara
muftaaḥ ššanta	safrit 'aḥmad
maktab lmudiir	mwaẓẓaf ḥukuume
si9r lmitir	mwaẓẓaf lḥukuume
9umr lbint likbiire	naa'ib 'unṣul
9umur bintak	mudiir bank
maktab ssiyaaḥa	ẓaabiṭ ṭayaraan

8. In each of the following sentences replace the expression in parentheses by a pronoun ending. The first two are completed.

(1) haadi saa9it ('aḥmad) ?	haadi saa9to ?
(2) šuu si9r (lbadle) ?	suu si9*i*rha ?
beet (lmudiir) hunaak.	šuu 9umr (lbint) ?
šuft sayyaarit (raašid) hoon ?	kiif šuġul (raašid) ?
kiif kaanat safrit (yuusif) ?	kiif ḥaal (wlaadak) ?
feen beet (ssayyid raašid) ?	beet (ssafiir) 'ariib min hoon.
šuu 9umr (lwalad) ?	

UNIT 15 • Speaking Arabic.

PATTERN SENTENCES

speak	ḥaka biḥki
You speak Arabic well, Mr. West.	btiḥki 9arabi mniiḥ, yaa mistir west.
Well, I speak a little bit.	ya9ni. baḥki šwayy.
tell	'aal bi'uul
learn	t9allam bit9allam
Tell me, where did you learn Arabic ?	'ulli. feen t9allamt l9arabi ?
university	jaam(i)9a
I learned it in an American university.	saddi'. t9allamto fii jaam9a 'ameerkaaniyye.
seem, appear	ẓahar biẓhar
school	madrase, pl. madaaris
teach	9allam bi9allim
It seems that you have a lot of schools that teach Arabic.	biẓhar fii 9indkum madaaris ktiire bit9allim 9arabi.
currently	9am-
be concerned	htamm bihtamm
Yes, they're very concerned these days.	na9am. 9ambihtammu ktiir haliyyaam.
read	'iri bi'ra
write	katab buktub
Do you read and write, too ?	bti'ra wibtuktub kamaan ?
reading	'raay(e)

Well, I'm not so bad in reading.	ya9ni. fili'raay miš baṭṭaal.
difficulty	ṣ9uube
writing	ktaabe
But I have difficulty in writing.	bass 9indi ṣ9uube filiktaabe.
teacher, professional man, maestro	'ustaaz
Who's the teacher that taught you?	miin l'ustaaz lli 9allamak?
an Arab	'ibin 9arab
An Arab or an American?	'ibin 9arab, willa 'ameerkaani?
An Arab.	'ibin 9arab.
name	'isim
What's his name?	šuu 'ismo?
His name's Abdallah Salem.	'ismo 9abda*ll*a saalim.
Do you know him?	bti9rafo?
hearing, having heard	saami9
I've heard about him.	saddi'. saami9 9anno.
personally	šaxṣiyyan
But I don't know him personally.	bass, maa ba9rafo šaxṣiyyan.
study	daras budrus
How long have you been studying Arabic?	'addeeš ṣarlak btudrus 9arabi?
approximately	ta'riiban
About two years.	ta'riiban santeen.

Additional vocabulary

language	luġa pl. -aat
dialect	lahje pl. -aat
colloquial (Arabic)	lluġa l9aammiyye *or* lluġa ddaarje
Classical (Arabic)	lluġa lfuṣḥa
English	'ingliizi
French	fransaawi
German	'a*l*m*a*ani
Italian	tilyaani
Russian	ruusi
Spanish	s*b*anyooli

STRUCTURE SENTENCES

1. Negative commands

don't go	laa truuḥ
Don't go with him.	laa truuḥ ma9o.
don't bother	laa tġallib
Don't bother yourself.	laa tġallib ḥaalak.
don't forget	laa tinsa
Don't forget to ask him.	laa tinsa tis'alo.
don't go	laa truuḥi
Don't go with him.	laa truuḥi ma9o.
don't bother	laa tġallbi
Don't bother yourself.	laa tġallbi ḥaalik.
don't forget	laa tinsi
Don't forget to ask him.	laa tinsi tis'alii(h).

don't go	laa truuḥu
Don't go with him.	laa truuḥu ma9o.
don't bother	laa tġallbu
Don't bother yourselves.	laa tġallbu ḥaalkum.
don't forget	laa tinsu
Don't forget to ask him.	laa tinsu tis'aluu(h).

GRAMMAR

1. Negative commands

A dependent prefix tense verb in the «you» form preceded by laa *no* has the meaning of a negative command : laa truuḥ ma9o *do not go with him !*

2. Place nouns

A given pattern may be associated with a specific added feature in such a way that it is best to regard the combination as a unit. Such a combination is called a pattern complex.

One very common added feature of this sort is a prefixed m-, which occurs with a variety of patterns: maktab, mašġuul, mwaẓẓaf, mit'assif, mudiir, mulḥaq, muftaaḥ.

One very common pattern complex of this sort is ma--a- (and its variant ma--i-), which often has the meaning «place of or for the action or state indicated by the root». This pattern, like most others, has variants depending on the root type. With this pattern may also occur the feminine ending -e/-a.

The following lists show *place nouns* that have occurred in Units 1-15, plus a few others that contain roots that have appeared in words in those Units.

(1) Regular roots : pattern ma--a- and ma--i-.

place noun		*root*	
mafra'	*cross roads*	fr'	*separating*
maktab	*office*	ktb	*writing*
mašġal	*workshop*	šġl	*working*
maṭ9am	*restaurant*	ṭ9m	*tasting*
maw'if	*stopping place*	w'f	*stopping*
ma9mal	*factory*	9ml	*doing*
madrase	*school*	drs	*studying*
maḥkame	*court*	ḥkm	*ruling*
maktabe	*library*	ktb	*writing*

(2) Doubled roots : pattern m(a)-a--.

maḥall	*place*	ḥll	*taking place of*
mḥaṭṭa	*station*	ḥṭṭ	*putting*

(3) Hollow roots : pattern ma-aa-.

maṭaar	*airport*	ṭyr	*flying*
mazaar	*shrine*	zwr	*visiting*

(4) Weak roots : pattern ma--a.

mamša	*corridor*	mšy	*walking*
mašta	*winter resort*	štw	*winter*

DRILLS

1. Give appropriate replies to the following sentences.

btiḥki 9arabi ?

feen t9allamt l9arabi ?

bti'ra wibtuktub kamaan?

miin 9allamak 9arabi ?

kam sane ṣarlak btit9allam 9arabi ?

fii 9indkum madaaris ktiire bit9allim 9arabi ?	kam sane ṣarlak btiḥki 9arabi?

2. Go through the following sentences, replacing -ak *you* (*m*) by -kum *you* (*pl*), changing anything in the rest of the sentence that needs to be changed. The first two are completed.

(1) 'alli biddo ysaa9dak.	'alli biddo ysaa9idkum.
(2) kam sane ṣarlak btiḥki 9arabi ?	kam sane ṣarlkum btiḥku 9arabi ?
'ayy wa't binaasbak ?	šufnaak fii maṣir.
miin 9allamak 9arabi ?	'eemta zaarak 'aḥmad ?
'aḥmad sa'alni 9annak.	'addeeš ṣarlak filjaam9a ?
baḥibb 'a9arrfak 9assayyid 9abda*ll*a.	barja9 'aaxdak ba9id saa9a.

3. Go through the following sentences, replacing -o/(-h) *him* by -hum *them*, changing anything in the rest of the sentence that needs to be changed. The first two are completed.

(1) 'ayy wa't binaasbo ?	'ayy wa't binaasibhum ?
(2) mumkin tsaa9do ?	mumkin tsaa9idhum ?
miin 9allamo 9arabi ?	mumkin tsaa9duu(h) ?
bti9rafli šii 9anno ?	mumkin taaxdo mnil'uteel ?
kam sane ṣarlo budrus 9arabi ?	feen laa'eeto ?
bti9rafo šaxṣiyyan ?	stanneeto filimḥaṭṭa.
saddi'. saami9 9anno.	nsiit 'ajiblo liktaab.
maa ba9rafo šaxṣiyyan.	sa'alt 'aḥmad 9anno ?
	'addeeš ṣarlo filmadrase ?

4. Change each of the following sentences into the negative, as illustrated in the first two.

(1) ruuḥ ma9o. — laa truuḥ ma9o.

(2) biḥki 9arabi mniiḥ. — maa biḥki 9arabi mniiḥ.

'ištri badle min 9ind raašid.

'is'al 9anno.

xud ljariide.

ḥakeet ma9o.

ba9rafo mniiḥ.

basadd'o.

'riit ljariide.

ḥuṭṭ ššanta 9aṭṭaawle.

stanna 9abda*ll*a.

ta9aal lyoom.

bi9allim 9arabi.

'akalt ktiir.

t9allamt ktiir.

5. In each of the following sentences change the « you (m) » verb form to the « you (pl)» form, as illustrated in the first two.

(1) 9ala 'ayy baaboor 'ijiit? — 9ala 'ayy baaboor 'ijiitu ?

(2) šuu bit'uul ? — šuu bit'uulu ?

fii 'ayy madrase ḥaṭṭeet wlaadak ?

leeš fataḥt lbaab ?

min feen štareet li'maaš ?

ma9 miin ruḥt 9ala beeruut?

fii 'ayy jaam9a t9allamt 9arabi ?

'riit ljaraayid ?

šuu 'ult ?

bti'ra wibtuktub kamaan ?

fii 'ayy madrase btit9allam 9arabi ?

btiḥki 9arabi mniiḥ.

ween darast 9arabi ?

šuù 9ambtudrus halla ?

ḥakeet ma9 l'ustaaz ?

6. In each of the following sentences change the «he» form of the verb to the «they» form. The first two are completed.

(1) daras 9arabi filmadrase.   darasu 9arabi filmadrase.

(2) šuu bi'uul ?   šuu bi'uulu ?

šuu 'aal ?   'iri ljariide.

katab la'aḥmad.   t9allam 9arabi fii 'ameerka.

ma9 miin raaḥ 9ala beeruut?   bi'ra wbuktub kamaan ?

fii 'ayy madrase ḥaṭṭ wlaado ?   biddo yiḥki ma9 lmudiir.

9ala 'ayy baaboor 'aja ?   miin 9allamo?

Unit 16 • Buying fruits and vegetables.

PATTERN SENTENCES

Good morning, Abu Khalil.	ṣabaaḥ lxeer, 'abu xaliil.
Good morning, Mr. West.	ṣabaaḥ nnuur, yaa mistir west.
health	ṣiḥḥa.
How's your health today?	kiif ṣiḥḥtak lyoom?
So-so.	maaši lḥaal.
Is business good?	nšaalla ššuġl mniiḥ?
good, fine	kwayyis
Fine, praise God.	kwayyis, lḥamdu lillaah.
We need a few vegetables.	laazimna šwayyit xuḍra.
What do you have that's new?	šuu fii 9indak šii jdiid?
fresh (invariable adj.)	ṭaaẓa
Everything I have is fresh.	kullši 9indi ṭaaẓa.
box	sanduu'
tomatoes	bandoora
as you wish	9ala keefak
I've just received a box of tomatoes that you'll like.	halla 'ajaani sanduu' bandoora 9ala keefak.
kilo	kiilo
ukiyeh (200 grams)	w'iyye
Fine. Put out two kilos for me.	ṭayyib. ḥuṭṭilli tneen kiilo.
Do you want something else?	btu'mur šii taani?
Yes, give me a kilo of squash.	na9am. 'a9ṭiini kiilo kuusa.
beans	luubya

And two kilos of beans.	witneen kiilo luubya.
cabbage	malfuuf
And three kilos of cabbage.	witlaate kiilo malfuuf.
Have you also got some good fruit?	fii 9indak kamaan fawaakih mniiḥa?
whatever	'eeš maa
Of course, of course. There's whatever you want.	ma9luum. ma9luum. fii 'eeš maa biddak.
a watermelon	baṭṭiixa
All right. Give me a small watermelon.	ṭayyib. 'a9ṭiini baṭṭiixa ẓġiire.
go up, come out, amount to	ṭili9 biṭla9
Now, how much does our account amount to?	halla, šuu biṭla9 ḥsaabna?
It amounts to three pounds and a quarter.	biṭla9 9aleek, tlat liiraat wrubu9.
send	ba9at bib9at
Please send them to the house.	min faḍlak, b9atli yyaahum 9albeet.
Gladly.	tikram.

Additional vocabulary

1. Vegetables

artichokes	'arḍi šooki
beans (dried)	faṣuulya
beans (Spanish beans)	fuul
beets	ša*m*andar

cabbage	malfuuf
carrots	jazar
cauliflower	'arnabiiṭ
chickpeas	ḥummuṣ
cucumbers	xyaar
eggplants	beetinjaan
garlic	tuum
lettuce	xass
mint	na9na9
okra	baamya
olives	zeetuun
onions	baṣal
parsley	ba'duunis
peas	bazeella
potatoes	baṭaaṭa
radishes	fijil
spinach	sabaanix
turnips	lift

2. Fruits

apricots	mišmiš
cherries	karaz
lemons	leemuun ḥaamiḍ
mulberries	tuut
oranges	burd'aan
peaches	durraa'

pears	njaaṣ
plums	xuux
strawberries	freez
tangerines	yuusif 'afandi, 'afandi

3. Meat and fish

beef	laḥim ba'ar
chickens	jaaj
ham	jamboon
lamb	laḥim xaruuf
liver	kibde
pork	laḥim xanziir
shrimp	'reedis
turkey	diik ḥabaš
veal	laḥim 9ijil

STRUCTURE SENTENCES

1. Collective nouns

Do you have watermelons?	fii 9indkum baṭṭiix?
We have fresh fish today.	fii 9inna lyoom samak ṭaaẓa.
Oranges are cheap these days.	lburd'aan rxiiṣ haliyyaam.
There are bananas and apples and grapes and figs.	fii mooz, wtuffaaḥ, w9inab, wtiin.
I don't like eggs.	maa baḥibb lbeeḍ.

2. Unit nouns

Give me a little watermelon.	'a9ṭiini baṭṭiixa ẓġiire.
Give me just one fish.	'a9ṭiini bass samake.
How many oranges did you take with you?	kam burd'aane 'axatt ma9ak?
Have an apple.	xood tuffaaḥa.
How many eggs do you give me for a pound?	kam beeḍa bta9ṭiini bliira?
Give me three watermelons.	'a9ṭiini tlat baṭṭiixaat.
Put out four fish for me.	ḥuṭṭilli 'arba9 samakaat.
Give me six oranges.	'a9ṭiini sitt burd'aanaat.
I ate three apples.	'akalt tlat tuffaaḥaat.
Six eggs for a pound.	sitt beeḍaat bliira.

3. Unit expressions

grain, seed, berry	ḥabbe
a tomato	ḥabbit bandoora
a cherry	ḥabbit karaz
an apricot	ḥabbit mišmiš
a fig	ḥabbit tiin
a grape	ḥabbit 9inab
Give me a tomato.	'a9ṭiini ḥabbit bandoora.
head	raas
an onion	raas basal
a radish	raas fijil
Give me an onion.	'a9ṭiini raas baṣal.

GRAMMAR

1. Collective nouns

Arabic has a class of nouns called *collectives.* These nouns indicate a species of object, not an individual specimen. An example is beeḍ *eggs.* The typical collective noun is masculine in gender (e.g. beeḍ) and has no plural.

Accompanying many collective nouns is a *unit noun.* This noun indicates an individual specimen, not the species as a whole. An example is beeḍa *an egg.* The typical unit noun is feminine in gender (e.g. beeḍa) and has a dual (beeṭṭeen) and a plural (beeḍaat). The plural is usually in -aat.

The collective noun with the prefix for «the» includes in its meaning *all* the specimens : bitḥibb lbeeḍ *do you like eggs?* Without the prefix for «the» it means *some* of the specimens : bitḥibb beeḍ *would you like some eggs ?*

Some collective nouns lack an accompanying unit noun (or have one that is not frequently used). These often use an annexion phrase to indicate an individual specimen : ḥabbit bandoora *a tomato*, raas baṣal *an onion.*

DRILLS

1. Give appropriate replies to the following sentences.

kiif ṣiḥḥtak ?	btu'mur šii taani ?
nšaa*ll*a ššuġl mniiḥ ?	fii 9indkum xass ?
šuu fii 9indak šii jdiid ?	šuu biṭla9 ḥsaabna ?

2. In each of the following sentences replace kuusa by the name of another vegetable or fruit.

laazimna šwayyit kuusa.	min ween bidjiib lkuusa ?

ḥuṭṭilli tneen kiilo kuusa.

min faḍlak, 'a9ṭiini tneen kiilo kuusa.

maa baḥibb lkuusa.

fii 9indak kuusa ?

3. In each of the following sentences replace the noun in parentheses by the appropriate pronoun ending. The first two are completed.

(1) jaabu (ssayyaara) ma9hum. — jaabuuha ma9hum.

(2) šufna ('abu xaliil) fii beeruut. — šufnaa fii beeruut.

sa'alu (l'ustaaz) 9an lmadrase.

ḥaṭṭu (wlaadhum) filmadrase.

9allamu ('aḥmad).

maa bi9rafu ('aḥmad) šaxṣiyyan.

zaaru (l'ustaaz).

šaafu (bintna) fil'uds.

leeš baa9u (lbeet) ?

maa laa'u ('aḥmad).

sa'alna (l'ustaaz) 9anno.

ḥaṭṭeena (lbint) filmadrase.

lissa maa zurna (l'ustaaz).

jibna (ssanduu') 9albeet.

laa'eena ('aḥmad) filbeet.

nsiina (ljaraayid).

'axadu (ssayyaara).

4. For each of the following verbs in the suffix tense «he» form give the prefix tense «he» form. The first example of each group is completed, and all the verbs within any one group work the same way.

samaḥ bismaḥ	'addam bi'addim	maša bimši
sa'al	'axxar	ḥaka
fataḥ	9allam	
	sakkar	

katab buktub	raaḥ biruuḥ	bi'i bib'a
'amar	zaar	nisi
šakar	šaaf	'iri
daras	kaan	
riji9 birja9	jaab bijiib	
širib	ṣaar	
9imil	baa9	
fihim		
9irif		
ṭili9		

UNIT 17 • Invalids.

PATTERN SENTENCES

(Visiting Abu Najib)

Abu Najib	'abu najiib
Good morning, Abu Najib.	ṣabaaḥ lxeer, yaa 'abu najiib.
Abu Akram	'abu 'akram
Good morning, Abu Akram.	ṣabaaḥ lxeeraat, 'abu 'akram.
your safety (an expression said to a person who is sick)	salaamtak
my brother (an informal term of address used among equals or to an inferior)	'axi
Your safety, my friend.	salaamtak, yaa 'axi.
May God keep you (in reply).	'a*ll*a ysallmak wyiḥfaẓak.
problem	mas'ale
It's nothing serious, I hope.	xeer nšaa*ll*a.
What's the matter ?	šuu lmas'ale ?
simple	baṣiiṭ
A simple matter, praise God.	baṣiiṭa, lḥamdilla.
cold	rašiḥ
I have a slight cold.	ma9i šwayyit rašiḥ.

better	'aḥsan
Are you better today?	nšaa*ll*a 'aḥsan lyoom?
Praise God. I'm a little better.	lḥamdilla, 'aḥsan šwayy.
fever	ḥaraara *or* sxuune
The fever went away today.	lyoom, raaḥat lḥaraara.
be upset	zi9il biz9al
when	lamma(n)
hear	simi9 bisma9
that you	'innak
sick	mariiḍ
Really, I was very upset when I heard that you were sick.	saddi'. z9ilt ktiir lamma smi9t innak mariiḍ.
bed	farše
How long have you been in bed?	'addeeš ṣarlak filfarše?
It's been two weeks.	ṣarli jum*i*9teen.
by God (here a mild interjection)	wa*ll*aahi, wa*ll*a
I just heard yesterday that you were ill.	wa*ll*aahi, bass mbaariḥ smi9t innak mariiḍ.
doctor	duktoor
Because they told me the doctor was at your place.	li'anno 'aaluuli dduktoor kaan 9indak.
yes	'aywa
strike	ḍarab buḍrub
needle	'ibre

give an injection	ḍarab 'ibre
Yes, he came and gave me an injection.	'aywa. 'aja ḍarabni 'ibre.
medicine	dawa
And gave me some medicine.	w'a9ṭaani šwayyit dawa.
get up	'aam bi'uum
I hope you'll be all right soon.	ṭayyib, nšaa*ll*a bit'uum 9assalaame.
Thank you (in reply).	'a*ll*a ysallmak.
(Inquiring about Abu Akram)	
How's Abu Akram's health ?	kiif ṣiḥḥit 'abu 'akram ?
He isn't very well.	saddi'. miš mniiḥ ktiir.
What's wrong with him ?	šuu maalo ?
influenza	'influwenza
He has the flu.	ma9o 'influwenza.
And he has a fever.	w9alee ḥaraara.
Well then, why doesn't he go to the hospital ?	'izan, leeš maa biruuḥ 9almustašfa ?
He *is* in the hospital.	maa huwwe filmustašfa.
And he's been there five days.	wṣarlo hunaak xamis tiyyaam.
Well, why didn't you tell me ?	ṭayyib, leeš maa 'ultilli ?
think	ftakar biftkir
Why, I thought that you knew.	wa*ll*aahi, ftakart 'innak bti9raf.

Additional vocabulary

pain, ache	waja9
ear ache	waja9 dineen

head ache	waja9 raas
stomach ache	waja9 mi9de, waja9 baṭin
tooth ache	waja9 snaan
upset stomach	talabbuk mi9de
pill	ḥabbe, pl. ḥbuub
thermometer	miizaan ḥaraara
have an operation	9imil 9amaliyye

STRUCTURE SENTENCES

1. Nisbe adjectives and nouns

The National Restaurant isn't bad.	lmaṭ9am lwaṭani miš baṭṭaal.
Do you like Arabic food ?	bitḥibb l'akl l9arabi ?
Do you know the military attaché ?	bti9raf lmulḥaq l9askari ?
Where's the American Embassy ?	ween ssafaara l'ameerkaaniyye?
Please direct me to the Arab Library.	min faḍlak, dillni 9almaktabe l9arabiyye.
Do you want a summer suit, or a winter suit ?	biddak badle ṣeefiyye, willa šatawiyye ?
He studied in the American University.	daras filjaam9a l'ameerkiyye.
Where did you study the Arabic language ?	ween darast lluġa l9arabiyye ?

Mr. West is a journalist.	mistir west ṣuḥufi.
Where is there a good watchmaker?	ween fii saa9aati mniiḥ ?
What's this in Arabic?	šuu haada bil9arabi ?
Do you speak French?	btiḥki fransaawi ?
Where's the English Consulate?	ween l'unṣliyye lingliiziyye ?

GRAMMAR

I. The nisbe

The suffix -i, meaning «of, pertaining to, connected with» makes adjectives out of nouns. (Compare the *-al* of English *personal*, the *-ar* of *consular*, the *-ic* of *economic*.) The Arabic grammatical term for this kind of word is nisbe *relation*, *proportion*. Following the Arabic practice, we shall call them *nisbe* adjectives.

The following lists show several types of nisbes, most of which have occurred in Units 1-17.

nisbe		*underlying noun*	
waṭani	*national*	waṭan	*homeland*
lubnaani	*Lebanese*	lubnaan	*Lebanon*
baladi	*municipal*	balad	*town*
maḥalli	*local*	maḥall	*place*
šaxṣi	*personal*	šaxṣ	*person*

The -e/-a of feminine T-nouns is regularly dropped before the nisbe suffix.

ḍaruuri	*necessary*	ḍaruura	*necessity*

ṣiḥḥi	*healthy*	ṣiḥḥa	*health*
ziraa9i	*agricultural*	ziraa9a	*agriculture*
ṣaḥaafi	*journalistic*	ṣaḥaafe	*journalism*

If the underlying noun regularly has the prefix for «the», this prefix is dropped in the nisbe.

šaami	*Damascene*	ššaam	*Damascus*
9iraaqi	*Iraqi*	l9iraaq	*Iraq*
'urduni	*Jordanian*	l'urdun	*Jordan*

Occasionally there is a change in the underlying stem.

'ameerkaani	*American*	'ameerka	*America*
fransaawi	*French*	fraansa	*France*
tilyaani	*Italian*	'iiṭaalya	*Italy*
šatawi	*winter*	šita	*winter*
sanawi	*annual*	sane	*year*

Occasionally the nisbe is formed from a plural noun.

saa9aati	*watchmaker*	saa9aat	*watches*
ṣuḥufi	*journalist*	ṣuḥuf	*newspapers*
9arabi	*Arab(ic)*	9arab	*Arabs*

The feminine of the nisbe always ends in -iyye, and the plural usually ends in -iyyiin, though other plurals occur.

masc.	*fem.*	*plural*	
waṭani	waṭaniyye	waṭaniyyiin	*national*
maḥalli	maḥalliyye	maḥalliyyiin	*local*
ṣeefi	ṣeefiyye	ṣeefiyyiin	*summer*
'ameerkaani	'ameerkaaniyye	'ameerkaan	*American*
'ingliizi	'ingliiziyye	'ingliiz	*English*

The feminine form of a nisbe is sometimes used as an independent noun, with a plural in -aat.

baladiyye	*municipality*
'unṣliyye	*consulate*
9amaliyye	*operation*
šaxṣiyye	*personality*

It is important to note that not all adjectives that end in -i are nisbes. For example, the final -i of ġaali *expensive* is part of the root ġly ; this is shown quite clearly in the feminine and plural forms : ġaalye, ġaalyiin.

DRILLS

1. Give appropriate replies to the following sentences.

xeer nšaa*ll*a. šuu lmas'ale ?	kiif lxidme filmustašfa ?
šuu maalak?	nšaa*ll*a bit'uum 9assalaame.
nšaa*ll*a 'aḥsan lyoom ?	šaafak dduktoor ?
'addeeš ṣarlak filmustašfa?	šuft dduktoor ?
9aleek ḥaraara ?	'eemta ṭli9t min lmustašfa ?
leeš maa 'ultilli 'innak mariiḍ?	

2. In each of the following sentences replace the pronoun ending -ha *her* by -o/(h) *him*, changing anything in the rest of the sentence that needs changing.

| ma9ha šwayyit rašiḥ. | 'aja wḍarabha 'ibre. |
| smi9t 'inha mariiḍa. | w'a9ṭaaha šwayyit dawa. |

’addeeš ṣar*l*lha filfarše ?

’aaluuli dduktoor kaan 9indha.

šuu maalha ?

ma9ha rašḥ t’iil.

w9aleeha ḥaraara.

3. In each of the following sentences replace the «she» form of the verb by the «he» form, changing anything in the rest of the sentence that needs changing. The first two are completed.

(1) bass mbaariḥ sim9at ’inno mariiḍ.	bass mbaariḥ simi9 inno mariiḍ.
(2) ’aalatli dduktoor kaan 9indo.	’alli dduktoor kaan 9indo.

sa’latni 9annak.

maa 9irfat ’innak hoon.

9imlat 9amaliyye.

fihmat kullši.

’a9ṭato šwayyit dawa.

ftakrat ’innak bti9raf.

bass mbaariḥ rij9at min lmustašfa.

maa xallato yruuḥ 9ala baġdaad.

nisyat t’ulli.

’iryat filjariide ’innak hoon.

t9allamt ’ingliizi fii ’ameerka.

šaafato fii beeruut.

’aalatli maa šaafat ḥasan.

’aalatli nisyat ’ismo.

ḥaṭṭathum fissayyaara.

štarat sayyaara jdiide.

ḥakat ma9 ’abu ’akram.

4. In each of the following sentences replace the word in parentheses by a different nisbe adjective or noun.

fii ’ayy jaami9a t9allamt (9arabi) ?

daras lluġa (l9arabiyye).

bitḥibb l’akl (l9arabi) ?

štareet badle (ṣeefiyye).	bti9raf lmulḥaq (l9askari) ?
btiḥki (fransaawi) ?	ween ssafaara
zaarna lyoom waaḥad	(l'ameerkaaniyye) ?
('ingliizi).	šuu haada (bil9arabi) ?

5. Give appropriate replies to the following.

'assalaamu 9alaykum.	tšarrafna.
kiif ḥaalak ?	tfaḍḍal zuurna filbeet.
tfaḍḍal striiḥ.	'ana mištaa'lak ktiir.
šukran.	šarraftuuna.
9an 'iznak.	daayme.
btismaḥli šwayy ?	miš ḍaruuri tġallib ḥaalak.
xaaṭrak.	hanii'an.
xaaṭirkum.	mabruuk.
marḥaba.	'a*ll*a yxalliilak yyaahum.
'ahlan wasahlan.	ma9 ssalaame.
ṣabaaḥ lxeer.	lḥamdilla 9assalaame.
masa lxeer.	salaamtak.

6. For each of the following verbs in the suffix tense «he» form give the prefix tense «he» form. The first example of each group is completed, and all the verbs in any one group work the same way.

'axad byaaxud	'aṭa9 bi'ṭa9	libis bilbas
'akal	fataḥ	lizim
	ḥafaẓ	simi9

katab	buktub	kaan	bikuun
ḍarab		'aal	
šakar			
'addam	bi'addim	tšarraf	bitšarraf
9arraf		tfaḍḍal	
šarraf		t9allam	
wa''af			
saa9ad	bisaa9id		
naasab			

UNIT 18 • A political figure.

PATTERN SENTENCES

Sulayman 'Abdo	sleemaan 9abdo
We're currently hearing a lot about Sulayman 'Abdo.	9ammnisma9 ktiir 9an sleemaan 9abdo.
article	maqaale, pl. -aat
And the newspapers have written a lot of articles about him.	wiljaraayid katbat 9anno maqaalaat ktiire.
that he	'inno
And they told me that he's from your town.	w'aaluuli 'inno min baladkum.
Do you know him personally?	bti9rafo šaxṣiyyan ?
meet	jtama9 bijtmi9
time	marra, pl. -aat
several times	9iddit marraat
Yes, I've met him several times.	na9am. jtama9t ma9o 9iddit marraat.
man	rijjaal
please	'a9jab bi9jib
And you'd like the man.	wirrijjaal bi9*i*jbak.
give a speech	xaṭab buxṭub
problem	mas'ale, pl. masaa'il

Listen to him give a speech on the national problems.	'isma9o yuxṭub filmasaa'il lwaṭaniyye.
move, shake	hazz bihizz
the world	ddinya
a moving, a shaking	hazz
He moves people profoundly.	bihizz ddinya hazz.
And the people like him very much.	winnaas biḥibbuu ktiir.
the second time	taani marra
elect	ntaxab bintxib
member	9uḍu
parliament	barlamaan
And this is the second time they've elected him member of parliament.	whaadi taani marra bintixbuu 9uḍu barlamaan.
interest	maṣlaḥa
people	ša9b
Because with him the interest of the people comes before everything else.	li'anno 9indo maṣlaḥt ššа9b 'abil kullši.
if (contrary to fact)	law
poor, unfortunate	maskiin
life	ḥayaah
suffer	t9azzab bit9azzab
And if you knew how much trouble the poor man has had in his life.	wlaw ti9raf 'addeeš lmaskiin t9azzab fii ḥayaato.

father	'ab
rich	ġani
poor	fa'iir
ground, land	'arḍ, pl. 'araaḍi
son	'ibin
in order to	ḥatta
His father was poor and sold his lands in order to educate his son.	abuu kaan fa'iir, wbaa9 'araaḍii ḥatta y9allim 'ibno.
educated	mit9allim
Tell me, where was he educated?	'ulli. feen mit9allim huwwe?
the first thing	'awwal šii
college	kulliyye
First of all he was educated in the Arab College.	'awwal šii, t9allam filkulliyye l9arabiyye.
England	blaad lingliiz, 'ingiltra
law	ḥuquuq, muḥaamaah
Later he went to England and studied law.	ba9deen raaḥ 9ablaad lingliiz, wdaras ḥuquuq.
work	štaġal bištġil
court	maḥkame
When he returned he worked in the court.	lamma riji9, štaġal filmaḥkame.
take place	ṣaar biṣiir
elections	'intixaabaat

And when the elections took place they elected him mayor.	wlamma ṣaarat lintixaabaat, ntaxabuu ra'iis baladiyye.
sincere	muxliṣ
like	mitil
The man was sincere and not like the others.	rrijjaal kaan muxliṣ, wmiš mitil ġeero.
be deceitful	tlaa9ab bitlaa9ab
He isn't deceitful.	maa bitlaa9ab.
if only	yaareet
responsible	mas'uul
thus, so	heek
we would be	lakunna
situation	ḥaale
If only all the responsible ones were like that, we'd be in a different situation.	yaareet kull lmas'uuliin heek, lakunna fii ġeer halḥaale.

Additional vocabulary

knowledge, science	9ilim, pl. 9uluum
Accounting	muḥaasabe
Agriculture	ziraa9a
Commerce	tijaara
Economics	'iqtiṣaaḍ
Education	tarbiye
Engineering	handase

History	taariix
Journalism	ṣaḥaafe
Literature	'adab, pl. 'aadaab
Medicine	ṭibb
Music	muusiiqa
Philosophy	falsafe
Political Science	9uluum siyaasiyye
Psychology	9ilm nnafs
Religion, Theology	9uluum diiniyye
Sociology	9ilm lijtimaa9

STRUCTURE SENTENCES

1. Ordinal numbers

This is the first time I've come here.	haadi 'awwal marra baaji lahoon.
This is the second school he's gone to.	haadi taani madrase raaḥ 9aleeha.
My office is the third office on your right.	maktabi taalit maktab 9ala 'iidak lyamiin.
This is the fourth article the newspaper has written.	haadi raabi9 maqaale katbatha ljariide.
Go to the third window.	ruuḥ 9aššubbaak ttaalit.
dwelling	saakin

floor, story	ṭaabi'
I'm living on the second floor.	'ana saakin fiṭṭaabi' ttaani.
Go to the fourth floor.	ruuḥ 9aṭṭaabi' rraabi9.

GRAMMAR

1. Ordinal numbers

The Arabic ordinal numbers are as follows:

masc.	*fem.*	
'awwal	'uula	*first*
taani	taanye	*second*
taalit	taalte	*third*
raabi9	raab9a	*fourth*
xaamis	xaamse	*fifth*
saadis	saadse	*sixth*
saabi9	saab9a	*seventh*
taamin	taamne	*eighth*
taasi9	taas9a	*ninth*
9aašir	9aašre	*tenth*

When these words follow the noun they modify, they behave as regular adjectives: ššubbaak ttaalit *the third window*, l'uuḍa ttaalte *the third room*. However, the ordinal frequently precedes the noun. In this case, the ordinal is always masculine singular: 'awwal marra *the first time*, taalit maktab *the third office*. No definite rules can be given about which construction is preferred.

DRILLS

1. Give appropriate replies to the following sentences.

bti9raf sleeman 9abdo ?

kam marra jtama9t ma9o ?

smi9to yuxṭub filmasaa'il lwaṭaniyye ?

biḥibbuu nnaas ?

kam marra ntaxabuu 9uḍu barlamaan ?

bti9raf šii 9an ḥayaato ?

feen t9allam huwwe ?

šuu daras fii blaad lingliiz ?

feen štaġal lamma riji9 min ngiltra ?

'eemta ṣaar ra'iis baladiyye ?

2. Give the Arabic equivalents of the following expressions, using the annexion construction. The first two are completed.

(1) a government school — madrasit ḥukuume

(2) the professor's name — 'ism l'ustaaz

a little medicine

a little work

a little food

the problem of the elections

the land problem

Ahmad's health

your children's health

your wife's health

several articles

the interest of the government

the interest of the country

the interest of the town

the name of the university

the name of the school

the name of the newspaper

the name of the hospital

your son's name

a box of tomatoes

several times	a cup of coffee
several newspapers	a kilo of squash
several maps	a member of parliament
several problems	a place name
the interest of the people	

3. In each of the following sentences replace the « he » forms of the verbs by the « I » forms. The first two are completed.

(1) t9allam filkulliyye l9arabiyye.	t9allamt filkulliyye l9arabiyye.
(2) ba9deen raaḥ 9ablaad lingliiz.	ba9deen ruḥt 9ablaad lingliiz.
sim9o yuxṭub filmasaa'il lwaṭaniyye.	bi9rafo šaxṣiyyan.
simi9 ktiir 9an sleemaan 9abdo.	ṣarlo santeen budrus ḥuquuq.
lamma riji9 štaġal filmaḥkame.	jtama9 ma9o 9iddit marraat.
kaan ġani.	daras ḥuquuq.
baa9 l'araaḍi.	biddo yudrus ḥuquuq filjaam9a.
'iri 9anno 9iddit maqaalaat.	lamma birja9 bištġil filmaḥkame.

4. For each of the following verbs in the suffix tense « he » form give the prefix tense « he » form. The first example of each group is completed, and all the verbs within any one group work the same way.

katab	buktub	ntaxab	bintxib
xaṭab		štaġal	
daras		jtama9	
		ftakar	
riji9	birja9	xalla	bixalli
simi9		kaffa	
9irif			
dall	bidill	jaab	bijiib
hazz		ṣaar	
ḥabb		baa9	

UNIT 19 • Friends. Higher numbers.

PATTERN SENTENCES

Welcome, Hanna.	'ahla wsahla, yaa ḥanna.
Welcome to you.	'ahla wsahla fiik.
How are you ?	kiif lḥaal ?
So-so.	maaši lḥaal.
sit	'a9ad bu'9ud
in order to	la-
time	zamaan
Good. Sit down and let's see.	ṭayyib, 'u'9ud lanšuuf.
I haven't see you for a long time.	min zamaan, maa šuftak.
family	'ahil
How's your family ?	kiif 'ahl lbeet ?
greet	sallam bisallim
They send greetings.	bisallmu 9aleek.
May God keep you (in reply).	'a*ll*a ysallmak.
news	'axbaar
friend	ṣaaḥib, pl. ('a)ṣḥaab
What's the news of our friends ?	šuu 'axbaar l'aṣḥaab ?
Well, who do you want to ask about ?	ya9ni, miin biddak tis'al 9anno?

Husayn and 'Ali and Samir and Ibrahim and Mahdi.	ḥseen, w9ali, wsamiir, wibraa-hiim, wmahdi.
Slowly. One by one.	šwayy, šwayy. waaḥad, waaḥad.
on his condition	9ala ḥaalo
Listen. Husayn is just as he was.	'isma9. ḥseen, lissaato 9ala ḥaalo.
teacher	m9allim
He's a teacher in the government school.	m9allim, fii madrast lḥukuume.
he wanted to go	kaan biddo yruuḥ
Didn't he want to go to Iraq?	maa kaan biddo yruuḥ 9al9iraaq?
but	laakin
Yes, but his wife wouldn't let him.	'aywa. laakin marto maa xallato.
weather, climate	ṭa'ṣ
She says the climate is too hot.	'aal ṭṭa'ṣ šoob ktiir.
All right. And 'Ali?	ṭayyib. w9ali?
leave	tarak bitrik
position, job	waẓiife
department	daa'ira
'Ali left his job in the Department of Health.	9ali, tarak waẓiifto fii daa'irt ṣṣiḥḥa.
clerk	kaatib
And now he's a petty clerk in the Orient Hotel.	whalla, kaatib ẓġiir fii 'uteel ššarq.

But does he like his work ?	bass, mabṣuuṭ bšuġlo ?
More or less.	ya9ni.
And Samir ?	wsamiir ?
promote	ra"a bira"i
As for Samir, I heard they intend to promote him because his work is good.	samiir, smi9t bidhum yra"uu. li'anno šuġlo kwayyis.
deserve	staḥa" bistiḥi"
Believe me, he deserves it.	saddi', bistḥi".
correct	maẓbuuṭ
That's correct.	haada maẓbuuṭ.
you had asked me	kunt sa'altni
You had asked me about Ibrahim.	kunt sa'altni 9an braahiim.
travel	saafar bisaafir
mother's brother	xaal
Ibrahim went to Damascus to his uncle's.	braahiim saafar 9aššaam, 9ind xaalo.
arrange	dabbar bidabbir
broadcasting (station)	'izaa9a
And his uncle got a job for him in the radio station.	wxaalo dabbarlo waẓiife fil'izaa9a.
And his wife went with him ?	wmarto raaḥat ma9o ?
Yes, and she works in the radio station, too.	'aywa. whiyye, kamaan, btištġil fil'izaa9a.

And what's the news of Mahdi?	wšuu 'axbaar mahdi ?
Has he got a job ?	nšaa*ll*a štaġal ?
As for Mahdi, I saw him in Beirut.	mahdi, šufto fii beeruut.
company	širke
He works for a tourist agency.	bištġil ma9 širkit siyaaḥa.
get ready	sta9add bist9idd
travel	safar
the United States	lwilaayaat lmuttáḥide
And he's getting ready to go to the United States.	w9ambist9idd lassafar, lalwilaayaat lmuttáḥide.
What's he going to do there ?	šuu biddo yi9mal hunaak ?
I think he's going to study.	baftkir biddo yudrus.
anyone	ḥad(a)
if	'iza
If you see any of them, say hello to them for me.	'iza bitšuuf ḥad minhum, sallimli 9alee(h).
May God keep you (in reply).	'a*ll*a ysallmak.

Additional vocabulary

Airline	širkit ṭayaraan
electricity	kahraba
Electric company	širkit kahraba
Oil Company	širkit zeet
steamship	baaxira, pl. bawaaxir
Steamship company	širkit bawaaxir

Higher numbers

One hundred and one	miyye wwaaḥad
One hundred and two	miyye witneen
One hundred and fifteen	miyye wxamis ṭa9š
One hundred and sixty	miyye wsittiin
One hundred and seventy-five	miyye wxamse wsab9iin
One thousand	'alf
Two thousand	'alfeen
Three thousand	tlat taalaaf
Twelve thousand	ṭna9šar 'alf
Thirty thousand	tlaatiin 'alf
Fifty-five thousand	xamse wxamsiin 'alf
One hundred thousand	miit 'alf
One million	malyoon
Two million	malyooneen
Three million	tlat malayiin
Twelve million	ṭna9šar malyoon

STRUCTURE SENTENCES

1. Strict agreement

Where is there a good restaurant?	ween fii maṭ9am mniiḥ?
This is a clean place.	haada maḥall nḍiif.
His father was poor.	'abuu kaan fa'iir.
Ali left his job.	9ali tarak waẓiifto.
The trip was good.	ssafra kaanat mniiḥa.

My watch needs fixing.	saa9ti bidha taṣliiḥ.
His wife went with him.	marto raaḥat ma9o.
The fever went away today.	lyoom, raaḥat lḥaraara.
Are your children big or little?	wlaadak kbaar, willa ẓġaar ?
The people like him very much.	nnaas biḥibbuu ktiir.
My family is very busy.	'ahli mašġuuliin ktiir.
There are a lot of people who work here.	fii naas ktiir bištiġlu hoon.
Two people taught me Arabic.	tneen 9allamuuni 9arabi.
There are two large bookstores here.	fii hoon maktabteen kbaar.
I bought two new suits.	štareet bad*i*lteen jdaad.

2. Deflected agreement

Things are at a standstill.	l'ašġaal waa'fe.
His prices are reasonable.	'as9aaro ma9'uule.
Do you have schools that teach Arabic ?	fii 9indkum madaaris bit9allim 9arabi ?
The newspapers have written a lot of articles about him.	ljaraayid katbat 9anno maqaalaat ktiire.
Listen to him give a speech on the national problems.	'isma9o yuxṭub filmasaa'il lwaṭaniyye.
People don't have any money.	nnaas maa fii ma9ha maṣaari.
I bought two summer suits.	štareet bad*i*lteen ṣeefiyye.

GRAMMAR

1. Compound numbers

In compound numbers above 20, the millions, thousands, hundreds, tens, and units are joined by w-/wi- *and.* A higher number precedes a lower one, except in combinations of units and tens, where the unit comes first : 'alf wtisi9 miyye wtamaanye wxamsiin *one thousand and nine hundred and eight and fifty* (*1958*).

2. Agreement

A formal system of *agreement* (also called *concord*) connects subordinate words (adjectives, verbs, and pronouns) to the nouns on which they depend. Arabic has two principal types of agreement : *strict* and *deflected.*

(1) Strict agreement : Subordinate words have the same gender (masculine or feminine) and number (singular or plural) as the noun on which they depend.

'abuu kaan fa'iir. *His father was poor.*

ssafra kaanat mniiḥa. *The trip was good.*

wlaadak kbaar, willa ẓġaar ? *Are your children big or little ?*

nnaas biḥibbuu ktiir. *The people like him very much.*

(2) Deflected agreement : The noun is plural but the subordinate words are feminine singular. With non-personal plurals (i.e. plurals that do not refer to human beings) deflected agreement is more common than strict agreement. Deflected agreement may also occur with some noun plurals that refer to human beings; one of these is naas *people.*

'as9aaro ma9'uule. *His prices are reasonable.*

ljaraayid katbat 9anno maqaalaat ktiire.	*The newspapers have written a lot of articles about him.*
nnaas maa fii ma9ha maṣaari.	*The people don't have any money.*

The dual is a kind of plural. It shows deflected agreement if the noun is non-personal and the adjective is a nisbe : bad*i*lteen ṣeefiyye *two summer suits.* Otherwise there is strict agreement : bad*i*lteen jdaad *two new suits*, ṣuḥufiyyeen 'ameerkaan *two American journalists.*

DRILLS

1. Give appropriate replies to the following sentences.

šuu bti9rafli 9an ḥseen ?	9ind miin raaḥ ?
feen bi9allim huwwe ?	šuu waẓiifto ?
leeš maa raaḥ 9al9iraaq ?	miin dabbarlo lwaẓiife ?
9ali, lissaato fii daa'irt ṣṣiḥḥa ?	marto raaḥat ma9o ?
feen bištġil halla ?	feen btištġil hiyye ?
laween saafar braahiim ?	

2. In each of the following sentences change the singular prefix tense verb form to the corresponding plural, making any other changes that may be necessary.

miin biddak tis'al 9anno ?	bukra bisaafir 9aššaam.
laazim 'atrik ba9id xamis tiyyaam.	biddo ydabbirlak šuġul.
'addeeš ṣarlak btudrus 9arabi ?	'addeeš ṣarlak btit9allam filjaam9a ?
	bištġil fii 'uteel ššarq.

kam yoom raḥtu'9ud hoon ?

bukra baruuḥ 9al9iraaq.

leeš maa bitruuḥ ma9i ?

'eemta biddak tsaafir ?

'addeeš ṣarlak btištġil hoon ?

saddi', bistḥi''.

'addeeš ṣarlo biḥki 9arabi ?

3. In each of the following sentences change the singular suffix tense verb form to the corresponding plural, making any other changes that may be necessary.

raaḥ 9al9iraaq 'abil santeen.

šaaf mahdi fii beeruut.

'alli 'inno raḥyiiji lahoon.

'eemta tarakt ššaam ?

tarak šuġlo.

kunt sa'altni 9an samiir.

dabbarlo waẓiife fii širkit siyaaḥa.

dabbartillo waẓiife kwayyse.

saafart 9aššaam.

saafar 9abeeruut 9ind xaalo.

štaġalt fil'izaa9a.

štaġal fii 'uteel ššarq.

jtama9t ma9o 9iddit marraat.

maa xallaa yruuḥ 9aššaam.

feen laa'a šuġul ?

'riit 9anno maqaalaat ktiire.

ḥakaali 9an ḥseen.

sta9addeet lassafar ?

4. In each of the following sentences change the prefix tense verb forms to the corresponding suffix tense forms.

ḥseen biruuḥ 9abeeruut.

marto maa bitruuḥ ma9o.

bizuur xaalo fiššaam.

bnirja9 9al'uds.

badrus ḥuquuq.

bidabbirli waẓiife filḥukuume.

binsaafir 9al9iraaq.

bisaa9id 'abuu.

baaxud lbaaboor min beeruut.

bnaaxud ṭṭayyaara labaġdaad.

bištġil ma9 širkit siyaaḥa.

bištiġlu fii 'uteel plaaza.

5, Give the Arabic equivalent of the following numbers.

21	71	93	54	632
102	726	81	91	1917
115	31	88	999	1929
140	550	228	425	1939
41	65	61	307	1941
400	51	75	650	1953

6. For each of the following verbs in the suffix tense « he » form give the prefix tense « he » form. The first example of each group is completed, and all the verbs within any one group work the same way.

fara'	bifri'	kaan	bikuun
tarak		raaḥ	
sallam	bisallim	šaaf	
dabbar		'aal	
9arraf		'aam	
saa9ad	bisaa9id	kaffa	bikaffi
saafar		xalla	
naasab		ra''a	

UNIT 20 • A radio station — I.

PATTERN SENTENCES

Persons : F : Fathi, the director of the station ; A ; 'Ali, his assistant ; W : Mr. West ; A group of Americans from the Embassy.

('Ali speaks to Mr. West and the group of Americans)

before	'abil maa
have (someone) visit	zawwar bizawwir
part, division, section	qisim, pl. 'aqsaam
A : Let's drink a cup of coffee before we have you visit the divisions of the broadcasting station.	xalliina nišrab finjaan 'ahwe, 'abil maa nzawwirkum 'aqsaam l'izaa9a.
In a little while the director will come, and I'll introduce you to him.	ba9d šwayy, biiji lmudiir, wba9arrifkum 9alee.

('Ali goes in to see the director)

Mr. Fathi, could you give us a few minutes of your time ?	yaa 'ustaaz fatḥi, mumkin ta9ṭiina min wa'tak kam d'ii'a?
Because we have some American visitors that work in the Embassy.	li'anno fii 9inna zuwwaar 'ameerkaan, bištiġlu fissafaara.
be introduced	t9arraf bit9arraf

	And they'd like to be introduced to you.	wbiḥibbu yit9arrafu 9ala ḥaḍirtak.
F :	They're very welcome. Have them come in.	'ahlan wasahlan. xalliihum yitfaḍḍalu.
	purpose	ġaraḍ
	Do you know what their purpose is?	bti9raf šuu ġaraḍhum?
	intention, object	ġaaye
	meet	'aabal bi'aabil
A :	I think their intention is first of all to meet you.	baftkir ġaayithum 'abil kullši, 'inhum y'aabluuk.
	look around, look over	tfarraj bitfarraj
	And then to look around the broadcasting station.	wba9deen yitfarraju 9al'izaa9a.
	very	jiddan
F :	But it's very necessary for us to give them more attention than other people.	bass ḍaruuri jiddan, nihtamm fiihum, 'aktar min ġeerhum.
	so that	laḥatta
	So that they'll leave here with a good impression.	laḥatta yiṭla9u min hoon bfikra mniiḥa.

('Ali returns to the group of Americans)

A :	Please come with me to the director.	tfaḍḍalu ma9i 9ind lmudiir.
	delighted	masruur
	visit	zyaara
	have a good time	nbaṣaṭ binbṣiṭ

F : Welcome. I'm delighted at your visit, and hope you'll have a good time here.	'ahlan wasahlan. 'ana masruur bizyaaritkum, winšaa*lla* btinbiṣṭu hoon.
brethren	'ixwaan
show	farja bifarji
Now 'Ali, let's go with the gentlemen, and show them whatever they want.	halla yaa 9ali, xalliina nruuḥ ma9 l'ixwaan, winfarjiihum šuu maa bidhum.
after	ba9id maa
finish	xallaṣ bixalliṣ
And after we've finished I shall be very delighted if you will come with me to lunch.	wba9id maa nxalliṣ bakuun masruur jiddan, 'iza btitfaḍḍalu ma9i 9alġada.
inconvenience	'iz9aaj
W: The honor is ours, only if it won't be an inconvenience for you.	'ilna ššaraf, bass 'iza maa bikuun fii 'iz9aaj laḥaḍritkum.
(not) at all	'abadan
F : No, there's no inconvenience at all. You're very welcome.	la'. maa fii 'iz9aaj 'abadan. 'ahlan wasahlan fiikum.

STRUCTURE SENTENCES

1. Relative sentences with ('i)lli

Where is the book ?	feen liktaab ?
It was on the table.	kaan 9aṭṭaawle.

Where is the book that was on the table?	feen liktaab lli kaan 9aṭṭaawle?
Do you know the man?	bti9raf rrijjaal?
He was across from us.	kaan 'baalna.
Do you know the man who was across from us?	bti9raf rrijjaal lli kaan 'baalna?
This is the restaurant.	haada lmaṭ9am.
I told you about it.	'ultillak 9anno.
This is the restaurant that I told you about.	haada lmaṭ9am lli 'ultillak 9anno.
What's the price of the car?	'addeeš ḥa" ssayyaara?
You want to buy it.	biddak tištriiha.
What's the price of the car that you want to buy?	'addeeš ḥa" ssayyaara lli biddak tištriiha?
Who is the teacher?	miin l'ustaaz?
He taught you.	9allamak.
Who's the teacher who taught you?	miin l'ustaaz lli 9allamak?
Who?	miin?
They visited the broadcasting station today	zaaru l'izaa9a lyoom.
Who are (the people) that visited the broadcasting station today?	miin lli zaaru l'izaa9a lyoom?

2. Relative sentences without ('i)lli

Do you have schools?	fii 9indkum madaaris?
She teaches Arabic.	bit9allim 9arabi.
Do you have schools that teach Arabic?	fii 9indkum madaaris, bit9allim 9arabi?
We have American visitors.	fii 9inna zuwwaar 'ameer-kaan.
They work in the Embassy.	bištiğlu fissafaara.
We have some American visitors that work in the Embassy.	fii 9inna zuwwaar 'ameerkaan, bištiğlu fissafaara.
This is the third job.	haadi taalit waẓiife.
He took it.	'axadha.
This is the third job he's taken.	haadi taalit waẓiife 'axadha.
There's a man here.	fii rijjaal hoon.
He wants to speak to you.	biriid yiḥki ma9ak.
There's a man here who wants to speak to you.	fii rijjaal hoon, biriid yiḥki ma9ak.
I have a friend.	fii 9indi ṣaaḥib.
I want to introduce you to him.	biddi 'a9arrfak 9alee(h).
I have a friend I want to introduce you to.	fii 9indi ṣaaḥib, biddi 'a9arrfak 9alee.

.3 The word ('i)lli as a pronoun

You want it.	biddak yyaa(h).
Choose what you want.	na''i lli biddak yyaa.
I know him.	ba9rafo.
As far as I know, he's not here.	'illi ba9rafo, 'inno miš hoon.
He wants me.	biddo yyaani.
He who wants me, let him come to me.	'illi biddo yyaani, yiiji la9indi.
You told me it.	'ultilli yyaa(h).
What you told me is right.	'illi 'ultilli yyaa, mažbuuṭ.

GRAMMAR

I. Relative sentences

A compound sentence like feen liktaab lli kaan 9aṭṭaawle? *where is the book that was on the table?* consists of two independent sentences: feen liktaab? *where is the book?* and kaan 9aṭṭaawle *it was on the table*, connected by the word ('i)lli *the one*.

The first sentence is called the *principal* sentence, the second the *relative* sentence. The relative sentence is like an adjective; it modifies or describes a noun, called the *antecedent*, in the principal sentence (in this case liktaab *the book*).

If the antecedent is definite (e.g. liktaab *the book*), the two sentences are linked by ('i)lli. If the antecedent is indefinite (e.g. rijjaal *a man*) there is no linking word, as in fii rijjaal hoon, biriid yiḥki ma9ak *there is a man here who wants to speak to you*.

The relative sentence almost always contains a cross-reference to the antecedent noun. This may be the subject marker of a verb, as in the sentences above; this is the case when the antecedent is the subject of the relative sentence. Or it may be a pronoun ending; this is the case when the antecedent is not the subject of the relative sentence. For example, in the compound sentence haada lmaṭ9am lli 'ultillak 9anno *this is the restaurant I told you about*, the pronoun ending -o *him* refers back to lmaṭ9am *the restaurant*.

In sentences like na''i lli biddak yyaa(h) *choose what you want*, the word ('i)lli is a pronoun. It is here the antecedent of the following relative sentence biddak yyaa(h) *you want it*; the pronoun -(h) refers back to ('i)lli.

2. Simple and complex verbs

The Arabic verb is divided into two main groups: *simple* verbs, having stems consisting of a root plus a simple pattern, and *complex* verbs, having stems consisting of a root plus a pattern complex.

Following the tradition of the native Arab grammarians, we distinguish nine classes or *Forms* of the complex verb, and mark them with the customary roman numerals, II–X, number I being reserved for the simple verb.

3. Verbs of Form I

The characteristic of verbs of Form I is that they have a simple pattern. There are four main variants, depending on the root type.

(1) Regular roots. Suffix tense may be -a-a- or -i-i-; prefix tense --a-, --i-, --u-.

root			
ftḥ	fataḥ	biftaḥ	*open*

s'l	**sa'al**	**bis'al**	***ask***
fr'	**fara'**	**bifri'**	***make a difference***
trk	**tarak**	**bitrik**	***leave***
drs	**daras**	**budrus**	***study***
ktb	**katab**	**buktub**	***write***
fhm	**fihim**	**bifham**	***understand***
šrb	**širib**	**bišrab**	***drink***
msk	**misik**	**bimsik**	***hold***

(2) Doubled roots. Suffix tense -a--; prefix tense -i--, -u--, -a-- (rare).

dll	**dall**	**bidill**	***direct***
ḥbb	**ḥabb**	**biḥibb**	***like***
ḥṭṭ	**ḥaṭṭ**	**biḥuṭṭ**	***put***
ṭmm	**ṭamm**	**biṭamm**	***remain***

(3) Hollow roots. Suffix tense -aa-; prefix tense -ii-, -uu-, -aa- (rare).

jyb	**jaab**	**bijiib**	***bring***
ṣyr	**ṣaar**	**biṣiir**	***become***
kwn	**kaan**	**bikuun**	***be***
zwr	**zaar**	**bizuur**	***visit***
nwm	**naam**	**binaam**	***sleep***

(4) Weak roots. Suffix tense may be -a-a or -i-i; prefix tense --a or --i.

bdy	bada	bibda	*begin*
ḥky	ḥaka	biḥki	*speak*
mšy	maša	bimši	*walk*
b'y	bi'i	bib'a	*remain*
nsy	nisi	binsa	*forget*

4. Verbs of Form II

The characteristic of verbs of Form II is doubling of the second consonant of the root. There are two variants of the pattern, depending on the root type.

(1) Regular, Doubled, and Hollow roots. Suffix tense -a--a-; prefix tense -a--i-.

root			
šrf	šarraf	bišarrif	*honor*
9lm	9allam	bi9allim	*teach*
9rf	9arraf	bi9arrif	*introduce*
jdd	jaddad	bijaddid	*renew*
xff	xaffaf	bixaffif	*lighten*
zwd	zawwad	bizawwid	*supply*
'yd	'ayyad	bi'ayyid	*support*

(2) Weak roots. Suffix tense -a--a; prefix tense -a--i.

r'y	ra''a	bira''i	*promote*
xly	xalla	bixalli	*keep, allow*

Many of these verbs have the meaning « cause something to happen » : 9arraf *make (someone) know, introduce*, beside 9irif *know;* fahham *make (someone) understand*, beside fihim *understand*; zawwar *have (someone) visit*, beside zaar *visit.*

5. Verbs of Form III

The characteristic of verbs of Form III is long *aa* between the first and second consonants of the root. There are two variants of the pattern, depending on the root type.

(1) Regular, Doubled, and Hollow roots. Suffix tense -aa-a- ; prefix tense -aa-i-.

root			
'bl	'aabal	bi'aabil	*meet*
sfr	saafar	bisaafir	*travel*
s9d	saa9ad	bisaa9id	*help*
'ṣṣ	'aaṣaṣ	bi'aaṣiṣ	*punish*
jwb	jaawab	bijaawib	*answer*

(2) Weak roots. Suffix tense -aa-a ; prefix tense -aa-i.

ḥky	ḥaaka	biḥaaki	*talk to*
l'y	laa'a	bilaa'i	*meet, find*

Many of these verbs have the meaning « reciprocal interaction or cooperation ».

DRILLS

1. Give appropriate replies to the following sentences.

miin mudiir l'izaa9a ?	feen bištiġlu humme ?
miin lli zaaru l'izaa9a lyoom ?	šuu kaan ġaraḏhum ?

2. In each of the following sentences replace the expression in parentheses by the appropriate pronoun ending.

zawwarna (l'ameerkaan) 'aqsaam l'izaa9a.	binfarji (zzuwwaar) šuu maa bidhum.
9arrafna (l'ameerkaan) 9almudiir.	xallaṣna (ššuġul).
	sa'alna (ḥasan) 9anno.
biḥibbu yit9arrafu 9a(lmudiir).	bti9rafu (lmudiir) ?
biḥibbu y'aablu (lmudiir).	šaafo (l'izaa9a) ?
'aabalu (l'ustaaz fatḥi).	baa9u (l'araaḍi).
'aabalna (l'ustaaz fatḥi).	ntaxabu (9ali) 9uḍu barlamaan.
'aabalna (mulḥaq ṭṭayaraan).	laa'eetu (9ali) fil'izaa9a ?
9arraftu (zzuwwaar) 9almudiir?	ra''u (ḥasan)?
'aabaltu (lmudiir) šaxṣiyyan ?	štareena (ssayyaara).
smi9tu (sleemaan 9abdo) yuxṭub ?	bnistanna (9ali) hoon.
	biḥibbu (9ali) ktiir.

3. In each of the following sentences change the prefix tense form of the verb to the corresponding suffix tense.

binzawwirhum l'izaa9a.	leeš maa bit'aablo šaxṣiyyan ?
ba9deen biiji l'ustaaz fatḥi.	ba9deen bitfarraju 9al'izaa9a.

ba9arrifhum 9alee.	binfarjiihum šuu maa bidhum.
bištiġlu fissafaara.	'eemtan bitxalliṣ šuġlak ?

4. Give the Arabic for the following.

Who's the teacher that taught him ?	He understands everything that I tell him.
This is the car he wants to sell.	This is the fourth time he's asked me.
Who's the man that came with you ?	I have a car that needs fixing.
Where's the bookstore you told me about ?	This is the first time I've seen him.
Is this the article I ought to read ?	We have several schools that teach Arabic.
Is this the hospital that Hasan went to ?	This is a problem that we have to study.
We have some visitors who want to meet the director.	I've heard that he has a house that he wants to sell.
I've read several articles that he wrote.	

5. For each of the following verbs in the suffix tense « he » form give the prefix tense « he » form. The first example of each group is completed, and all the verbs within any one group work in the same way.

fihim	bifham	saa9ad	bisaa9id	'aal	bi'uul
širib		naasab		kaan	
9irif		'aabal		'aam	

sakkar bisakkir	tšarraf bitšarraf
zawwar	tfaḍḍal
9arraf	t9arraf
xallaṣ	t9allam
faḍḍal	tfarraj
	t9azzab

UNIT 21 • A radio station — II.

PATTERN SENTENCES

begin	bada bibda
room	ġurfe
F: All right, 'Ali, let's begin with the news room.	ṭayyib, yaa 9ali. xalliina nibda bġurfit l'axbaar.
agency	wakaale, pl. -aat
supply	zawwad bizawwid
We have several agencies that supply us with news.	fii 9inna 9iddit wakaalaat bidzawwidna bil'axbaar.
for example	matalan
Reuters	wakaalit rooytar
the Arab News Agency	wakaalt l'anbaa' l9arabiyye
For example, Reuters and the Arab News Agency and others.	matalan, wakaalit rooytar, wwakaalt l'anbaa' l9arabiyye, wġeerhum.
editing	taḥriir
translation	tarjame
The division of editing and translation is in the next room.	qism ttaḥriir wittarjame, fil-ġurfe ttaanye.
take turns at	tnaawab bitnaawab
work	9amal

night and day	ṭuul lleel winnhaar
And we have there five employees that take turns at the work night and day.	w9inna hunaak xams mwaẓẓafiin, bitnaawabu l9amal, ṭuul lleel winnhaar.
bulletin	našra, pl. -aat
news (adj.)	'ixbaari
broadcast	'azaa9 bizii9
W : How many news bulletins do you broadcast per day ?	kam našra 'ixbaariyye bidzii9u filyoom ?
morning (adj.)	ṣabaaḥi
evening (adj.)	masaa'i
F : We have a morning bulletin at seven o'clock.	fii 9inna našra ṣabaaḥiyye, ssaa9a sab9a.
afternoon	ba9d ḍḍuhur
Then there's the two o'clock afternoon bulletin.	ba9deen, fii našrit ssaa9a tinteen ba9d ḍḍuhur.
And there are two bulletins in the evening.	wfii naš*i*rteen filmasa.
One at six o'clock and the other at ten o'clock.	waḥde ssaa9a sitte, wittaanye ssaa9a 9ašra.
All of these bulletins are in the Arabic language.	haadi nnašraat kullha, filluġa l9arabiyye.
suppose	ẓann biẓunn
And I suppose that you hear our English bulletin at 5 : 30.	w'aẓunn 'inkum btisma9u našritna lingliiziyye, ssaa9a xamse wnuṣṣ.

Now excuse me for a little while.	halla btismaḥuuli šwayy.
appointment	maw9id
ministry, cabinet	wazaara
the prime minister	ra'iis lwazaara
Because I have an appointment with the Prime Minister.	li'anno 9indi maw9id ma9 ra'iis lwazaara.
I hope I'll see you in an hour.	nšaa*ll*a bašuufkum ba9id saa9a.
have (someone) go around	dawwar bidawwir
'Ali, have them go around the other divisions.	yaa 9ali. dawwirhum 9al'aqsaam ttaanye.
program	barnaamaj
child	ṭifil, pl. 'aṭfaal
And let them hear the children's program.	wxalliihum yisma9u barnaamaj l'aṭfaal.
studio	stuudyo
recording	tasjiil
And then take them to the recording studio.	wxudhum ba9deen 9astuudyo ttasjiil.
party	ḥafle
music (adj.)	muusiiqi
So that they may hear our music recital.	laḥatta yisma9u ḥaflitna lmuusiiqiyye.

STRUCTURE SENTENCES

1. The comparative

bigger, older	'akbar
He's older than I am.	huwwe 'akbar minni fil9umur.
farther	'ab9ad
Which is farther from here? Baghdad or Cairo?	miin 'ab9ad min hoon? baġdaad, willa lqaahira?
better	'aḥsan
He speaks Arabic better than I do.	biḥki 9arabi 'aḥsan minni.
more	'aktar
He knows more French than his wife does.	bi9raf fransaawi 'aktar min marto.
nicer	'aḥla
There's nothing nicer than that.	'aḥla min heek, maa fii.
better for you	'aḥsanlak
It's better for you to come with me.	'aḥsanlak tiiji ma9i.
He's the youngest of them.	huwwe 'aẓġar waaḥad fiihum.
more important	'ahamm
The most important problem of today is the problem of the elections.	'ahamm mas'ale lyoom, mas'alt lintixaabaat.

middle	'awṣaṭ
I studied the history of the Middle East.	darast taariix ššarq l'awṣaṭ.
near	'adna
This is a map of the Near East.	haadi xaarṭa laššarq l'adna.
far	'aqṣa
I don't know much about the Far East.	maa ba9raf ktiir 9an ššarq l'aqṣa
supreme	'a9la, f. 9ulya
His father works in the Supreme Court.	'abuu bištġil filmaḥkame l9ulya.
busier	mašġuul 'aktar
I'm busier than you are.	'ana mašġuul 'aktar minnak.

2. Comparative after maa

How nice she is !	maa 'aḥlaaha.
How big it is !	maa 'akbaro.

GRAMMAR

1. The comparative

Arabic has a class of words called *comparatives*. The typical comparative correlates with an underlying adjective, has the same root as the adjective, has a predictable pattern, and has a meaning closely related to the meaning of the adjective.

(1) With Regular and Hollow roots the comparative has the pattern 'a--a-.

root	comparative		underlying adjective	
kbr	'akbar	*bigger*	kbiir	*big*
ẓġr	'aẓġar	*smaller*	ẓġiir	*small*
b9d	'ab9ad	*farther*	b9iid	*far*
'rb	'a'rab	*nearer*	'ariib	*near*
ṭyb	'aṭyab	*tastier*	ṭayyib	*tasty*

(2) With Doubled roots the pattern is 'a-a-- (occasionally 'a--a-, as above).

jdd	'ajadd	*newer*	jdiid	*new*
xff	'axaff	*lighter*	xafiif	*light*
hmm	'ahamm	*more important*	muhimm	*important*

(3) With Weak roots the pattern is 'a--a.

ḥlw	'aḥla	*nicer*	ḥilu	*nice*
ġly	'aġla	*more expensive*	ġaali	*expensive*
9ly	'a9la	*higher*	9aali	*high*

All the above are either masculine or feminine in gender. There is a special pattern that is feminiue only: -u--a. This is quite rare, is restricted to a few roots, and chiefly appears in expressions borrowed from the written language.

kbr	kubra	*major*
ṣġr	ṣuġra	*minor*
wṣṭ	wuṣṭa	*central*
fṣḥ	fuṣḥa	*pure*
9ly	9ulya	*supreme*

Most adjectives with a pattern complex do not form the comparative by a pattern, but by a phrase with 'aktar *more* : mašġuul 'aktar *busier*; mit9allim 'aktar *more educated.* One adjective, mniiḥ *good*, has a suppletion root: 'aḥsan *better*.

The Arabic comparative is the equivalent of both the English comparative (*nearer, more important*) and superlative (*nearest, most important*). When two objects or classes are compared the usual translation is the English comparative: beeruut 'akbar min 9ammaan *Beirut is larger than Amman*; the Arabic equivalent of *than* is min. When more than two objects are compared, or when an absolute statement is made, the usual translation is the English superlative: lmaḥkame l9ulya *the supreme court*, 'ahamm mas'ale *the most important problem.*

A very common construction consists of the comparative immediately followed by an indefinite singular noun : 'ahamm mas'ale *the most important problem.* This is generally translated by a definite superlative, although the Arabic construction is grammatically indefinite.

A special use of the comparative is in a construction following unstressed maa. The meaning is exclamatory: maa 'akbaro *how big it is!*

2. Verbs of Form IV

The characteristic of verbs of Form IV is a prefixed 'a- in the suffix tense; this element drops in the prefix tense. There are four variants of the pattern, depending on the root type.

(1) Regular roots. Suffix tense 'a--a-; prefix tense --i-.

root			
9jb	'a9jab	bi9jib	*please*
z9j	'az9aj	biz9ij	*disturb*

(2) Doubled roots. Suffix tense 'a-a--; prefix tense -i--.

ṣrr	'aṣarr	biṣirr	*insist*

(3) Hollow roots. Suffix tense 'a-aa-; prefix tense -ii-.

zy9	'azaa9	bizii9	*broadcast*

(4) Weak roots. Suffix tense 'a--a; prefix tense --i.

9ṭy	'a9ṭa	bya9ṭi	*give*

Verbs of Form IV are very rare in spoken Arabic.

3. Verbs of Form V

The characteristics of verbs of Form V are two: doubling of the second consonant of the root, and prefixed t-. There are two variants of the pattern, depending on the root type.

(1) Regular, Doubled, and Hollow roots. Suffix and prefix tense patterns identical : t-a--a-.

root			
šrf	tšarraf	bitšarraf	*be honored*
9lm	t9allam	bit9allam	*be taught, learn*
9rf	t9arraf	bit9arraf	*be introduced*
'ss	t'assas	bit'assas	*be established*
jwz	djawwaz	bidjawwaz	*be married*

(2) Weak roots. Suffix and prefix tense patterns identical : t-a--a.

r'y	tra''a	bitra''a	*be promoted*

Many of these verbs have the meaning « the subject is being acted upon », often translated by the English passive phrase.

Form V stands in a reciprocal relation to Form II. When the Form II verb means «cause (something)», the corresponding Form V verb means «be caused»: šarraf *honor*, beside tšarraf *be honored.*

4. Verbs of Form VI

The characteristics of verbs of Form VI are two: long *aa* between the first and second consonants of the root, and prefixed t-. There are two variants of the pattern, depending on the root type.

(1) Regular, Doubled, and Hollow roots. Suffix and prefix tense patterns identical: t-aa-a-.

root			
l9b	tlaa9ab	bitlaa9ab	*be deceitful*
s9d	tsaa9ad	bitsaa9ad	*be helped*
'ṣṣ	t'aaṣaṣ	bit'aaṣaṣ	*be punished*
nwb	tnaawab	bitnaawab	*take turns at*

(2) Weak roots. Suffix and prefix tense patterns identical: t-aa-a.

l'y	tlaa'a	bitlaa'a	*meet together*

Some of these verbs have the meaning «reciprocal action by more than one actor», and are usually in the plural: bitnaawabu l9amal *they take turns at the work.*

Others have the meaning «the subject is being acted upon», much like verbs of Form V.

Form VI stands in a reciprocal relation to Form III. When the Form III verb means «do (something)», the corresponding Form VI verb means «be done»: saa9ad *help*, tsaa9ad *be helped*

DRILLS

1. Give appropriate replies to the following sentences.

šuu 'awwal šii šaafuu ?

min feen btiiji 'axbaar l'izaa9a?

kam mwaẓẓaf fii qism ttaḥriir wittarjame ?

kam našra 'ixbaariyye bizii9u filyoom ?

'ayy saa9a nnašra ṣṣabaaḥiyye?

'eemta bizii9u našrit ba9d ḍḍuhur ?

kam našra bizii9u filmasa ?

b'ayy luġa bizii9u našraat l'axbaar ?

'ayy barnaamaj sim9u ba9id maa tarakhum lmudiir ?

9ala 'ayy stuudyo raaḥu ?

šuu sim9u hunaak ?

2. In each of the following sentences change the suffix tense form of the verb to the corresponding prefix tense.

zawwarnaahum 'aqsaam l'izaa9a.

9arrafnaahum 9almudiir.

'aabaluu šaxṣiyyan.

bada bġurfit l'axbaar.

'ayy saa9a badat l'izaa9a ?

zawwaduuha bil'axbaar.

tnaawabna l9amal.

kam našra 'azaa9u filyoom ?

b'ayy luġa 'azaa9u našraat l'axbaar?

dawwarthum 9al'aqsaam ttaanye.

'axadnaahum 9ala qism ttaḥriir.

3. Give the Arabic for the following, using the noun annexion construction.

the news of the friends

the news of our friends

the director's visit

the news room

news of Samir	the recording room
a government school	the children's program
the government school	several divisions
the health department	several agencies
a tourist agency	the sections of the radio station
an airline (an aviation company)	the translation section
	the editing section

4. For each of the following verbs in the suffix tense « he » form give the prefix tense « he » form. The first example of each group is completed, and all the verbs within any one group work the same way.

riji9	birja9	tlaa9ab	bitlaa9ab
simi9		tnaawab	
fihim			
9imil			
'addam	bi'addim	ḥaṭṭ	biḥuṭṭ
zawwar		ẓann	
dawwar			
zawwad			

UNIT 22 • Filling out applications.

PATTERN SENTENCES

(Farid is talking to a secretary in the Consulate)

coming, having come	jaay
present	'addam bi'addim
request	ṭalab
I've come to present a request for a job in the Consulate.	'ana jaay 'a'addim ṭalab šuġul fil'unṣliyye.
Who should I see?	miin laazim 'ašuuf?
Please wait a moment.	min faḍlak, stanna šwayy.
(The secretary goes out and returns)	
In five minutes the consul would like to meet you personally.	ba9id xamis da'aayi', l'unṣul biḥibb y'aablak šaxṣiyyan.
(Farid goes in to see the consul)	
sort	noo9
What sort of work do you want?	šuu noo9 ššuġl lli biddak yyaa?
pertaining to writing	kitaabi

typing	ṭibaa9a
or	'aw
accounting	m(u)ḥaasabaat
Oh, a secretarial position such as translating and typing or accounting.	ya9ni. waẓiife kitaabiyye, mitil tarjame, wṭibaa9a, 'aw muḥaa-sabaat.
fill out	9abba bi9abbi
official, formal	rasmi
Fine. But you'll have to fill out a formal application.	ṭayyib, bass, laazim t9abbi ṭalab rasmi.
I'm ready.	ḥaaḍir.
information	ma9luumaat
Well then, could you give me the necessary information ?	mumkin 'izan ta9ṭiini lma9luumaat llaazme ?
reply, answer	jawaab
prompt, quick	musta9jal
Because I'd like to give you a prompt reply.	li'anno baḥibb 'a9ṭiik jawaab musta9jal.
generous	kariim
What's your name ?	l'ism lkariim ?
Farid Hanna Abu Salman.	fariid ḥanna 'abu salmaan.
How old are you ?	'addeeš 9umrak ?
Twenty-five.	xamse w9išriin sane.
date	taariix
birth	wilaade

What's the date of your birth?	šuu taariix lwilaade ?
February fourth, 1933.	'arba9a šbaaṭ, sant 'alf wtisi9 miyye witlaate witlaatiin.
place	makaan
All right. Where's your place of birth ?	ṭayyib. makaan lwilaade, feen?
Bethlehem.	beet laḥim.
father	waalid
Your father's name ?	'ism lwaalid ?
Hanna Abu Salman.	ḥanna 'abu salmaan.
address	9unwaan
Your father's address ?	9unwaan lwaalid ?
street	šaari9
star	najme
Star Street, Bethlehem.	šaari9 nnajme, beet laḥim.
mother	waalde
Your mother's name ?	'ism lwaalde ?
Huda Abu Salman.	huda 'abu salmaan.
self, same	nafs *or* zaat
I suppose it's also the same address, isn't it ?	'aẓunn kamaan nafs l9unwaan, miš heek ?
Yes.	na9am.
Your nationality ?	ljinsiyye ?
Jordanian	'urduni.
certificate, testimony	šhaade, pl. -aat

pertaining to knowledge	9ilmi
What are your diplomas ?	šuu šhaadaatak l9ilmiyye ?
I have a B. A. from the American University in Beirut.	ma9i bii 'ee mniljaam9a l'ameerkiyye fii beeruut.
be graduated	txarraj bitxarraj
What year were you graduated?	'ayy sane txarrajt ?
The year 1954.	sant 'alf witisi9 miyye w'arba9a wxamsiin.
specialty	taxaṣṣuṣ
What was your major ?	šuu kaan taxaṣṣuṣak ?
Accounting.	m(u)ḥaasabe.
Where did you work after you graduated ?	feen štaġalt ba9id maa txarrajt?
I was working in the Accounting Department of the Government.	kunt 'aštġil fii daa'irat lmuḥaasabe ma9 lḥukuume.
Why did you leave your work?	leeš tarakt šuġlak ?
wages, salary	ma9aaš
small, slight	'aliil
My salary was low.	ma9aaši kaan 'aliil.
hope	t'ammal bit'ammal
And I hope to find a better job.	wbat'ammal 'alaa'i waẓiife 'aḥsan.
authority, reference	marja9, pl. maraaji9
Could you give us three references ?	mumkin ta9ṭiina tlat maraaji9 ?

dean	9amiid
Yes. The Dean of the University of Beirut, and the director of the Accounting Department, and the mayor of Bethlehem.	na9am. 9amiid jaami9at beeruut, wmudiir daa'irat lmuḥaasabe, wra'iis baladiyyit beet laḥim.
thankful, grateful	mamnuun
Fine. Thank you very much.	ṭayyib. mamnuunak ktiir.
return, send back	radd birudd
I hope to send you an answer in two weeks.	nšaa*ll*a baruddillak jawaab, ba9id 'usbuu9een.

Additional vocabulary

1· The months of the year

January	kaanuun taani, kaanuun ttaani
February	šbaaṭ
March	'aaḍaar
April	niisaan
May	'ayyaar
June	ḥzeeraan
July	tammuuz
August	'aab
September	'ayluul
October	tišriin 'awwal, tišriin l'awwal
November	tišriin taani, tišriin ttaani
December	kaanuun 'awwal, kaanuun l'awwal

2. Occupations and professions

Accountant	m(u)ḥaasib
Contractor	mit9ahhid
Editor	m(u)ḥarrir
Engineer	m(u)handis
Judge	'aaḍi
Lawyer	m(u)ḥaami
Merchant	taajir
Translator	m(u)tarjim

STRUCTURE SENTENCES

I. Connective maa

Where were you living before you came here ?	feen kunt saakin, 'abil maa 'ijiit lahoon ?
Where did you work after you were graduated ?	feen štaġalt ba9id maa txarrajt?
I'll give you as much as you want.	ba9ṭiik 'add maa biddak.
As you wish.	mitil maa biddak.
I'll go wherever I find work.	feen maa balaa'i šuġul, baruuḥ.
Let him do whatever he wants to.	xallii yi9mal šuu maa biddo.
Come here whenever you want to.	ta9aal lahoon, 'eemta maa biddak.

Do it however you want to.	'i9malo kiif maa biddak.
Whenever you want, I'll go with you.	wa't maa biddak, baruuḥ ma9ak.
The day that you come here we'll go visit him.	yoom maa btiiji lahoon, binruuḥ nzuuro.
I went to Egypt the year that I got my diploma.	ruḥt 9ala maṣir, sant maa 'axatt ššhaade.
I'll eat at the place where you eat.	maḥall maa btaakul baakul.

GRAMMAR

I. Connective maa

Connective maa occurs after prepositions, question words, and certain nouns of time or place. Here this particle is a connective between the preposition, question word, etc. and an immediately following sentence.

After prepositions, this particle has no convenient translation ; both ba9id and ba9id maa mean « after. » Connective maa simply converts the preposition into a conjunction joining two separate sentences : feen kunt saakin 'abil maa 'ijiit lahoon? *where were you living before you came here ?*

After question words, maa can be translated as «-ever» : feen maa *wherever*, šuu maa *whatever*, kiif maa *however* : ta9aal lahoon 'eemta maa biddak *come here whenever you want to*.

After nouns of time, maa means « when » or « that » : yoom maa *the day when ;* sant maa *the year that*. After nouns of place it means « where » or « that » : maḥall maa *the place where*, saa9it maa *the hour that*.

Note that before connective maa feminine T-nouns appear in the combining form : sant maa, saa9it maa.

2. Verbs of Form VII

The characteristic of verbs of Form VII is a prefixed n-. There are four variants of the pattern, depending on the root type.

(1) Regular roots. Suffix tense n-a-a-; prefix tense n-(i)-i-.

root			
bṣṭ	nbaṣaṭ	binbṣiṭ	*be happy*
ftḥ	nfataḥ	binftiḥ	*be opened*

(2) Doubled roots. Suffix and prefix tense patterns identical : n-a--.

ḥbb	nḥabb	binḥabb	*be liked*
9dd	n9add	bin9add	*be counted*

(3) Hollow roots. Suffix and prefix tense patterns are identical : n-aa-.

'wl	n'aal	bin'aal	*be said*
zwr	nzaar	binzaar	*be visited*

(4) Weak roots. Suffix tense n-a-a ; prefix tense n--i, or n-a-a (identical with the prefix tense), depending on the verb.

ḥky	nḥaka	binḥaka	*be said*
ṭwy	nṭawa	binṭwi	*be folded*

Matching most Form I verbs that are regularly accompanied by a direct object (e.g. fataḥo *he opened it*) is a Form VII verb that indicates the subject as being acted upon (e.g. nfataḥ *it was opened*). Used in the negative, these verbs often have the meaning « not able to be done » : lbaab maa binftiḥ *the door can't be opened.*

3. Verbs of Form VIII

The characteristic of verbs of Form VIII is an infixed -t- after the first consonant of the root. There are four variants of the pattern, depending upon the root type.

(1) Regular roots. Suffix tense -ta-a- ; prefix tense -t(i)-i-.

root			
šġl	štaġal	bištġil	*work*
jm9	jtama9	bijtmi9	*meet*
nxb	ntaxab	bintxib	*elect*

(2) Doubled roots. Suffix and prefix tense patterns identical : -ta--.

hmm	htamm	bihtamm	*be concerned*

(3) Hollow roots. Suffix and prefix tense patterns identical : -taa-.

ḥwj	ḥtaaj	biḥtaaj	*need*
šw'	štaa'	bištaa'	*long for*

(4) Weak roots. Suffix tense -ta-a ; prefix tense -t-i.

šry	štara	bištri	*buy*

(5) With roots whose first consonant is w, the combination wt becomes tt.

wf'	ttafa'	bittfi'	*agree*
wḥd	ttaḥad	bittḥid	*be united*

Form VIII verbs have no apparent systematic correlations of meaning, either within the class, or with other verbs.

4. Verbs of Form IX

The characteristic of verbs of Form IX is doubling of the last consonant of the root. There are no variants of the pattern.

(1) Regular and Hollow roots (Doubled and Weak do not occur). Suffix and prefix tense patterns identical : --a--.

root			
ḥmr	ḥmarr	biḥmarr	*become red*
swd	swadd	biswadd	*become black*
byḍ	byaḍḍ	bibyaḍḍ	*become white*

The meanings of Form IX verbs relate to colors and physical defects.

5. Verbs of Form X

The characteristic of verbs of Form X is prefixed sta- before the first consonant of the root. There are four variants of the pattern, depending on the root type.

(1) Regular roots. Suffix tense sta--a-; prefix tense sta--i-.

root			
9ml	sta9mal	bista9mil	*use*

(2) Doubled roots. Suffix tense sta-a--; prefix tense st-i--.

ḥ"	staḥa"	bistḥi"	*deserve*
9dd	sta9add	bist9idd	*get ready*

(3) Hollow roots. Suffix tense sta-aa-; prefix tense st(a)-ii-.

rwḥ	staraaḥ	bistriiḥ	*rest*
šwr	stašaar	bistašiir	*consult*

(4) Weak roots. Suffix tense sta--a ; prefix tense sta--i.

ḥlw staḥla bistaḥli *find nice*

Form X verbs have no apparent systematic correlations of meaning, either within the class, or with other verbs.

6. Summary of the verb

The following is a schematic summary of the ten Forms of the verb, showing the suffix tense and prefix tense. For illustration we use the imaginary root fks, which stands for any occurring Regular root.

I	fakas	bifkas, bifkus, bifkis
II	fakkas	bifakkis
III	faakas	bifaakis
IV	'afkas	bifkis
V	tfakkas	bitfakkas
VI	tfaakas	bitfaakas
VII	nfakas	binfkis
VIII	ftakas	biftkis
IX	fkass	bifkass
X	stafkas	bistafkis

DRILLS

1. Give appropriate replies to the following questions.

šuu 'ism lli 'addam ṭalab šuġul fil'unṣliyye ?

feen t9allam ?

šuu ma9o šhaadaat ?

šuu lwaẓiife lli biddo yyaaha?	'eemta txarraj?
'addeeš 9umro?	šuu kaan taxaṣṣuṣo?
min feen huwwe?	feen štaġal ba9id maa txarraj?
šuu jinsiyyto?	leeš tarak šuġlo?

2. In the following sentences change the suffix tense verb forms to the corresponding prefix tense.

'addam ṭalab šuġul.	'eemta txarraj?
miin šaaf bil'awwal?	šuu kaan taxaṣṣuṣo?
l'unṣul 'aabalo šaxṣiyyan.	'eemta 'ajaa jawaab?
9abba ṭalab rasmi.	

3. For each of the following verbs in the suffix tense « he » form give the prefix tense «he» form. The first example of each group is completed, and all the verbs within any one group work the same way.

tšarraf	bitšarraf	xalla	bixalli
t9allam		ra''a	
tfarraj		9abba	
t'ammal		kaffa	
jtama9	bijtmi9	ḥaṭṭ	biḥuṭṭ
štaġal		ẓann	
ntaxab		radd	
ftakar			

UNIT 23 • Goods and services.

PATTERN SENTENCES

1. At the hotel	**fil'uteel**
person	šaxṣ
bath(room)	ḥammaam
private	xuṣuuṣi
I want a room for two with private bath.	biddi 'uuḍa lašaxṣeen, ma9 ḥammaam xuṣuuṣi.
wake	fayya' bifayyi'
the morning	ṣṣubuḥ
Wake me at seven o'clock in the morning.	fayyi'ni ssaa9a sab9a ṣṣubuḥ.
2. With the maid	**ma9 lxaadme *or* ma9 ṣṣaan9a**
wash	ġassal biġassil
sheet	šaršaf, pl. šaraašif
Wash the sheets.	ġassli ššaraašif.
hang up	9alla' bi9alli'
roof	ṣaṭiḥ
Hang the wash on the roof.	9all'i lġasiil 9aṣṣaṭiḥ.
sweep	kannas bikannis
kitchen	maṭbax

Sweep the kitchen.	kannsi lmaṭbax.
clean	naḍḍaf binaḍḍif
Clean the house.	naḍḍfi lbeet.
prepare	ḥaḍḍar biḥaḍḍir
Prepare dinner for eight o'clock.	ḥaḍḍri l9aša lassaa9a tamaanye.
throw out	zatt bizitt
basket	salle
garbage	zbaale
Throw this into the garbage can.	zitti haadi bsallt zzbaale.
wipe off	masaḥ bimsaḥ
floor	'arḍ
Wipe off the floor.	'imsaḥi l'arḍ.
wash down	šaṭaf bušṭuf
Wash down the floor.	'uš*u*ṭfi l'arḍ.
iron	kawa bikwi
Iron the shirts.	'ikwi l'umṣaan.
turn	daar bidiir
attention	baal
Take care of the child.	diiri baalik 9aṣṣabi.

3. At the barber's

9ind lḥallaa'

cut	'aṣṣ bi'uṣṣ
hair	ša9ir
How do you want me to cut your hair?	kiif biddak 'a'uṣṣillak ša9rak?

lighten	xaffaf bixaffif
above	foo'
please (lit. by your life)	biḥyaatak
Please shorten it a bit on top.	biḥyaatak, xaffifli yyaa šwayy min foo'.
comb	maššaţ bimaššiţ
dry	naašif
Please comb it dry.	min faḍlak, maššţo 9annaašif.
shave	ḥala' biḥli'
beard	da'in *or* liḥye
Do you want a shave?	biddak tiḥli' da'nak?
favor	ma9ruuf
If you please.	'iza bti9mal ma9ruuf.
No, thanks.	la'. mamnuun.
May it be to your pleasure (expression said to someone who has just had a haircut, a shave, or a bath).	na9iiman.
May God favor you (in reply).	'a*ll*a yin9im 9aleek.

4. At the presser's — 9ind lkawwa

laundry	ġasiil
ironing, pressing	kawi
I have five shirts to be washed and ironed.	fii 9indi xamis 'umṣaan, ġasiil wkawi.
And three pairs of pants to be cleaned and pressed.	witlat banţaloonaat, tanḍiif wkawi.

When do you want them?	'eemta biddak yyaahum?
The day after tomorrow, if possible.	ba9id bukra, 'iza mumkin.
All right. Would you like me to send them to your house or will you come and get them?	ṭayyib, ḥaaḍir. bitḥibb 'ab9atlak yyaahum 9albeet, willa btiiji taaxudhum?
while, when	w-/wi-
returning	raaji9
about	ḥawaali
I'll come and get them on my way back from work, say about five o'clock.	baaji 'aaxudhum, w'ana raaji9 min ššuġul. ya9ni, ḥawaali ssaa9a xamse.

5. At the post office — filboosṭa

stamp	ṭaabi9, pl. ṭawaabi9
regular, ordinary	9aadi
airmail	bariid jawwi
Please give me five regular stamps and ten airmail stamps.	min faḍlak, 'a9ṭiini xamis ṭawaabi9 9aadiyye, w9ašar ṭawaabi9 bariid jawwi.
registered	msajjal *or* msoogar
I have an airmail letter that I want to send registered to America.	fii ma9i maktuub ṭayyaara, biddi 'ab9ato msajjal la'ameerka.
need	ḥtaaj biḥtaaj

How much will it need in the way of stamps?	'addeeš biḥtaaj ṭawaabi9?

STRUCTURE SENTENCES

1. Active participles of simple verbs

Where are you staying?	feen-naazil?
Where were you living?	feen kunt saakin?
I've heard about him.	'ana saami9 9anno.
We need some vegetables.	laazimna šwayyit xuḍra.
He's a clerk at the Embassy.	huwwe kaatib fissafaara.
What school did he put his children in?	fii 'ayy madrase ḥaaṭiṭ wlaado?
I'm going home.	'ana raayiḥ 9albeet.
I'm not free now.	miš faaḍi halla.
This hotel is very expensive.	haada l'uteel ġaali ktiir.
He's coming tomorrow.	huwwe jaay bukra.

2. Active participles of complex verbs

He is a teacher in the government school.	huwwe m9allim fii madrast lḥukuume.
He's going tomorrow.	huwwe msaafir bukra.
That's not possible.	haada miš mumkin.

The important thing is for me to see him today.	lmuhimm 'ašuufo lyoom.
Who's the director of the company?	miin mudiir šširke?
I'm sorry.	'ana mit'assif.
I came late.	'ijiit mit'axxir.
I was thinking that you were coming.	kunt miftkir 'innak jaay.
Why are you in a hurry?	leeš mista9jil?
I'm ready.	'ana mist9idd.

GRAMMAR

1. Participles

Arabic has a class of words called *participles.* The typical participle correlates with an underlying verb, has the same root as the verb, has a predictable pattern, and has a verb-like meaning. There are two kinds of participles : *active* and *passive.* Not every verb has both.

Participles are typically adjectives, but sometimes function as nouns, often with a specialized meaning and a plural different from the adjective plural. Occasionally they function as verbs.

2. The active participle

The active participle of the simple verb has the pattern -aa-i-. This pattern has three variants, depending on the root type.

(1) Regular and Doubled roots : -aa-i-.

root			*underlying verb*	
ktb	kaatib	*writing*	katab	*write*
rj9	raaji9	*returning*	riji9	*return*
ḥṭṭ	ḥaaṭiṭ	*putting*	ḥaṭṭ	*put*
'ṣṣ	'aaṣiṣ	*cutting*	'aṣṣ	*cut*

(2) Hollow roots : -aayi-.

rwḥ	raayiḥ	*going*	raaḥ	*go*
šwf	šaayif	*seeing*	šaaf	*see*
by9	baayi9	*selling*	baa9	*sell*

(3) Weak roots: -aa-i.

b'y	baa'i	*remaining*	bi'i	*remain*
mšy	maaši	*walking*	maša	*walk*

Active participles of complex verbs have a stem pattern that is identical with the pattern of the prefix tense, except for Forms V and VI, where the stem vowel is *i*. To this stem is prefixed m-/mi- (occasionally mu-).

Form			*underlying verb*	
II	m9allim	*teacher*	bi9allim	*teach*
	muḥarrir	*editor*	biḥarrir	*edit*
III	msaafir	*traveling*	bisaafir	*travel*
	muḥaasib	*accountant*	biḥaasib	*reckon*
IV	mumkin	*possible*	bimkin	*be possible*
	muhimm	*important*	bihimm	*concern*

	mudiir	*director*	bidiir	*direct*
V	mit'axxir	*late*	bit'axxar	*be late*
	mit9allim	*educated*	bit9allam	*be taught*
VIII	miftkir	*thinking*	biftkir	*think*
	mištaa'	*longing*	bištaa'	*long for*
X	mista9jil	*in a hurry*	bista9jil	*hurry*
	mist9idd	*ready*	bist9idd	*get ready*

Active participles function as verbal adjectives, as nouns, and occasionally as verbs. As adjectives, they have the usual masculine, feminine and plural forms.

masc.	*fem.*	*plural*
kaatib	kaatbe	kaatbiin
ḩaaţiţ	ḩaaţţa	ḩaaţţiin
raayiḩ	raayḩa	raayḩiin
baa'i	baa'ye	baa'yiin
msaafir	msaafre	msaafriin
mit9allim	mit9allme	mit9allmiin
mista9jil	mista9*i*jle	mista9*i*jliin

Some active participles indicate an action taking place in the present and to be continued in the future, or going to take place in the future: ween raayiḩ? *where are you going?* These mostly correlate with verbs that mean motion or remaining in one place.

Other active participles indicate an action that began or took place in the past: 'ana saami9 9anno *I've heard about him.* Here the participle is (apparently) equivalent to a suffix tense verb.

Functioning as nouns, they frequently mean «the one who

does so-and-so », and sometimes have a plural different from the adjective.

kaatib	kuttaab	*writer*
ẓaabiṭ	ẓubbaaṭ	*officer*
9aamil	9ummaal	*worker*
m9allim	m9allmiin	*teacher*
msaa9id	msaa9diin	*assistant*
muḥaami	muḥaamiin	*lawyer*
mudiir	mudara(a')	*director*

DRILLS

1. Go through the following sentences changing the masculine singular active participles first to feminine singular and then to plural, changing anything in the rest of the sentence that needs changing.

huwwe saami9 9anni.

feen naazil huwwe ?

'eemtan raaji9 9abeeruut ?

feen raayiḥ ?

huwwe waa'if hoon.

'eemtan bitkuun ḥaaḍir ?

'eemtan msaafir 9al'uds ?

'aja mit'axxir.

feen mit9allim huwwe ?

huwwe mista9jil ktiir.

'ana mit'assif.

2. Give the active participle for each of the following verbs. The first example of each group is completed, and all the participles within any one group work the same way.

katab	kaatib	lizim	laazim
'a9ad		libis	

daras		riji9	
fataḥ		simi9	
sakan		ṭili9	
tarak		9imil	
ẓahar		9irif	
ḥaṭṭ	ḥaaṭiṭ	maša	maaši
’aṣṣ		bada	
ḥabb		ḥaka	
raaḥ	raayiḥ	fiḍi	faaḍi
’aal		’iri	
daar		bi’i	
jaab		ġili	
šaaf		nisi	
zaar			
9allam	m9allim	xalla	mxalli
ḥaḍḍar		9abba	
maššaṭ			
naḍḍaf			
sadda’		t9allam	mit9allim
sakkar		t’ammal	
šarraf		t’assaf	
wa’’af		t’axxar	
xallaṣ		txarraj	
9arraf		t9azzab	

UNIT 24 • From New York to Beirut.

PATTERN SENTENCES

When did you get here ?	'eemta 'ijiit lahoon ?
I've been here three days.	ṣarli tlat tiyyaam.
coming out	ṭaali9
How long has it been since you left America ?	'addeeš ṣarlak ṭaali9 min 'ameerka ?
past	maaḍi
I left on the eighteenth of last month.	tarakt fii taman ṭa9š ššahr lmaaḍi.
How did you come ? By airplane or by boat ?	kiif 'ijiit ? fiṭṭayyaara, willa filbaaxira ?
journey	riḥle
varied	mnawwa9
Well, the journey was mixed.	wa*ll*aahi, rriḥle kaanat mnawwa9a.
ride	rikib birkab
I flew from New York to Paris.	rkibt ṭṭayyaara min nyuu yoork labaariiz.
train	treen
Then I took the train to Marseilles.	ba9deen 'axalt ttreen lamarsiilya.
And from Marseilles I took the boat to Beirut.	wmin marsiilya, řkibt lbaaxira labeeruut.

Tell me, did you like Paris?	'ulli. 'a9jábatak baariiz?
be visited	nzaar binzaar
Really, that's a town to be visited.	saddi', haadi balad btinzaar.
truth	ḥa'ii'a
The truth is that it's a very lovely town.	lḥa'ii'a, 'inha balad ḥilwe ktiir.
full	malyaan
garden	bustaan, pl. basatiin
And filled with gardens.	wmalyaane basatiin.
trees	šajar
side	janb, pl. jawaanib
road	ṭarii', pl. ṭuru'
And trees on the sides of all the streets.	wiššajar 9ala jawaanib kull ṭṭuru'.
street	šaari9, pl. šawaari9
well arranged	mrattab
Also its streets are clean and well arranged.	kamaan, šawaari9ha nḍiife wimrattabe.
thing	šii, pl. 'ašyaa'
be able	'idir bi'dar
And Paris has lots of things that one can see and ought to see.	wbaariiz, fiiha 'ašyaa' ktiire, bi'dar lwaaḥad yšuufha, wlaazim yšuufha.
Like what, for instance?	mitil 'eeš, ya9ni?
palace	'aṣir

One should see, for example, the Palace of Versailles.	laazim yšuuf, matalan, 'aṣir verṣaay.
museum	matḥaf
And the Louvre museum.	wmatḥaf lluuvr.
grave, tomb	'abir
And Napoleon's tomb.	w'abir naabilyoon.
memorial, monument	tizkaar
And the Bastille.	wtizkaar lbastiil.
tower	burj
And the Eiffel Tower.	wburj 'iifil.
How many days did you stay in Paris ?	kam yoom 'a9att fii baariiz ?
I stayed in Paris twenty four hours.	'a9att fii baariiz 'arba9a w9išriin saa9a.
And I would have liked to stay longer.	wkunt baḥibb 'a'9ud 'aktar.
And how's Marseilles ?	wkiif marsiilya ?
Well, it's not bad.	wa*ll*aahi, miš baṭṭaale.
But I didn't have a very good time there.	laakin 'ana maa nbaṣaṭṭ fiiha ktiir.
And where did you stop next?	wba9deen, feen wa"aftu ?
cemetery	ma'bara
We stopped in Genoa for ten hours during which we visited the cemetery.	wa"afna fii janawa 9ašir saa9aat, zurna fiiha lma'bara.

And on the way we also visited	wzurna kamaan fiṭṭarii',
Naples and Athens.	naabuli w'atiina.
And then we came on to Beirut.	wba9deen, 'ijiina labeeruut.

STRUCTURE SENTENCES

1. Passive participles of simple verbs

He's not well.	huwwe miš mabṣuuṭ.
I'm busy now.	'ana mašġuul halla.
What he says, goes.	kil*i*mto masmuu9a.
That's correct.	haada maẓbuuṭ.
I got an airmail letter today.	'ajaani lyoom maktuub ṭayyaara.
Leave the door open, please.	xalli lbaab maftuuḥ, min faḍlak.
I'd be very much obliged.	bakuun mamnuun ktiir.
This house is sold.	haada lbeet mabyuu9.
Bring me stuffed squash.	jibli kuusa maḥši.
Is the shirt ironed ?	l'amiiṣ makwi ?

2. Passive participles of complex verbs

Why is the door closed ?	leeš lbaab msakkar ?
The journey was mixed.	rriḥle kaanat mnawwa9a.

The house is well arranged.	lbeet mrattab.
This is not filled out correctly.	haada miš m9abba maẓbuuṭ.
name	'isim, pl. 'asmaa'
elected	muntaxab, pl. -iin
Do you know the names of those who were elected?	bti9raf 'asmaa' lmuntaxabiin?
I'd like to give you a prompt reply.	baḥibb 'a9ṭiik jawaab musta9jal.

GRAMMAR

I. The passive participle

The passive participle of the simple verb has the pattern ma--uu-. This pattern has two variants, depending on the root type.

(1) Regular, Doubled, and Hollow roots : ma--uu-.

root			*underlying verb*	
fth̩	maftuuḥ	*open*	fataḥ	*open*
sm9	masmuu9	*heard*	simi9	*hear*
'ṣṣ	ma'ṣuuṣ	*cut*	'aṣṣ	*cut*
ḥṭṭ	maḥṭuuṭ	*placed*	ḥaṭṭ	*put*
by9	mabyuu9	*sold*	baa9	*sell*

(2) Weak roots : ma--i.

ḥšy	maḥši	*stuffed*	ḥaša	*stuff*
kwy	makwi	*ironed*	kawa	*iron*

Passive participles of complex verbs have a stem pattern that is identical with the pattern of the suffix tense. To this stem is prefixed m-/mu- (occasionally mi-). Verbs of Forms V, VI, and VII rarely have passive participles. Note that Form IV loses the prefixed 'a-.

Form			*underlying verb*	
II	m'addam	*presented*	addam	*present*
	mrattab	*well arranged*	rattab	*put in order*
	m9abba	*filled out*	9abba	*fill out*
III	mbaarak	*blessed*	baarak	*bless*
IV	mulḥaq	*annexed*	'alḥaq	*annex*
VIII	muntaxab	*elected*	ntaxab	*elect*
X	musta9jal	*hurried*	sta9jal	*hurry*

These words are typically adjectives, with the usual masculine, feminine, and plural forms.

masc.	*fem.*	*plural*
maftuuḥ	maftuuḥa	maftuuḥiin
m9abba	m9abbaay	m9abbayiin
maḥši	maḥšiyye	maḥšiyyiin
mrattab	mrattabe	mrattabiin
mbaarak	mbaarake	mbaarakiin
mulḥaq	mulḥaqa	mulḥaqiin
muntaxab	muntáxabe	muntaxabiin
musta9jal	musta9jale	musta9jaliin

Occasionally these words function as nouns with a specialized meaning, and sometimes with a plural different from the adjective.

maktuub	makatiib	*letter*
mašruub	mašruubaat	*alcoholic beverage*
mwaẓẓaf	mwaẓẓafiin	*official*
maḥši	maḥaaši	*stuffed vegetable*
mulḥaq	mulḥaqiin	*attaché*
mustašaar	mustašaariin	*counselor*

Occasionally no singular exists.

ma'kuulaat	*things to eat*
ma9luumaat	*information*

DRILLS

1. Give appropriate replies to the following questions based on the Pattern Sentences of this Unit.

'eemta 'aja min 'ameerka ?

kiif saafar min nyuu yoork labaariiz ?

kiif saafar min baariiz lamarsiilya ?

nbaṣaṭ fii baariiz ?

šuu bi'dar lwaaḥad yšuuf fii baariiz ?

kam saa9a 'a9ad fii baariiz ?

nbaṣaṭ kamaan fii marsiilya ?

wfeen wa''af fiṭṭarii', been marsiilya wbeeruut ?

2. In the following sentences change the suffix tense verb forms to the corresponding prefix tense.

tarakt nyuu york yoom ssabt. 'a9att fii baariiz yoomeen.

rkibt ṭṭayyaara min nyuu
york labaariiz.
ba9deen 'axatt ttreen
lamarsiilya
wmin marsiilya rkibt lbaaxira
labeeruut.

wa''afna fii janawa sitt
saa9aat.
zurna fiṭṭarrii' naabuli
w'atiina.

3. For each of the following verbs in the suffix tense « he » form give the prefix tense « he » form. The first example of each group is completed, and all the verbs within any one group work the same way.

katab	buktub	'akal	byaakul	kaan	bikuun
šakar		'axad		šaaf	
daras				zaar	
				'aal	
				'aam	

fihim	bifham	dabbar	bidabbir	jaab	bijiib
ṭili9		zawwar		ṣaar	
9irif		wa''af		baa9	
rikib		xallaṣ			
simi9					
'idir					

4. Give the passive participle for each of the following verbs. The first example of each group is completed, and all participles within any one group work the same way.

katab	maktuub	simi9	masmuu9
fataḥ		9imil	

'aṭa9		9irif	
samaḥ		fihim	
sa'al			
ḥaṭṭ	maḥṭuuṭ	ḥaḍḍar	mḥaḍḍar
'aṣṣ		naḍḍaf	
ḥabb		sadda'	
radd		9alla'	
		sakkar	
		'addam	
		faṣṣal	

UNIT 25 • The program of the new cabinet — I

PATTERN SENTENCES

program	minhaaj, pl. manaahij
I heard the program of the new cabinet on the two o'clock news bulletin.	smi9t minhaaj lwizaara jjdiide, fii našrit ssaa9a tinteen.
appearing	ẓaahir
And it looks like a good program.	wiẓẓaahir 'inno minhaaj kwayyis.
pass by	faat bifuut
loss	xsaara
What a shame ! I missed hearing it.	yaa xsaara. faatni 'asma9o.
Could you tell me what was most important in it ?	mumkin t'ulli, šuu 'ahamm maa fii ?
plan	xiṭṭa, pl. xiṭaṭ
support	'ayyad bi'ayyid
cause, question	qaḍiyye, pl. qaḍaaya
The plan of the government is to support the Arab cause.	xiṭṭit lḥukuume, 'iṇha t'ayyid lqaḍaaya l9arabiyye.
maintain	ḥaafaẓ biḥaafiẓ
relation	9alaa'a, pl. 9alaa'aat
state, nation	dawle, pl. duwal

major	kubra
And at the same time to maintain good relations with the great powers.	wfii nafs lwa't, tḥaafiẓ 9al9alaa'aat ṭṭayybe, ma9 dduwal lkubra.
informal term of address (lit. our master)	yaa siidna
mention	zakar buzkur
project	mašruu9, pl. mašaarii9
And then, sir, they mentioned the new projects that they intend to carry out.	wba9deen, yaa siidna, zakaru lmašaarii9 jjdiide lli bidhum yi9maluuha.
arming	tasliiḥ
army	jeeš, pl. jyuuš
constructing	'inšaa'
factory, plant	ma9mal, pl. ma9aamil
For example, arming the army, and constructing war plants.	matalan, tasliiḥ ljeeš, w'inšaa' ma9aamil 9askariyye.
organizing	tanẓiim
department	daa'ira, pl. dawaa'ir
reviving	'in9aaš
industry	ṣinaa9a
And organizing the government departments, and reviving the national industry.	wtanẓiim dawaa'ir lḥukuume, w'in9aaš ṣṣinaa9a lwaṭaniyye.
expanding	tawsii9

movement	ḥarake
commercial	tijaari
economic	'iqtiṣaadi
And expanding commercial and economic activity.	wtawsii9 lḥarake ttijaariyye wiliqtiṣaadiyye.
lowering	taxfiiḍ
tax	ḍariibe, pl. ḍaraa'ib
And lowering taxes.	wtaxfiiḍ ḍḍaraa'ib.
program	barnaamaj, pl. baraamij
teaching	ta9liim
Then they spoke about the education programs.	ba9deen ḥaku 9an baraamij tta9liim.
promise	wa9ad byuu9id
industrial	ṣinaa9i
agricultural	ziraa9i
They promised to open industrial and commercial and agricultural schools.	wa9adu yiftaḥu madaaris ṣinaa9iyye, wtijaariyye, wziraa9iyye.
compulsory	'ijbaari
And to make education compulsory.	wiyxallu tta9liim 'ijbaari.

STRUCTURE SENTENCES

I. Verbal nouns : Form I verbs

I have trouble in writing.	9indi ṣ9uube filiktaabe.

I'm not so bad in reading.	fili'raay, miš baṭṭaal.
I'm very pleased at your visit.	'ana masruur jiddan bizyaaritkum.
They take turns at the work.	bitnaawabu l9amal.
The shirt needs ironing.	l'amiiṣ biddo kawi.
I'm honored to have met you.	tšarrafna mma9riftak.

2. Verbal nouns : Form II verbs

The car needs repairing.	ssayyaara bidha taṣliiḥ.
The watch needs cleaning.	ssaa9a bidha tanḍiif.
He works in the editing division.	bištġil fii qism ttaḥriir.
Arming the army.	tasliiḥ ljeeš.
Organizing the government departments.	tanẓiim dawaa'ir lḥukuume.
Expanding commercial activity.	tawsii9 lḥarake ttijaariyye.
Where is the Ministry of National Education ?	feen wizaart ttarbiye lwaṭaniyye ?

GRAMMAR

1. Verbal nouns

Arabic has a class of words called *verbal nouns.* The typical verbal noun correlates with an underlying verb, has the same root as the verb, has (with statable exceptions) a predictable pattern, and has a verb-like meaning.

Many verbal nouns have two kinds of meaning. One is the abstract activity of the verb without reference to time: zyaara *visiting*; in this usage it has no plural. The other is a more concrete meaning: zyaara *a visit*; in this usage it has a plural: zyaaraat *visits.*

The verbal noun may be translated by an English infinitive, participle, or noun: ssayyaara bidha taṣliiḥ *the car needs to be repaired,...needs repairing,...needs repair.*

2. Verbal nouns of simple verbs

Verbal nouns of simple verbs may have any one of a large number of patterns. There is no predictability.

verbal noun		*underlying verb*	
ktaabe	*writing*	katab	*write*
zyaara	*visiting*	zaar	*visit*
'raay(e)	*reading*	'iri	*read*
9amal	*work*	9imil	*do*
hazz	*shaking*	hazz	*shake*
kawi	*ironing*	kawa	*iron*
ma9rife	*knowing*	9irif	*know*

3. Verbal nouns of complex verbs : Form II

Verbal nouns of complex verbs are very regular. For Form II the pattern is ta--ii-, with two variants, depending on the root type.

(1) **Regular, Doubled, and Hollow roots : ta- -ii-.**

root			*underlying verb*	
nḍf	tanḍiif	*cleaning*	naḍḍaf	*clean*
ṣlḥ	taṣliiḥ	*repairing*	ṣallaḥ	*repair*
ḥrr	taḥriir	*editing*	ḥarrar	*edit*
zwd	tazwiid	*supplying*	zawwad	*supply*

(2) **Weak roots : ta- -iye.**

rby	tarbiye	*education*	rabba	*educate*

UNIT 26 • The program of the new cabinet — II

PATTERN SENTENCES

side, aspect	naaḥye, pl. nawaaḥi
helping	m(u)saa9ade
fallah, peasant	fallaaḥ, pl. -iin
And another side of the program is helping the fallahin.	wnaaḥye taanye filminhaaj, musaa9adat lfallaaḥiin.
loan	qirḍ, pl. quruuḍ
financial	maali
The government has promised to give them financial loans.	wa9dat lḥukuume ta9ṭiihum quruuḍ maaliyye.
hope	'amal
improving	taḥsiin
season	mawsim
In the hope of improving the harvest.	9ala 'amal taḥsiin lmawsim zziraa9i.
irrigation	rayy
And then they have projects for irrigation.	wba9deen, 9indhum mašaarii9 lirrayy.
rail	sikke, pl. sikak
iron	ḥadiid
harbor, port	miina, pl. mawaani

And repairing the railways and the harbors.	wtaṣliiḥ sikak lḥadiid, wilmawaani.
concern	'ihtimaam
matter, affair	'amir, pl. 'umuur
And concern for matters of health.	wilihtimaam fii 'umuur ṣṣiḥḥa.
increase	zaad biziid
number	9adad
And they're going to increase the number of hospitals.	wraayḥiin yziidu 9adad lmustašfayaat.
combat	kaafaḥ bikaafiḥ
disease	maraḍ, pl. 'amraaḍ
contagious	saari
And combat contagious diseases.	wiykaafḥu l'amraaḍ ssaarye.
shortly, soon	9an 'ariib
carry out	'ajra bijri
amendment, modification	ta9diil, pl. -aat
law	qaanuun, pl. qawaaniin
parliamentary	niyaabi
And soon they're going to carry out amendments to the parliamentary election laws.	w9an 'ariib, raayḥiin yijru ta9diilaat fii qawaaniin lintixaabaat nniyaabiyye
free	ḥurr
So that the elections will be free.	laḥatta tkuun lintixaabaat ḥurra.

magnificent	9aẓiim
That certainly is a magnificent plan.	saddi'. haada minhaaj 9aẓiim.
apply, put into practice	ṭabba' biṭabbi'
application	taṭbii'
practical	9amali
But I hope they'll put it into actual practice.	bass nšaa*ll*a yṭabb'uu taṭbii' 9amali.

STRUCTURE SENTENCES

1. Verbal nouns : Form III verbs

Ahmad works in the Accounting Department.	'aḥmad bištġil fii daa'irat lmuḥaasabe.
Helping the fallahin.	musaa9adat lfallaaḥiin.
Combating diseases.	mukaafaḥat l'amraaḍ.

2. Verbal nouns: Form IV verbs

It's no inconvenience at all.	maa fii 'iz9aaj 'abadan.
Reviving the national industry.	'in9aaš ṣṣinaa9a lwaṭaniyye.
Constructing war plants.	'inšaa' ma9aamil 9askariyye.

3. Verbal nouns: Form V verbs

He has an upset stomach.	ma9o talabbuk mi9de.
What was your specialty ?	šuu kaan taxaṣṣuṣak ?

4. Verbal nouns: Form VIII verbs

Today the elections begin.	lyoom btibda lintixaabaat.
Reviving the national economy.	'in9aaš liqtiṣaaḍ lwaṭani.
Concern for matters of health.	lihtimaam fii 'umuur ṣṣiḥḥa.

GRAMMAR

1. Verbal nouns of complex verbs: Forms III—X

Verbal nouns of Forms III—X are relatively rare in the kind of Arabic described in this book. The following list illustrates only the patterns that occur with Regular and Doubled roots.

Form			*underlying verb*	
III	musaa9ade	*helping*	saa9ad	*help*
IV	'in9aaš	*reviving*	'an9aš	*revive*
V	taxaṣṣuṣ	*specialization*	txaṣṣaṣ	*specialize*
VI	talaa9ub	*being deceitful*	tlaa9ab	*be deceitful*
VII	'infijaar	*exploding*	nfajar	*explode*
VIII	'ijtimaa9	*meeting*	jtama9	*meet*
IX	'iḥmiraar	*redness*	ḥmarr	*become red*
X	'istiqlaal	*independence*	staqall	*be independent*

UNIT 27 • Telephone conversations.

PATTERN SENTENCES

1. B : Mr. Batte ; H : Mr. Haddad ; M : Maid

M :	Hello ? Who's speaking ?	haloo ? miin 9ambiḥki ?
B :	Is this Mr. Haddad's house ?	hoon beet ssayyid ḥaddaad ?
M :	Yes, who do you want ?	na9am. miin bitriid ?
B.	I'd like to speak to Mr. George Haddad.	baḥibb 'aḥki ma9 ssayyid joorj ḥaddaad.
M :	Who wants him ?	miin biddo yyaa ?
B :	William Batte. I'm an attaché at the American Embassy.	wilyam baat. 'ana mulḥaq fissafaara l'ameerkiyye.
	present	mawjuud
	Is Mr. George at home ?	ssayyid joorj mawjuud ?
M :	One minute. I'll see.	d'ii'a lašuuf.
B :	If you please.	min faḍlik.
H :	Hello, Mr. Batte. How are you ?	haloo, mistir baat. kiif ḥaalak ?
B :	Fine, thanks. How are *you* ?	mabṣuuṭ, lḥamdilla. kiif ḥaalak 'inte ?
H :	Fine, praise God.	nuškur 'a*ll*a. mabṣuuṭ.

	telephone	talfan bitalfin
B :	I've called you several times, but there wasn't any answer.	talfantillak 9iddit marraat, bass maa kaan fii jawaab.
	vacation	furṣa
H :	Well, I was on vacation last week, and I wasn't here.	saddi'. kaan 9indi furṣa l'usbuu9 lmaaḍi, wmaa kunt hoon.
B :	I'd like very much to see you, if possible.	baḥibb ktiir 'ašuufak, 'iza mumkin.
H :	Come visit us whenever you want.	tfaḍḍal zuurna wa't maa bitriid.
	You're most welcome.	'ahlan wasahlan fiik.
	evening	l9ašiyye
B :	I'll come tomorrow evening about eight o'clock.	baaji bukra l9ašiyye, ḥawaali ssaa9a tamaanye.
H :	Fine.	bitšarrif.
B :	Good-by.	ma9 ssalaame.
H :	Good-by.	'a*ll*a ysallmak.

2. K : Mr. Key ; M : Maid

K :	Hello ?	haloo ?
M :	Hello ? Who's this ?	haloo ? miin ḥaḍ*i*rtak ?
K :	I'm Major Key. Is this Mr. Salameh's house ?	'ana meejar kii. hoon beet ssayyid salaame ?

	number	numra
	wrong (invariable adj.)	ġalaṭ
M :	I'm sorry. Wrong number.	mit'assfe. numra ġalaṭ.

3. B : Mr. Black ; K : Khalil ; O : Operator ; M : Maid

B :	Hello, hello ? This is Mr. Black.	haloo, haloo ? hoon mistir blaak.
	Please give me 59378.	'a9ṭiini, min faḍlik, xamse tis9a tlaate sab9a tamaanye.
	answer	radd birudd
	try	jarrab bijarrib
O :	One minute, please.	d'ii'a, min faḍlak.
	I've telephoned twice, Mr. Black, but they don't answer.	talfant marrteen, mistir blaak, bass maa biruddu.
	If you'll wait a little longer, I'll try again.	'iza btistanna šwayy, bajarrib marra taanye.
B :	If you please.	'i9mali ma9ruuf.
O :	Mr. Black, go ahead now.	mistir blaak, tfaḍḍal 'iḥki.
B :	Hello. Is Mr. Khalil there?	haloo. ssayyid xaliil mawjuud?
M:	Yes. One minute, please.	na9am. d'ii'a, min faḍlak.
K :	Hello ? Who's speaking ?	haloo ? miin 9ambiḥki ?
	father's brother	9amm
	request	ṭalab buṭlub
	arrive	wiṣil byuuṣal

B : I'm James Black, a friend of your cousin Elias in Detroit.	'ana jeemz blaak, ṣaaḥib ibin 9ammak lyaas fii ditrooyt.
And he asked me to call you when I arrived in Beirut.	whuwwe ṭalab minni 'atalfinlak lamma buuṣal labeeruut.
(The connection is suddenly cut off)	
B : Hello, hello, hello?	haloo, haloo, haloo ?
(To the operator)	
line	xaṭṭ
Why did you cut off the line ?	leeš 'aṭa9ti lxaṭṭ ?
O : I'm sorry. I thought you'd finished.	mit'assfe. ftakartak xallaṣt.
One minute, I'll give you the line again.	d'ii'a halla ba9ṭiik lxaṭṭ min jdiid.

4. O : Mr. Oakes; S: Secretary

S : Hello ? Who's speaking ?	haloo ? miin 9ambiḥki ?
O : This is Fred Oakes.	'ana fredd 'ooks.
I'd like to speak to Mr. Munir Al-Halabi.	baḥibb 'aḥki ma9 ssayyid muniir lḥalabi.
S : He's not here now.	huwwe miš mawjuud halla.
O : When will he be back ?	'eemta birja9 ?

	message	xabar
S :	He'll be back at three.	birja9 ssaa9a tlaate.
	Would you like to leave a message for him ?	bitriid titriklo xabar ?
O :	Yes, I'd like to make an appointment with him for tomorrow morning.	na9am. baḥibb 'a9mal maw9id ma9o labukra ṣṣubuḥ.
S :	Would ten o'clock be all right ?	ssaa9a 9ašra, mniiḥ ?
O :	Very good. Thank you.	ktiir mniiḥ. mamnuun.

5. B : Mr. Batte ; S : Secretary

	electricity	kahraba
S :	Hello ? This is the Electric Company.	haloo ? hoon širkit lkahraba.
B :	I'd like to speak to Mr. Nadim Haddad, please.	baḥibb 'aḥki ma9 ssayyid nadiim ḥaddaad, min faḍlik.
	transfer	ḥawwal biḥawwil
S :	Mr. Nadim is on another line.	ssayyid nadiim 9axaṭṭ taani.
	I'll transfer you to him.	halla baḥawwlak 9alee.

UNIT 28 • A Juha story.

PATTERN SENTENCES

world	9aalam
donkey	ḥmaar
The world and Juha's donkey.	l9aalam wiḥmaar juḥa.
monk	raahib, pl. ruhbaan
There were three monks who were traveling.	fii tlat ruhbaan, kaanu msaafriin.
whenever	kull maa
discuss	tbaaḥas bitbaaḥas
learned man	9aalim, pl. 9ulama
And every time they arrived at a town they used to hold discussions with the learned men there .	wkull maa wiṣlu labalad, kaanu yitbaaḥasu ma9 l9ulama lli fiiha.
famous	mašhuur
One time they arrived at a town that they had heard was famous for its learned men.	marra wiṣlu labalad, sim9u 'inha mašhuura b9ulamaaha.
sultan	ṣulṭaan
They went and visited the sultan there.	raaḥu zaaru ṣṣulṭaan fiiha.
minister of state	waziir, pl. wuzara

propose	qtaraḥ biqtriḥ
call	naada binaadi
dispute	jaadal bijaadil
One of the ministers in the palace proposed to the sultan that he call Juha to dispute with them.	waaḥad min lwuzara fil'aṣir, qtaraḥ 9aṣṣulṭaan, 'inno ynaadi juḥa yjaadilhum.
joke, witty remark	nukte, pl. nukat
intelligence	zaka
lightness	xiffe
spirit	ruuḥ
Because Juha was famous for his witty remarks and his intelligence and his lightness of spirit.	li'anno juḥa kaan mašhuur bnukato, wzakaa, wxiffit ruuḥo.
banquet	9aziime
courtyard	saaḥa
The sultan made them a great banquet in the courtyard of the palace.	ṣṣulṭaan 9imillhum 9aziime kbiire fii saaḥt l'aṣir.
invite	9azam bi9zim
And invited Juha to it.	w9azam 9aleeha juḥa.
riding	raakib
Juha came, riding his famous donkey.	'aja juḥa raakib ḥmaaro lmašhuur.
dine	t9ašša bit9ašša

proclaim	'a9lan bi9lin
beginning	'ibtidaa'
dispute	mujaadale
After they had all dined, the sultan proclaimed the beginning of the dispute.	ba9id maa lkull t9aššu, 'a9lan ṣṣulṭaan btidaa' lmujaadale.
The first monk began and asked Juha :	'aam rraahib l'awwal, wsa'al juḥa.
sheikh	šeex
middle	nuṣṣ
« Can you tell me, sir, where is the middle of the world ? »	bti'dar t'ulli, yaa šeex, ween nuṣṣ ddinya ?
hold, seize	misik bimsik
stick	9aṣa
point out	'aššar bi'aššir
Juha seized his stick and pointed with it to the place where his donkey had put his right hoof, and said :	'aja juḥa, misik 9aṣaato, w'aššar fiiha maḥall maa kaan ḥmaaro ḥaaṭiṭ 'iido lyamiin, w'aal.
« Here is the middle of the world. »	hoon nuṣṣ ddinya.
The monk asked him :	sa'alo rraahib.
prove	barhan bibarhin
« But how can you prove that this is the middle of the world ? »	bass. kiif bitbarhin 'inno hoon nuṣṣ ddinya ?

measure	'aas bi'iis
He said to him : « If you don't believe me, go measure the world. »	'allo. 'iza maa bitsaddi'ni, ruuḥ 'iis ddinya.
talk	kalaam
increase	zyaade
deficiency	nu'ṣaan
liar	kazzaab
«And if there is any exaggeration or deficiency in what I have said, I shall be a liar.»	w'iza kaan fii kalaami zyaade willa nu'ṣaan, 'ana bakuun kazzaab.
The second monk began and asked :	'aam rraahib ttaani, wsa'al.
star	najme, pl. njuum
sky	sama
«All right, what is the number of the stars of the sky ? »	ṭayyib. 'addeeš 9adad njuum ssama ?
answer	jaawab bijaawib
Juha answered : « As many as there are hairs on my donkey.»	juḥa jaawab, 'add maa 9ala ḥmaari ša9ir.
be astonished	t9ajjab bit9ajjab
The monk was astonished and said :	t9ajjab rraahib, w'aal.
proof	burhaan
«And what's your proof ? »	wšuu burhaanak ?

count	9add bi9idd
Juḥa said to him : « If you don't believe me, go count them. »	'allo juḥa. 'iza maa bitsaddi'ni, ruuḥ 9iddha.
exceed	zaad biziid
decrease	na'aṣ bun'uṣ
right	ḥa"
I owe you, I promise you	'ilak 9alayy
« And if there should be one too many or one too few, you will be right, and I will owe you whatever you want. »	w'iza kaan bidziid willa btun'uṣ waḥde, lḥa" bikuun ma9ak. w'ilak 9alayy šuu maa biddak.
be countable	n9add bin9add
The monk answered and said: «All right, but the donkey's hairs, can they be counted ? »	riji9 rraahib, w'aal. ṭayyib. bass ša9ir liḥmaar, huwwe bin9add ?
Juha said to him : « That's for you to say. Are you asking me ? All right, how can the stars of the sky be counted ? »	'allo juḥa. 'uul laḥaalak. jaay tis'alni ? ṭayyib, kiif btin9add njuum ssama ?
a hair	ša9ra
After this, the third monk began and asked him : « How many hairs are there in my beard ?	ba9*i*dha, 'aam rraahib ttaalit, wsa'alo. kam ša9ra fii liḥ*i*yti ?

tail	danab
Juha said to him : « As many as there are hairs in my donkey's tail. »	'allo juḥa. 'add maa fii danab ḥmaari ša9ir.
The monk answered and said: « And what's your proof ? »	riji9 rraahib w'aal. wšuu burhaanak ?
Juha said to him : «That's a simple matter. »	'allo juḥa. haadi mas'ale baṣiiṭa.
pluck	nataf bintif
«We'll begin plucking out the hairs of your beard, hair by hair. »	bnibda nintif ša9ir liḥ*i*ytak, ša9ra ša9ra.
remove	'aam bi'iim
«And every time we remove a hair from your beard, we'll remove a hair from the donkey's tail. Then we'll see.»	wkull maa bin'iim ša9ra min liḥ*i*ytak, bin'iim ša9ra min danab liḥmaar. ba9deen binšuuf.
agree	ttafa' bittfi'
total	majmuu9
divorce	ṭalaa'
triple divorce	ṭṭalaa' bittlaate
my stepmother	mart 'abuuy
« If the two totals don't agree, I shall have to divorce my stepmother».	'iza maa ttafa' lmajmuu9een, 9alayy ṭṭalaa' bittlaate min mart abuuy.

laugh	ḍiḥik biḍḥak
answer	jawaab, pl. jawabaat *or* 'ajwibe
pleasant	laṭiif
All who were in the palace laughed and were astonished at Juha's pleasant answers.	kull lli fil'aṣir ḍiḥku, wit9ajjabu min jawabaat juḥa llaṭiife.
clap the hands	za''af biza''if
become tired	ti9ib bit9ab
two hands	'ideen
And applauded him until their hands were tired.	wza''afuulo laḥatta ti9bat 'ideehum.

EXPLANATORY NOTES

Juha is the hero of an enormous number of stories of wit and stupidity, in which he is frequently accompanied by his donkey. Who Juha was, and when he lived, is uncertain. Some accounts say he was a learned man of the time of Harun ar-Rashid (766 ? - 809) ; others place him variously in the 12th century, the 13th century, and the 15th century. One scholar says that Arabic droll stories about a certain Juha were current in large numbers at the end of the 10th century. Juha is also frequently identified with, or possibly confused with, Khodja, an Imam (Moslem religious leader) who lived, according to some accounts, in Anatolia during the 13th century, about whom similar stories are told. In any case, Juha's curious mixture of wit and stupidity have become proverbial among the Arabs.

The phrase ṭṭalaa' bittlaate *the threefold divorce* refers to a prescription in the Shari'a (šarii9a *religious law of Islam*) concerning divorce. Under this law the husband, and not the wife, has the right to break, by repudiation, a validly contracted marriage. A man may divorce his wife merely by saying « You are divorced.» He may do this twice, and each time take her back without any ceremony. One utterance of this formula is called simple repudiation ; two utterances constitute double repudiation. But if the man says the formula a third time, or repudiates his wife with a triple formula in one sentence, this is known as repudiation through the triple formula, and the divorce is final.

UNIT 29 • A village.

PATTERN SENTENCES

1. An invitation

My family would like to meet you, Mr. West, before you return to America.	'ahli biḥibbu y'aabluuk, yaa mistir west, 'abil maa tirja9 la'ameerka.
spend (time)	'aḍa bi'ḍi
village	'arye, pl. qura
And I wanted to ask you if you could come with me and spend three or four days with them in the village.	wḥabbeet 'as'alak, 'iza mumkin tiiji ma9i, ni'ḍi tlat arba9 tiyyaam 9indhum fil'arye.
up to now	laḥadd halla
be available	ṣaḥḥ bisiḥḥ
opportunity	furṣa
Really, I'd like to very much, because up to now I haven't had a chance to get acquainted with the life of the fallahin in the villages.	saddi'. baḥibb ktiir. li'anno laḥadd halla, maa ṣaḥḥilli furṣa 'at9arraf fiiha 9ala ḥayaat lfallaaḥiin filqura.

2. In the village

go around, turn around	daar biduur

together	sawa
Now we'll go together and go around for two or three hours, and I'll show you the most important things here.	halla binruuḥ sawa, wbindur*i*l-na saa9teen tlaate, bafarjiik fiiha 'ahamm maa fii hoon.
mosque	jaami9
church	kniise
First of all I'd like to show you the mosque, and then we'll go see the church.	'awwal šii, baḥibb 'afarjiik 9aljaami9, wba9deen binruuḥ nšuuf likniise.
mixed	maxluuṭ
Christian	masiiḥi, pl. masiiḥiyye
Moslem	mislim, pl.-iin
Our town is mixed. About half Christian and half Moslem.	baladna maxluuṭa. ta'riiban nnuṣṣ fiiha masiiḥiyye, winnuṣṣ ttaani mis*i*lmiin.
wedding	9urs
Today the Christians are having a wedding, and if you'd like to we'll go watch it for a couple of hours.	lyoom fii 9urs 9ind lmasiiḥiyye. w'iza bitḥibb, binruuḥ nitfarraj 9alee saa9teen zamaan.
evening party	sahra
This evening we'll go to the evening party if you'd like to.	l9ašiyye binruuḥ 9assahra, 'iza bitḥibb.
What do they do at the evening party?	šuu bi9malu bissahra?
dancing	ra'ṣ
dabke (a folk dance)	dabke
singing	ġina

drinking	šurub
good time	basṭ
There's dancing and dabke and singing and drinking and a good time.	fii ra'ṣ, wdabke, wġina, wšurb, wbasṭ.

3. The headman

vineyard, orchard	karm, pl. kruum
And what do you think of going with me today to the vineyards and fig orchards?	wšuu ra'yak truuḥ ma9i lyoom, 9akruum l9inab wittiin?
she is undertaking it	bit'uum fiiha
And while we're on the way we'll look at the new agricultural projects that the government is undertaking.	wniḥna raayḥiin fiṭṭarii', bnitfarraj 9almašaarii9 zziraa9iyye jjdiide, lli 9ambit'uum fiiha lḥukuume.
mukhtar (headman)	muxtaar
Then we'll introduce you, after we come back, to the mukhtar of the town.	ba9deen bin9arrfak, lamma nirja9, 9amuxtaar lbalad.
guest	ḍeef, pl. ḍyuuf
Really, he's a fine man, and he likes to be introduced to the guests of the town.	saddi'ni, huwwe rijjaal ṭayyib. wbiḥibb yit9arraf 9aḍyuuf lbalad.
dearer, dearest	'aḥabb

And what he likes most of all is to talk to them about the town.	w'aḥabb maa 9alee, 'inno yiḥkiilhum 9an lbalad.
Wait till you go to his place.	stanna latruuḥ 9indo.
be founded	t'assas bit'assas
He'll tell you the history of the town from the day it was founded up to today.	biḥkiilak taariix lbalad, min yoom maa t'assasat, laḥadd lyoom.
explain	šaraḥ bišraḥ
politics	siyaase
internal, domestic	daaxli
He'll also explain to you the internal politics of the town.	wbišraḥlak kamaan siyaast lbalad ddaaxliyye.
explain	fahham bifahhim
products	mantuujaat
sources of income	daxil
expenditures	xarj
He'll explain to you about the products of the town, and its sources of income, and its expenditures, and whatever you want.	bifahhmak 9an mantuujaat lbalad, wdaxilha, wxarjha, wšuu maa biddak.
always	daayman
Whenever I bring guests here I always introduce them to him.	'ana lamma bajiib ḍyuuf, daayman ba9arrifhum 9alee.

And he explains to them all about the town.	whuwwe bišraḥilhum kullši 9an lbalad.
Because I don't know very much about it.	li'anno 'ana maa ba9raf ktiir 9anha.
it happens that	ḥaakim
outside	barra
feast day	9iid, pl. 'a9yaad
relative	'ariib, pl. 'araayib
It happens that I've spent most of my time away from here and I only come to the town on feast days to visit my family and relatives.	ḥaakim 'aḍeet 'aktar wa'ti barra. wmaa baaji 9albalad ġeer 9al'a9yaad, laḥatta 'azuur l'ahil wil'araayib.
question	su'aal, pl. -aat, 'as'ile
I have a lot of questions about life in the villages.	fii 9indi 'as'ile ktiire 9an lḥayaa filqura.
compose, write	'allaf bi'allif
personal observation	mušaahade, pl. -aat
I want to write a book about what I've seen in the Near East when I get back to America.	biddi 'a'allif ktaab 9an mušaahadaati fiššarq l'adna, lamma 'arja9 la'ameerka.
be printed	nṭaba9 binṭbi9
copy	nusxa
And after it's printed I'll send you a copy.	wba9id maa yinṭbi9, bab9atlak nusxa.
I'd be very grateful.	bakuun mamnuun ktiir.

Additional vocabulary

1. Feast Days and Holidays

Birthday	9iid miilaad
Christmas	9iid lmiilaad
Easter	9iid lfiṣiḥ
Independence	9iid listiqlaal
New Year's	9iid raas ssane
Birthday of the Prophet	9iid lmawlid
Breaking of the fast of Ramadan	9iid lfiṭir
Feast of the Sacrifice	9iid l'aḍḥa.

2. General Feast Day and Holiday Greetings

May you be safe and sound every year.	kull sane w'inte saalim.
And may you be safe and sound (in reply).	w'inte saalim.

3. Kinship terms

These are terms of reference and are listed from the point of view of Ego, i.e., my father, etc. The term without the ending -i is given in parentheses.

my father	'abuuy	('ab)
my mother	'immi	('imm)

my brother	'axuuy	('ax)
my sister	'uxti	('uxt)
my husband	zooji	(zooj)
	joozi	(jooz)
my wife	zoojti	(zooje)
	marti	(mara)
my son	'ibni	('ibin)
my daughter	binti	(bint)
my grandfather (either side)	siidi	(siid)
	jiddi	(jidd)
my grandmother (either side)	sitti	(sitt)
my stepfather	jooz 'immi	(jooz 'imm)
my stepmother	mart 'abuuy	(mart 'ab)
my father's brother	9ammi	(9amm)
my father's sister	9ammti	(9amme)
my mother's brother	xaali	(xaal)
my mother's sister	xaalti	(xaale)
my brother's son	'ibin 'axuuy	('ibin 'ax)
my brother's daughter	bint 'axuuy	(bint 'ax)
my sister's son	'ibin 'uxti	('ibin 'uxt)
my sister's daughter	bint 'uxti	(bint 'uxt)
my father's brother's son	'ibin 9ammi	('ibin 9amm)
my father's brother's daughter	bint 9ammi	(bint 9amm)
my father's sister's son	'ibin 9ammti	('ibin 9amme)

my father's sister's daughter	bint 9ammti	(bint 9amme)
my mother's brother's son	'ibin xaali	('ibin xaal)
my mother's brother's daughter	bint xaali	(bint xaal)
my mother's sister's son	'ibin xaalti	('ibin xaale)
my mother's sister's daughter	bint xaalti	(bint xaale)

Kinship terms

Terms like jiddi *my grandfather* and 'ibin 9ammi *my father's brother* that designate a relative are known as *kinship terms.* The Arabic kinship system is not very different from our own and employs terms similar to ours.

There are some uses of Arabic kinship terms that are different from Western usage. For instance, it is customary for parents to be called by the name of their first-born son : 'abu 'akram *the father of Akram* ; 'imm 'akram *the mother of Akram.* This is a common term of address and reference and is used by persons both inside and outside the kinship group.

UNIT 30 • Going home.

PATTERN SENTENCES

pack	ḍabb biḍubb
Have you packed everything, Mr. West, or do you need some help?	ḍabbeet kullši yaa mistir west, willa biddak m(u)saa9ade?
packed	maḍbuub
rest	raaḥa
Thank you, everything's packed. I only want you to rest.	šukran. kullši maḍbuub. maa biddi 'illa raaḥtak.
make (something) come down	nazzal binazzil
under	taḥt
All right, then. I'll come help you take the suitcases downstairs.	ṭayyib, 'izan. baaji 'asaa9dak nnazzil ššantaat lataḥt.
see (someone) off	wadda9 biwaddi9
And then we'll go see you off at the harbor.	wba9deen, binruuḥ nwadd9ak 9almiina.
But don't forget us, Mr. West, while you're in America.	bass laa tinsaana yaa mistir west, w'inte fii 'ameerka.
line	ṣaṭir, pl. 'asṭur

Write us two or three lines when you arrive.	ktub*i*lna ṣaṭreen tlaate, lamma tuuṣal.
keep (someone) informed	ṭamman biṭammin
And always keep us informed about yourself.	wdaayman ṭamminna 9an ḥaḍ*i*rtak.
It's inconceivable that I should forget you, Ahmad, after all the kindness you've shown me.	miš ma9'uul 'ansaakum, yaa 'aḥmad, ba9id kull lma9ruuf lli 9miltuu ma9i.
forgiveness, pardon	9afu
embarrass	xajjal bixajjil
gratitude	mamnuuniyye
Don't mention it, Mr. West. You embarrass me. What have I done for you that I should deserve all this gratitude?	l9afu, yaa mistir west. xajjaltna. šuu 9milnaalak, laḥatta nistḥi" kull halmamnuuniyye?
kindness, favor	faḍil, pl. 'afḍaal
I won't forget your kindness all my life.	faḍ*i*lkum, maa bansaa ṭuul ḥayaati.
If you or any of your relatives come to America, you must come to visit me at my home. My house is your house (an expression extending hospitality).	biḥyaatak, 'iza 'ijiit 'inte, 'aw ḥad min 'araaybak 9a'ameerka, laazim tiiju zzuuruuni filbeet. lbeet beetkum.
be safe	silim bislam
owner	ṣaaḥib, pl. ('a)ṣḥaab

May the house and its owners be safe (in reply).	yislam lbeet w'aṣḥaabo.
I hope to send my oldest boy to America to be educated,	nšaa*ll*a raḥ'ab9at 'ibni likbiir 9a'ameerka, ḥatta yit9allam.
and he will come to visit you.	whuwwe biiji yzuurkum.
gift, present	hadiyye, pl. hadaaya
Before I forget, Mr. West. I have a small gift I want you to take to your family.	abil maa 'ansa, yaa mistir west, fii ma9i hadiyye ẓġiire, biddi taaxudha lal9eele.
Why bother, Ahmad ?	leeš halġalabe, yaa 'aḥmad ?
duty	waajib
It's no bother. It's a duty.	maa fii ġalabe. haada waajib.
I beg forgiveness of God (a reply to a compliment)	'astaġfiru *ll*aa, staġfara*ll*a
overwhelm	ġamar buġmur
kindness	luṭuf
Not at all. You've overwhelmed me with your kindness.	'astaġfiru *ll*aa. ġamartuuna bluṭ*u*fkum.
make (someone) arrive	waṣṣal biwaṣṣil
I think I have to go back now.	baftkir laazim 'arja9 halla.
Good luck, and may God be with you and bring you back safely to your family.	mwaffa', nšaa*ll*a. w'a*ll*a ykuun ma9ak, wiywaṣṣlak 9ind 'ahlak bissalaame.
May God keep you.	'a*ll*a ysallmak.

VOCABULARY I • Arabic-English.

This Vocabulary is arranged alphabetically, according to the transcription used in the text. The ordinary letters and special symbols appear in the following order : ' a b *b* d ḍ e f g ġ h ḥ i j k l *l* m *m* n o p q r *r* s ṣ š t ṭ u v w x y z ẓ 9.

Verbs are entered in the third person masculine singular (the « he » form) of the suffix tense, followed by the third person masculine singular of the prefix tense. They are translated by the English infinitive without « to ».

Nouns are entered in the singular, followed by the plural, if any. Plurals are not entered separately, except for the relatively few plurals that lack a singular. Singular nouns ending in -a or -e are feminine, unless otherwise marked ; all other singular nouns are masculine.

Adjectives are entered in the masculine singular, followed by the feminine singular, and the plural, if any.

The abbreviations are the same as those used elsewhere in the book.

'

'a'rab	*nearer, nearest*
'aab	*August*
'aabal bi'aabil	*meet*
'aaḍaar	*March*
'aaḍi 'uḍa(a) *or* quḍaat	*judge*
'aal bi'uul	*tell, say*
'aam bi'iim	*remove*

'aam bi'uum	*get up*
'aam fii	*undertake*
'aas bi'iis	*measure*
'aaṣaṣ bi'aaṣiṣ	*punish*
'aaṣiṣ 'aaṣṣa 'aaṣṣiin	*cutting*
'ab 'abbayaat *or* 'aabaa'	*father*
'abadan	(*not*) *at all*
'abil	*before, ago*
'abil maa (+ verb)	*before*
'abir 'buur	*grave, tomb*
'abyaḍ beeḍa biiḍ	*white*
'ab9ad	*farther, farthest*
'adaar bidiir	*direct*
'adab 'aadaab	*literature*
'add	*as much as*
'add maa (+ verb)	*as much as, as many as, whatever*
'addaaḥa 'addaaḥaat	*lighter*
'addam bi'addim	*advance, present*
'addeeš	*how much, how long*
'adna	*nearer, nearest*
'aḍa bi'ḍi	*spend* (*time*)
'aḍḥa (m)	*sacrifice*
'afaad bifiid	*be useful*
'afandi	*effendi* (*a term of address*)
'afandi	*tangerines*
'aġla	*more expensive, most expensive*
'ahamm bihimm	*concern*

'ahamm	*more important, most important*
'ahil (pl)	*family*
'ahla wsahla	*welcome !*
'ahlan wasahlan	*welcome!*
'ahwe	*coffee*
'ahwe 'ahaawi	*coffee shop*
'aḥabb	*dearer, dearest*
'aḥla	*nicer, nicest*
'aḥmar ḥamra ḥumur	*red*
'aḥsan	*better, best*
'aja biiji	*come*
'ajadd	*newer, newest*
'ajra bijri	*carry out*
'akal byaakul	*eat*
'akbar kubra	*bigger, biggest; older, oldest*
'akil	*food*
'aktar	*more, most*
'ala bi'li	*fry*
'alam 'laam	*pencil, pen*
'alam ḥibir	*fountain pen*
'alf 'aalaaf/taalaaf *or* 'uluuf	*thousand*
'alfeen	*two thousand*
tlat taalaaf	*three thousand*
'alḥaq bilḥiq	*annex*
'aliil 'aliile 'aliiliin *or* 'laal	*small, slight*
'allaf bi'allif	*compose, write*
'a*ll*a	*God*
'a*ll*a ysallmak	*may God keep you* (*m*) (*in reply to* ma9 ssalaame)

nuškur 'a*ll*a	*let us thank God*
'a*lm*aani 'a*lm*aaniyye 'a*lm*aan	*German*
'amal 'aamaal	*hope*
'amar bu'mur	*order, command*
'ameerka	*America*
'ameerkaani 'ameerkaaniyye 'ameerkaan	*American*
'amiiṣ 'umṣaan	*shirt*
'amir 'awaamir	*command*
'amrak	*yes, indeed (lit. your command)*
'amir 'umuur	*matter, affair*
'amkan bimkin	*be possible*
'ana	*I*
'anbaa' (pl)	*news*
'anniine 'anaani	*bottle*
'an9am bin9im	*favor*
'a*ll*a yin9im 9aleek	*may God favor you (in reply to* na9iiman *)*
'an9aš bin9iš	*revive*
'aqṣa	*farther, farthest*
'arba9a / 'arba9	*four*
'arba9 sniin	*four years*
'arba9 ṭa9š / 'arba9 ṭa9šar	*fourteen*
'arba9 ṭa9šar sane	*fourteen years*
'arb9iin	*forty*
'arḍ (f)	*floor*
'arḍ (f) 'araaḍi	*ground, land*
'arḍi šooki	*artichokes*

'ariib 'ariibe 'raab	*close, near*
'ariib min	*close to*
'ariib 'araayib	*relative*
'arnabiiṭ	*cauliflower*
'arye qura	*village*
'asaas 'asaasaat	*foundation*
'aswad sooda suud	*black*
'aṣaaṣ 'aṣaaṣaat	*punishment*
'aṣarr biṣirr	*insist*
'aṣfar ṣafra ṣufur	*yellow*
'aṣir 'ṣuur	*palace*
'aṣṣ bi'uṣṣ	*cut*
'aššar bi'aššir	*point out*
'atiina	*Athens*
'aṭa9 bi'ṭa9	*cut*
'aṭṭa9 bi'aṭṭi9	*cut to pieces*
'aṭyab	*tastier, tastiest*
'aw	*or*
'awṣaṭ wuṣṭa	*middle, central*
'awwal 'uula 'awaa'il	*first*
'awwal šii	*first of all*
'ax 'ixwe	*brother*
'axi	*my brother (an informal term of address)*
'axuuy	*my brother*
'axad byaaxud	*take*

'axaff	*lighter, lightest*
'axḍar xaḍra xuḍur	*green*
'axxar bi'axxir	*delay*
'ayluul	*September*
'aywa	*yes*
'ayy	*what, which, any*
'ayyaar	*May*
'ayyad bi'ayyid	*support*
'azaa9 bizii9	*broadcast*
'azra' zar'a zuru'	*blue*
'az9aj biz9ij	*disturb*
'aẓġar	*younger, youngest; smaller, smallest*
'a9ad bu'9ud	*sit*
'a9jab bi9jib	*please*
'a9la 9ulya	*higher, highest*
'a9lan bi9lin	*proclaim*
'a9ṭa bya9ṭi	*give*
'a9zab 9izbaan	*bachelor*
'baal	*across from*
'eemta(n)	*when*
'eemta maa (+ verb)	*whenever*
'eeš	*what*
'eeš maa (+ verb)	*whatever*
'ibin wlaad	*son*
'ibin 9arab	*Arab (m)*
'ibre 'ubar	*needle*

'ibtidaa'	*beginning*
'ideen	*two hands*
'idir bi'dar	*be able*
'ihtimaam	*concern*
'iḥmiraar	*redness*
'iid 'ayaadi	*hand*
'ideen	*two hands*
'iiṭaalya	*Italy*
'ijbaari 'ijbaariyye 'ijbaariyyiin	*compulsory*
'ijtimaa9 'ijtimaa9aat	*meeting, society*
'illa	*except, minus*
'illi	*that, which, who, the one*
'imm (f) 'immayaat	*mother*
'infijaar	*exploding*
'influwenza	*influenza*
'ingiltra	*England*
'ingliizi 'ingliiziyye 'ingliiz	*English*
'inno	*that, that he*
'inšaa'	*constructing*
'inte	*you (m)*
'inti	*you (f)*
'intixaab	*electing*
'intixaabaat	*elections*
'intu	*you (pl)*

'in9aaš	*reviving*
'iqtiṣaaḍ	*economics*
'iqtiṣaaḍi 'iqtiṣaaḍiyye 'iqtiṣaaḍiyyiin	*economic*
'iri bi'ra	*read*
'irš 'ruuš	*piastre*
'isim 'asmaa'	*name*
'istiqlaal	*independence*
'ixbaari 'ixbaariyye 'ixbaariyyiin	*news* (*adj.*)
'ixwaan	*brethren*
'iza	*if*
'izaa9a 'izaa9aat	*broadcasting ; radio station*
'izan	*then*
'izin 'zuune *or* 'uzuunaat	*leave, permission*
'iz9aaj 'iz9aajaat	*inconvenience*
'maaš	*cloth*
'raay(e)	*reading*
'reedis	*shrimp*
'uddaam	*in front of*
'unṣliyye 'unṣliyyaat	*consulate*
'unṣul 'anaaṣil	*consul*
'urduni 'urduniyye, 'urduniyyiin *or* 'urduniyye	*Jordanian*
'usbuu9 'asabii9	*week*

'ustaaz 'asaatze	*teacher, maestro professional man*

'ustaaz 'asaatze	*teacher, maestro*
	professional man
'uteel 'uteelaat	*hotel*
'uṭun	*cotton*
'uuḍa 'uwaḍ	*room*
'uxt (f) xawaat	*sister*
'yaas 'yaasaat	*measurement*

B

b- / bi-	*in*
bhaliblaad	*in this country*
bil9arabi	*in Arabic*
ba'ar	*cows*
ba'ara ba'araat	*a cow*
ba'duunis	*parsley*
ba'laawe	*baklava*
baa'i baa'ye baa'yiin	*remaining*
baab bwaab	*door*
baaboor bawabiir	*boat*
baal	*attention*
baamye	*okra*
baarak bibaarik	*bless*

'a*ll*a ybaarik fiik	*may God bless you (in reply to* mabruuk)
baaṭaḥ bibaaṭiḥ	*wrestle*
baaxira bawaaxir	*steamship*
baayi9 baay9a baay9iin	*selling*
baa9 bibii9	*sell*
bada bibda	*begin*
badle badlaat	*suit*
baġdaad (f)	*Baghdad*
baḥri baḥriyye baḥriyyiin	*naval*
bakkiir	*early*
bala	*without*
balaaš	*no need*
balad (f) blaad	*town*
baladi baladiyye	*municipal*
baladiyye baladiyyaat	*municipality*
bala9 bibla9	*swallow*
bana bibni	*build*
bandoora	*tomatoes*
bank bnuuk	*bank*
banna (m) bannayiin	*mason*
bard	*coldness*
barhan bibarhin	*prove*
bariid	*mail*
bariid jawwi	*airmail*

barlamaan barlamaanaat	*parliament*
barnaamaj baraamij	*program*
barra	*outside*
bass	*but*
baṣal	*onions*
baṣiiṭ baṣiiṭa baṣiiṭiin	*simple*
baṣṭ	*good time*
batt bibitt	*decide*
baṭaaṭa	*potatoes*
baṭaḥ bibṭaḥ	*throw down*
baṭin bṭuun	*belly*
baṭṭ	*ducks*
baṭṭa baṭṭaat	*a duck*
baṭṭaal baṭṭaale baṭṭaaliin	*bad*
baṭṭiix	*watermelons*
baṭṭiixa baṭṭiixaat	*a watermelon*
bazeella	*peas*
ba9at bib9at	*send*
ba9d	*up to now*
ba9deen	*later on*
ba9id / ba9d	*after*
ba9d ḍḍuhur	*afternoon*
ba9id maa (+verb)	*after*
beeḍ	*eggs*
beeḍa beeḍaat	*an egg*

been	*between*
beeruut (f)	*Beirut*
beet byuut	*house*
beet *mayy*	*toilet*
beetinjaan	*eggplants*
beetinjaane beetinja(a)naat	*an eggplant*
beet laḥim (f)	*Bethlehem*
bi'i bib'a	*stay, remain*
bid- / bidd-	*want*
bidkum	*you (pl) want*
bidna	*we want*
biddak	*you (m) want*
biḥyaatak	*please (lit. by your life)*
biira	*beer*
binni binniyye binniyyiin	*brown*
bint (f) banaat	*daughter, girl*
bint 9arab	*Arab (f)*
blaad (f)	*country ; countries*
blaad lingliiz	*England*
bluuze bluuzaat	*blouse*
booṣṭa booṣṭaat	*post office*

D

d'ii'a da'aayi'	*minute*
da'in d'uun	*beard*
daa'ira dawaa'ir	*department*
daan dineen	*ear*
daar bidiir	*turn*
diir baalak	*take care*
daar biduur	*go around, turn around*
daarij daarje daarjiin	*current*
daawa bidaawi	*treat medically*
ḍaaxli daaxliyye daaxliyyiin	*internal, domestic*
daayman	*always*
daayme	*always (expression said after drinking coffee and returning the cup)*
dabbar bidabbir	*arrange*
dabbuus dababiis	*pin*
dabke dabkaat	*dabke (a folk dance)*
daftar dafaatir	*notebook*
dall bidill	*direct*
danab dnaab	*tail*

daras budrus	*study*
dawa (m) 'adwiye	*medicine*
dawle duwal	*state, nation*
dawwar bidawwir	*have (someone) go around*
daxil	*sources of income*
diik dyuuk	*rooster*
diik ḥabaš	*turkey*
diinaar dananiir	*dinar*
diini diiniyye diiniyyiin	*religious*
dinya	*world*
djawwaz bidjawwaz	*be married*
draa9 'adru9 / tudru9	*drā' (an arm's length)*
tlat tudru9	*three drā's*
duġri	*straight ahead*
duktoor dakaatra	*doctor*
durraa'	*peaches*

D

ḍabb biḍubb	*pack*
ḍall biḍall	*stay*
ḍarab buḍrub	*strike*
ḍarab 'ibre	*give an injection*

ḍariibe ḍaraa'ib	*tax*
ḍaruura ḍaruuraat	*necessity*
ḍaruuri ḍaruuriyye ḍaruuriyyiin	*necessary*
ḍḍahraan (f)	*Dhahran*
ḍeef ḍyuuf	*guest*
ḍiḥik biḍḥak	*laugh*
ḍuhur	*noon*

F

fa'iir fa'iire fu'ara	*poor*
faa' bifii'	*wake up*
faadi	*savior*
faaḍ bifiiḍ	*overflow*
faaḍi faaḍye faaḍyiin	*free, empty*
faat bifuut	*pass by*
faatiḥ faatḥa faatḥiin	*open*
faḍḍal bifaḍḍil	*prefer*
faḍil 'afḍaal	*favor, kindness*
fahham bifahhim	*explain*
fallaaḥ fallaaḥiin	*fallah, peasant*
falsafe falsafaat	*philosophy*

fara' bifri'	*make a difference*
farja bifarji	*show*
farše faršaat	*bed*
faṣṣal bifaṣṣil	*cut out a garment*
faṣuulya	*dried beans*
fataḥ biftaḥ	*open*
fawaakih	*fruit*
fayya' bifayyi'	*wake*
feen	*where*
feen maa (+verb)	*wherever*
fiḍi bifḍa	*be free, be vacant*
fihim bifham	*understand*
fii	*there is, there are*
fii / fii- / fi-	*in*
fijil	*radishes*
fikra fikar	*idea*
filfil	*pepper*
finjaan fanajiin	*cup*
fiṣiḥ	*Easter*
fiṭir	*breaking fast*
foo'	*above*
fraansa	*France*
fransaawi fransaawiyye fransaawiyyiin	*French*
freez	*strawberries*

ftakar biftkir	*think*
fṭuur	*breakfast*
furṣa furaṣ	*vacation, opportunity*
fuṣḥa	*pure*
fuṣṭaan faṣaṭiin	*dress*
fuul	*Spanish beans*
fuuṭa fuwaṭ	*napkin*

G

gravaat (f) gravattaat	*necktie*
gumruk gamaarik	*customs*

Ġ

ġaab biġiib	*be absent*
ġaali ġaalye ġaalyiin	*expensive*
ġaaye ġaayaat	*object, intention*
ġaazal biġaazil	*flirt*
ġada (m)	*midday meal*

ġalab biġlib	*overcome*
ġalabe ġalabaat	*trouble, bother*
ġalaṭ (invariable adj.)	*wrong*
ġallab biġallib	*bother*
ġamar buġmur	*overwhelm*
ġani ġaniyye 'aġniya	*rich*
ġaraḍ 'aġraaḍ	*purpose*
ġasiil	*laundry, wash*
ġassal biġassil	*wash*
ġazal biġzil	*spin*
ġeebe ġeebaat	*absence*
ġeeme ġeemaat *or* ġyuum	*cloud*
ġeer	*other than, different*
ġili biġla	*be expensive*
ġina (m)	*singing*
ġurfe ġuraf	*room*

H

ha-	*this (m, f), these*
haada	*this (m)*
haadi	*this (f)*
habb bihibb	*blow*

hadam bihdim	*destroy*
hadd bihidd	*demolish*
hadiyye hadaaya	*gift, present*
hadool	*these*
haḍam bihḍim	*digest*
halla	*now*
haloo	*hello (on telephone)*
handase handasaat	*engineering*
hanii'an	*may it do you good (said to someone who has just drunk some water)*
hanna bihanni	*give joy*
'a*ll*a yhanniik	*may God give you joy (in reply to* hanii'an)
hawiyye hawiyyaat	*identity card*
hayy	*here is, here are*
hazz bihizz	*move, shake*
hazz	*a moving, a shaking*
heek	*thus, so*
hiyye	*she*
hoon	*here*
htamm bihtamm	*be concerned*
humme	*they*
hunaak	*there*
huwwe	*he*

H

ḥa"	*price*
ḥa" ḥ'uu'	*right*
ḥa'ii'a ḥa'aayi'	*truth*
ḥaaḍir ḥaaḍra ḥaaḍriin	*ready, present*
ḥaafaẓ biḥaafiẓ	*maintain*
ḥaafiz ḥawaafiz	*stimulus*
ḥaafiẓ ḥaafẓa ḥaafẓiin	*keeper*
ḥaaka biḥaaki	*talk to*
ḥaakim	*it happens that*
ḥaal 'aḥwaal	*condition*
ḥaal	*self*
ḥaale ḥaalaat	*situation*
ḥaamiḍ ḥaamḍa ḥaamḍiin	*sour*
ḥaasab biḥaasib	*reckon*
ḥaaṭiṭ ḥaaṭṭa ḥaaṭṭiin	*putting*
ḥabb biḥibb	*like, love*
ḥabbe ḥabbaat	*grain, seed, berry*
ḥabbit bandoora	*a tomato*
ḥabbit zeetuun	*an olive*
ḥabbit 9inab	*a grape*

ḥabbe ḥbuub	*pill*
ḥabiib ḥabiibe ḥabaayib	*loved one*
ḥad(a)	*anyone*
ḥadd ḥduud	*boundary*
ḥadiid	*iron*
ḥaḍḍar biḥaḍḍir	*prepare*
ḥaḍra ḥaḍraat	*presence*
ḥaḍ*i*rtak	*your presence (a term of address)*
ḥafaẓ biḥfaẓ	*keep*
'al*l*a yiḥfaẓak	*may God keep you*
ḥafle ḥaflaat	*party*
ḥaka biḥki	*speak*
ḥala' biḥli'	*shave*
ḥalab (f)	*Aleppo*
ḥaliib	*milk*
ḥallaa' ḥallaa'iin	*barber*
ḥammaam ḥammaamaat	*bath, bathroom*
ḥaraara	*fever*
ḥarake ḥarakaat	*movement*
ḥaram	*sanctuary*
ḥariir	*silk*
ḥarram biḥarrim	*forbid*
ḥarrar biḥarrir	*edit*
ḥaša biḥši	*stuff*

ḥatta	*in order to*
ḥaṭṭ biḥuṭṭ	*put*
ḥawaali	*about*
ḥawwal biḥawwil	*transfer*
ḥayaa(h) (f)	*life*
ḥayy ḥayye 'aḥyaa'	*alive*
ḥazz biḥizz	*sever*
ḥaẓẓ ḥẓuuẓ	*luck*
ḥda9š / ḥda9šar	*eleven*
ḥda9šar sane	*eleven years*
ḥeeṭ ḥiiṭaan	*wall*
ḥibir	*ink*
ḥilu ḥilwe ḥilwiin	*sweet, nice*
ḥmaar ḥamiir	*donkey*
ḥmarr biḥmarr	*become red*
ḥsaab	*bill, account*
ḥtaaj biḥtaaj	*need*
ḥubb	*love*
ḥukuume ḥukuumaat	*government*
ḥummuṣ	*chickpeas*
ḥuquuq	*law*
ḥurr ḥurra 'aḥraar	*free*
ḥzeeraan	*June*

J

jaab bijiib	*bring*
jaadal bijaadil	*dispute*
jaaj	*chickens*
jaaaje jaajaat	*a chicken*
jaamal bijaamil	*be courteous to*
jaami9 jawaami9	*mosque*
jaam(i)9a jaam(i)9aat	*university*
jaari jaarye jaaryiin	*flowing*
jaa*r* jiiraan	*neighbor*
jaawab bijaawib	*answer*
jaay jaaye jaayiin	*coming, having come*
jaddad bijaddid	*renew*
jakeet jake(e)taat	*jacket*
jamal jmaal	*camel*
jama9 bijma9	*add*
jamb	*next to*
jamboon	*ham*
jamma9 bijammi9	*collect*
janb	*next to*
janb jawaanib	*side*

jariide jaraayid	*newspaper*
jarrab bijarrib	*try*
jawaab jawaabaat *or* 'ajwibe	*answer*
jawwi jawwiyye jawwiyyiin	*air (adj.)*
jazar	*carrots*
jdiid jdiide jdaad	*new*
jeeb jyaab	*pocket*
jeeš jyuuš	*army*
jibne	*cheese*
jidd jduud	*grandfather*
jiddan	*very*
jins jnaas	*kind, sort*
jinsiyye jinsiyyaat	*nationality*
jooz jwaaz	*husband*
jooz 'imm	*stepfather*
jtama9 bijtmi9	*meet*
jum9a juma9	*week*

K

kaaf	*the Arabic letter kāf*
kaafaḥ bikaafiḥ	*combat*
kaan bikuun	*be*

kaanuun (l)'awwal	*December*
kaanuun (t)taani	*January*
kaas kaasaat	*glass*
kaatab bikaatib	*correspond*
kaatib kaatbe kaatbiin	*writing*
kaatib kuttaab	*writer, clerk*
kabbar bikabbir	*enlarge*
kaffa bikaffi	*be enough*
kahraba	*electricity*
kakaaw (f)	*hot chocolate*
kalaam	*talk*
kalsaat (pl)	*socks*
kalsoon kalsoonaat	*undershorts*
kam	*how many ; some, a few*
kamaan	*also, too*
kannas bikannis	*sweep*
karaz	*cherries*
kariim kariime kurama	*generous*
karm kruum	*vineyard, orchard*
katab buktub	*write*
kawa bikwi	*iron*
kawi	*ironing, pressing*
kawwa (m) kawwayiin	*presser*
kazzaab kazzaabiin	*liar*
kbiir kbiire kbaar	*big ; old*

keef	*wish*
kibde	*liver*
kibriite kibriitaat	*box of matches*
kiif	*how*
kiif ḥaalak ?	*how are you ?*
kiif maa (+verb)	*however*
kiilo kilowaat	*kilo*
kilme kilmaat	*word*
kilme waḥde	*bottom price*
kitaabi kitaabiyye	*pertaining to writing*
kittaan	*linen*
kniise kanaayis	*church*
koola	*cola*
ktaab kutub	*books*
ktaabe ktaabaat	*writing*
ktiir ktiire ktaar	*much, a lot ; too much*
kubra	*major*
kull	*all, every*
kull maa (+verb)	*whenever*
kulliyye kulliyyaat	*college*
kundara kanaadir	*pair of shoes*
kursi karaasi	*chair*
kuštbaan kašaatbiin	*thimble*
kuusa (m)	*squash*
kwayyis kwayyse kwayysiin	*good, fine*

L

l'aḥad	*Sunday*
l'arba9a	*Wednesday*
l'uds (f)	*Jerusalem*
l'urdun	*Jordan*
la'	*no*
laa	*no, not*
laa'a bilaa'i	*find, meet*
laakin	*but*
laazim laazme laazmiin	*necessary*
lahje lahjaat	*dialect*
laḥatta	*so that*
laḥim	*meat*
laḥim ba'ar	*beef*
laḥim xanziir	*pork*
laḥim xaruuf	*lamb*
laḥim 9ijil	*veal*
laḥme	*meat*
lamma(n)	*when*
lamma9 bilammi9	*polish*
laṭiif laṭiife laṭiifiin *or* luṭafa	*pleasant*

law	*if (contrary to fact)*
leel	*nighttime*
leele layaali	*night*
leele sa9iide	*good night*
lleele	*tonight*
leemuun (ḥaamiḍ)	*lemons*
leeš	*why ; because*
lḥamdilla	*praise be to God*
li'anno	*because*
libis bilbas	*put on*
lift	*turnips*
liḥye liḥa *or* liḥyaat	*beard*
liira liiraat	*pound (currency)*
liista liistaat	*menu*
lissa	*up to now*
lizim bilzam	*be necessary*
ljum9a	*Friday*
lla	*except, minus*
lli	*that, which, who ; the one*
loon 'alwaan	*color*
lqaahira	*Cairo*
lqur'aan	*the Koran*
lubnaan	*Lebanon*
lubnaani lubnaaniyye lubnaaniyyin	*Lebanese*

luġa luġaat	*language*
lluġa ddaarje	*the colloquial language*
lluġa lfuṣḥa	*the pure language (i. e. Classical Arabic)*
lluġa l9aammiyye	*the colloquial language*
luṭuf 'alṭaaf	*kindness*
luubya	*beans*
lxamiis	*Thursday*
l9iraaq	*Iraq*

M

m'addam m'addame m'addamiin	*presented*
m'aṣṣ m'aṣṣaat	*scissors*
ma'bara ma'aabir	*cemetery*
ma'kuulaat (pl)	*things to eat*
ma'li ma'liyye ma'liyyiin	*fried*
ma'ṣuuṣ ma'ṣuuṣa ma'ṣuuṣiin	*cut*
maa	*not*
maa	*(see Grammar of Unit 22)*
maa	*that which*

maa	*how !*
maa 'aḥlaaha	*how nice she is !*
maa 'akbaro	*how big it is !*
maaḍi maaḍye	*past ; last*
maali maaliyye	*financial*
maaši maašye maašyiin	*walking*
maaši lḥaal	*so-so*
maaza	*hors d'œuvres (with drinks)*
mabruuk mabruuke mabruukiin	*blessed*
mabṣuuṭ mabṣuuṭa mabṣuuṭiin	*well*
mabyuu9 mabyuu9a mabyuu9iin	*sold*
madrase madaaris	*school*
maḍbuub maḍbuube maḍbuubiin	*packed*
mafra' mafaari'	*cross roads*
maftuuḥ maftuuḥa maftuuḥiin	*opened*
maġluuṭ maġluuṭa maġluuṭiin	*wrong*
mahil	*slowness*
maḥall maḥallaat	*place*

maḥalli maḥalliyye maḥalliyyiin	*local*
maḥbuub maḥbuube maḥbuubiin	*loved*
maḥkame maḥaakim	*court*
maḥrame maḥaarim	*handkerchief*
maḥši maḥšiyye maḥšiyyiin	*stuffed*
maḥši maḥaaši	*stuffed vegetable*
maḥṭuuṭ maḥṭuuṭa maḥṭuuṭiin	*placed*
majalle majallaat	*magazine*
majmuu9 majmuu9aat	*total*
makaan 'amkine	*place*
maktab makaatib	*office*
maktabe maktabaat	*bookstore, library*
maktuub makatiib	*letter*
makwi makwiyye makwiyyiin	*ironed*
malfuuf	*cabbage*
malfuufe malfuufaat	*a cabbage*
malyaan malyaane malyaaniin	*full*
malyoon malayiin	*million*
mamnuun mamnuune mamnuuniin	*thankful, grateful*
mamnuunak	*thank you*
mamuuuniyye	*gratitude*

mamša (m) mamaaši	*corridor*
mansuub mansuube mansuubiin	*attributed to*
manṣuub manṣuube manṣuubiin	*suspended*
mantuujaat (pl)	*products*
maqaale maqaalaat	*article*
mara niswaan	*wife, woman*
mart 'ab	*stepmother*
mara' bumru'	*pass*
maraḍ 'amraaḍ	*disease*
marduud marduude marduudiin	*rejected*
marḍuuḍ marḍuuḍa marḍuuḍiin	*bruised*
marḥaba	*hello*
marḥabteen	*hello (in reply)*
mariiḍ mariiḍa marḍa	*sick*
marja9 maraaji9	*authority, reference*
marra marraat	*time*
mas'ale masaa'il	*problem*
mas'uul mas'uule mas'uuliin	*responsible*
masa	*evening*
masa lxeer	*good evening*

masa nnuur	*good evening (in reply)*
masaa'i masaa'iyye	*evening (adj.)*
masaḥ bimsaḥ	*wipe off*
masiiḥi masiiḥiyye masiiḥiyyiin *or* masiiḥiyye	*Christian*
maskiin maskiine masakiin	*poor, unfortunate*
masluu' masluu'a masluu'iin	*boiled*
masmuu9 masmuu9a masmuu9iin	*heard*
masruur masruura masruuriin	*delighted*
maṣaari	*money*
maṣir (f)	*Egypt*
maslaḥa maṣaaliḥ	*interest*
maša bimši	*walk*
mašġal mašaaġil	*workshop*
mašġuul mašġuule mašġuuliin	*busy*
mašhuur mašhuura mašhuuriin	*famous*
mašruub mašruubaat	*alcoholic beverage*
mašruu9 mašaarii9	*project*
maššaṭ bimaššiṭ	*comb*
mašta (m) mašaati	*winter resort*
mašwi mašwiyye mašwiyyiin	*broiled*

matalan	*for example*
matḥaf mataaḥif	*museum*
maṭaar maṭaaraat	*airport*
maṭbax maṭaabix	*kitchen*
maṭ9am maṭaa9im	*restaurant*
maw'if mawaa'if	*stopping place*
mawjuud mawjuude mawjuudiin	*present*
mawlid	*birth*
mawsim mawaasim	*season*
maw9id mawaa9iid	*appointment*
maxluuṭ maxluuṭa maxluuṭiin	*mixed*
mazaar mazaaraat	*shrine*
maẓbuuṭ maẓbuuṭa maẓbuuṭiin	*correct*
ma9	*with*
ma9 ssalaame	*good-by*
ma9ak	*you have*
ma9'uul ma9'uule ma9'uuliin	*reasonable*
ma9aaš ma9aašaat	*wages, salary*
ma9aleeš	*it doesn't matter*
ma9la'a ma9aali'	*spoon*
ma9luum	*of course, certainly*
ma9luumaat (pl)	*information*
ma9mal ma9aamil	*factory, plant*
ma9rife	*knowing*

ma9ruuf	*favor*
mbaarak mbaarake mbaarakiin	*blessed*
mbaariḥ	*yesterday*
mhandis mhandsiin	*engineer*
mḥaami muḥaamiin	*lawyer*
mḥaasib mḥaasbiin	*accountant*
mḥaḍḍar mḥaḍḍara mḥaḍḍariin	*prepared*
mḥammar mḥammara mḥammariin	*roasted*
mḥarrir mḥarririin	*editor*
mḥaasabaat (pl)	*accounting*
mḥaasabe	*accounting*
mḥaṭṭa mḥaṭṭaat	*station*
miftkir miftikre miftikriin	*thinking*
mijjawwiz mijjawwze mijjawwziin	*married*
miilaad	*birth*
miin	*who, whom, whose*
miina (m) mawaani	*harbor, port*
miizaan mayaziin	*scale*
miizaan ḥaraara	*thermometer*
miliḥ	*salt*
min / min- / minn- / mni-	*from ; than*

min faḍlak	*please (to a man, speaker requesting something)*
min šaan	*for the sake of*
min šaan xaaṭrak	*for your sake*
minhum	*from them*
minnak	*from you*
mnilbalad	*from the town*
huwwe 'akbar minni	*he is older than I am*
minhaaj manaahij	*program*
misik bimsik	*hold, seize*
mislim mis*i*lme mis*i*lmiin	*Moslem*
mista9jil mista9*i*jle mista9*i*jliin	*in a hurry*
mist9idd mist9idde mist9iddiin	*ready*
miš	*not*
miš baṭṭaal	*not bad*
miš heek ?	*isn't it so ?*
mišmiš	*apricots*
mištaa' mištaa'a mištaa'iin	*longing*
mit'assif mit'assfe mit'assfiin	*sorry*
mit'axxir mit'axxre mit'axxriin	*late*
mitil	*like*
mitil maa (+ verb)	*as, as much as*

mitir mtaar	*meter*
mit9ahhid mit9ahhdiin	*contractor*
mit9allim mit9allme mit9allmiin	*educated*
miyye / miit / mit-	*hundred*
miit 'alf	*one hundred thousand*
miteen	*two hundred*
mi9de mi9ad *or* mi9daat	*stomach*
mnawwa9 mnawwa9a mnawwa9iin	*varied*
mniiḥ mniiḥa mnaaḥ	*good*
mooz	*bananas*
mrattab mrattabe mrattabiin	*well arranged*
msaafir msaafre msaafriin	*traveling*
msaa9ade msaa9adaat	*helping*
msaa9id msaa9diin	*assistant*
msajjal msajjale msajjaliin	*registered*
msakkar msakkara msakkariin	*closed*
msoogar msoogara msoogariin	*registered*
mtarjim mtar*i*jmiin	*translator*
mudiir mudara(a')	*director, manager*
muftaaḥ mafatiiḥ	*key*
muhandis muhandisiin	*engineer*
muhimm muhimme muhimmiin	*important*

muḩaamaah (f)	*law*
muḩaami muḩaamiin	*lawyer*
muḩaasabaat (pl)	*accounting*
muḩaasabė	*accounting*
muḩaasib muḩaasbiin	*accountant*
muḩarrir muḩarririin	*editor*
mujaadale mujaadalaat	*dispute*
mukaafaḩa	*combating*
mulḩaq mulḩaqa mulḩaqiin	*annexed*
mulḩaq mulḩaqiin	*attaché*
mumkin	*possible*
muntaxab muntáxabe muntaxabiin	*elected*
musaa9ade	*helping*
mustašaar mustašaariin	*counselor*
mustašfa (m) mustašfayaat	*hospital*
musta9jal musta9jale musta9jaliin	*prompt, quick, hurried*
mušaahade mušaahadaat	*personal observation*
mutarjim mutarjimiin	*translator*
muttaḩid muttáḩide muttaḩidiin	*united*
muusiiqa	*music*
musiiqi musiiqiyye	*music (adj.)*
muxliṣ muxilṣa muxilṣiin	*sincere*
muxtaar maxatiir	*mukhtar (headman)*

mwaffa' mwaffa'a mwaffa'iin	*prosperous, successful*
mwaẓẓaf mwaẓẓafiin	*official*
m9abba (m) m9abbaay (f) m9abbayiin	*filled out*
m9allim m9allmiin	*teacher*

M

*m*ayy (f)	*water*
*m*ayyitna	*our water*

N

n'aal bin'aal	*be said*
na"a bina"i	*choose*
na'aṣ bun'uṣ	*decrease*
naa'ib nuwwaab	*deputy*
naa'ib 'unṣul	*vice consul*
naabuli (f)	*Naples*
naada binaadi	*call*
naafas binaafis	*compete*

naaḥye nawaaḥi	*side, aspect*
naam binaam	*sleep*
naas (pl)	*people*
naasab binaasib	*be convenient, be suitable*
naašif naašfe naašfiin	*dry*
naayib nuwwaab	*deputy*
naayib 'unṣul	*vice consul*
naazil naazle naazliin	*staying*
naḍḍaf binaḍḍif	*clean*
nafas	*breath*
nafs	*self ; soul ; same*
nafs lwa't	*the same time*
najaḥ binjaḥ	*succeed*
najjaḥ binajjiḥ	*make succeed*
najme njuum	*star*
nasiib nasaayib	*relative*
naṣiib	*lot*
našra našraat	*bulletin*
nataf bintif	*pluck*
nazzal binazzil	*make (something) come down*
na9am	*yes*
na9iiman	*may it be to your pleasure (expression said to someone who has just had a haircut, a shave, or a bath)*
na9na9	*mint*

nbaṣat binbṣiṭ	*have a good time, be happy*
nbiid	*wine*
nḍiif nḍiife nḍaaf	*clean*
nfajar bin*i*fjir	*explode*
nfataḥ bin*i*ftiḥ	*be opened*
nhaar	*daytime*
nḥabb binḥabb	*be liked*
nḥaka binḥaka	*be said*
niḥna	*we*
niisaan	*April*
nisi binsa	*forget*
niswaan (pl).	*women, wives*
niyaabi niyaabiyye niyaabiyyiin	*parliamentary*
njaaṣ	*pears*
noo9 'anwaa9	*sort*
nšaa*ll*a	*if God wills*
ntaxab bintxib	*elect*
nṭaba9 binṭbi9	*be printed*
nṭawa binṭwi	*be folded*
nu'ṣaan	*deficiency*
nukte nukat	*joke, witty remark*
numra numar	*number*
nusxa nusax	*copy*
nuṣṣ nṣaaṣ	*half, middle*

nuur 'anwaar *light*

nzaar binzaar *be visited*

n9add bin9add *be counted, be countable*

P

proova proovaat *fitting*

Q

qaḍiyye qaḍaaya *cause, question*

qaanuun qawaaniin *law*

qirḍ quruuḍ *loan*

qisim 'aqsaam *part, division, section*

qtaraḥ biqtriḥ *propose*

R

ra"a bira"i *promote*

ra'i 'aaraa' *opinion*

ra'iis ru'asa(a')	*head man*
ra'iis baladiyye	*mayor*
ra'iis wazaara	*prime minister*
ra'ṣ	*dancing*
raabi9 raab9a	*fourth*
raad biriid	*want*
raafa' biraafi'	*accompany*
raafa9 biraafi9	*defend*
raahib ruhbaan	*monk*
raaḥ biruuḥ	*go*
raaḥa	*rest*
raaji9 raaj9a raaj9iin	*returning*
raakib raakbe raakbiin	*riding*
raas ruus	*head*
raas baṣal	*an onion*
raas fijil	*a radish*
raayiḥ raayḥa raayḥiin	*going*
rabba birabbi	*educate*
rabii9	*spring*
radd birudd	*return, send back, answer*
raḥ- / raayiḥ	*going to, will, shall*
ramaadi ramaadiyye ramaadiyyiin	*gray*
rasmi rasmiyye rasmiyyiin	*formal, official*
rašiḥ	*a cold*

rattab birattib	*put in order*
rayy	*irrigation*
riḥle riḥlaat	*journey*
riji9 birja9	*return*
rijjaal rjaal	*man*
rikib birkab	*ride*
rubu9 rbaa9	*quarter*
ruuḥ 'arwaaḥ	*spirit*
ruusi ruusiyye ruus	*Russian*
ruzz	*rice*
rxiiṣ rxiiṣa rxaaṣ	*inexpensive*

S

sa'al bis'al	*ask*
saada (invariable adj.)	*plain*
saabi9 saab9a	*seventh*
saadis saadse	*sixth*
saafar bisaafir	*travel*
saaḥa saaḥaat	*courtyard*
saaḥib saaḥbe saaḥbiin	*pulling*
saakin saakne saakniin	*dwelling*
saami9 saam9a saam9iin	*hearing, having heard*

saari saarye	*contagious*
saa9a saa9aat	*hour, watch*
saa9a mnabbih	*alarm clock*
saa9aati pl. saa9aatiyye	*watchmaker*
saa9ad bisaa9id	*help*
sabaanix	*spinach*
saba9 ṭa9š / saba9 ṭa9šar	*seventeen*
saba9 ṭa9šar sane	*seventeen years*
sabb bisibb	*curse*
sab9a / sabi9 / sab9	*seven*
sabi9 tušhur	*seven months*
sab9 sniin	*seven years*
sab9iin	*seventy*
sadda' bisaddi'	*believe*
safaara safaaraat	*embassy*
safar	*travel*
safiir sufara(a')	*ambassador*
safra safraat	*trip*
sahra sahraat	*evening party*
sakan buskun	*dwell*
sakkan bisakkin	*house*
sakkar bisakkir	*close*
salaam	*peace*
'assalaamu 9alaykum	*the peace upon you*
salaame	*safety*

salaamtak	*your safety (an expression said to a person who is sick)*
sallam bisallim	*keep safe ; greet*
'a*ll*a ysallmak	*may God keep you (in reply to* ma9 ssalaame)
sallimli 9alee(h)	*say hello to him for me*
salle sallaat	*basket*
sama	*sky*
samaḥ bismaḥ	*permit*
btismaḥli bsiigaara ?	*may I take a cigarette ?*
samak	*fish*
samake samakaat	*a fish*
sanduu' sanadii'	*box*
sanawi sanawiyye	*annual*
sane sniin	*year*
sawa	*together*
sayyaara sayyaaraat	*car*
sayyid	*Mr.*
sa9al bus9ul	*cough*
sa9iid sa9iide su9ada	*happy*
sa9iide mbaarake	*good night (in reply)*
s*b*anyooli s*b*anyooliyye s*b*anyool	*Spanish*
seef syuuf	*sword*
sifir ṣfaar	*zero*
siid syaad	*grandfather ; master*
siigaara siigaaraat *or* sagaayir	*cigarette*

sikke sikak	*rail*
sikkit ḥadiid	*railway*
sikkiin sakakiin	*knife*
silim bislam	*be safe*
simi9 bisma9	*hear*
sinama sinamaat	*movie, movie house*
sinn snaan	*tooth*
sinn tuum	*a clove of garlic*
sitt (f) sittaat	*grandmother*
sitte / sitt	*six*
sitt sniin	*six years*
sittiin	*sixty*
sitt ṭa9š / sitt ṭa9šar	*sixteen*
sitt ṭa9šar sane	*sixteen years*
siyaaḥa	*tourism*
siyaase	*politics*
siyaasi siyaasiyye	*political*
si9ir 'as9aar	*price*
ssabt	*Saturday*
ssu9uudiyye	*Saudi Arabia*
staġfar bistaġfir	*seek forgiveness*
'astaġfiru *llaa* *or* staġfara*lla*	*I beg forgiveness of God (a reply to a compliment)*
staḥa" bistḥi"	*deserve*
staḥla bistaḥli	*find nice*

stanna bistanna	*wait*
staqall bistqill	*be independent*
staraaḥ bistriiḥ	*rest*
stašaar bistašiir	*consult*
sta9add bist9idd	*get ready*
sta9jal bista9jil	*hurry*
sta9mal bista9mil	*use*
stuudyo stuudyowaat	*studio*
su'aal su'aalaat *or* 'as'ile	*question*
sukkar	*sugar*
suruur	*pleasure*
suu' (f) swaa'	*market*
suuriyya	*Syria*
su9aal	*coughing*
swadd biswadd	*become black*
sxuune	*fever*

Ṣ

ṣaabuun	*soap*
ṣaaḥib ('a)ṣḥaab	*friend ; owner*
ṣaan9a ṣaan9aat	*maid*
ṣaar biṣiir	*become ; take place*

ṣabaaḥ	*morning*
ṣabaaḥ lxeer	*good morning*
ṣabaaḥ lxeeraat	*good morning (in reply)*
ṣabaaḥ nnuur	*good morning (in reply)*
ṣabaaḥi ṣabaaḥiyye	*morning (adj.)*
ṣaaḍar biṣaaḍir	*confiscate*
ṣabb biṣubb	*pour*
ṣabi ṣubyaan	*boy, child*
ṣaḍar buṣḍur	*come out*
ṣaḍḍar biṣaḍḍir	*export*
ṣaḥaafe	*journalism*
saḥaafi ṣaḥaafiyye	*journalistic*
ṣaḥḥ biṣiḥḥ	*be available*
ṣaḥḥteen	*two healths (in reply to* daayme*)*
ṣaḥiife ṣuḥuf	*newspaper*
ṣaḥin ṣḥuun	*plate*
ṣalaṭa ṣalaṭaat	*salad*
ṣallaḥ biṣalliḥ	*repair*
ṣaṭiḥ ṣṭuuḥ	*roof*
ṣaṭir 'aṣṭur / tuṣṭur *or* ṣṭuur	*line*
tlạt tuṣṭur	*three lines*
ṣeef	*summer*
ṣeefi ṣeefiyye	*summer (adj.)*
ṣeefiyye ṣeefiyyaat	*summertime*
ṣiḥḥa	*health*

ṣiḥḥi ṣiḥḥiyye	*healthy*
ṣinaa9a ṣinaa9aat	*industry*
ṣinaa9i ṣinaa9iyye	*industrial*
ṣooṭ ('a)ṣwaaṭ	*voice*
ṣṣubuḥ	*the morning*
ṣuġra	*minor (f)*
ṣuḥufi ṣuḥufiyyiin	*journalist*
ṣulṭaan ṣalaṭiin	*sultan*
ṣuuf	*wool*
ṣ9uube ṣ9uubaat	*difficulty*

S

ša'fe šu'af	*piece*
šaaf bišuuf	*look, see*
šaami šaamiyye šwaam	*Damascene*
šaan	*matter, concern*
šaari9 šawaari9	*street*
šaay	*tea*
šaayif šaayfe šaayfiin	*looking, seeing*
šabah	*resemblance*
šabaḥ 'ašbaaḥ	*phantom*

šahir 'ašhur / tušhur	*month*
tlat tušhur	*three months*
šajar	*trees*
šakar buškur	*thank*
šamandar	*beets*
šanta šantaat	*suit case, brief case*
šaraf	*honor*
šaraḥ bišraḥ	*explain*
šarii9a	*religious law of Islam*
šarq	*east*
ššarq l'awṣaṭ	*the Middle East*
ššarq l'adna	*the Near East*
ššarq l'aqṣa	*the Far East*
šarraf bišarrif	*honor*
šaršaf šaraašif	*sheet*
šatawi šatawiyye	*winter (adj.)*
šatawiyye šatawiyyaat	*wintertime*
šaṭaf bušṭuf	*wash down*
šaxar bušxur	*snore*
šaxṣ 'ašxaaṣ	*person*
šaxṣi šaxṣiyye	*personal*
šaxṣiyyan	*personally*
šaxṣiyye šaxṣiyyaat	*personality*
ša9b	*people*
ša9ir	*hair*

ša9ra ša9raat	*a hair*
šbaaṭ	*February*
šeex šyuux	*sheikh*
šhaade šhaadaat	*certificate, testimony, diploma*
šii 'ašya(a')	*thing, something*
širib bišrab	*drink*
širke širkaat	*company*
širkit ṭayaraan	*airline*
šita (m)	*winter*
šmaal	*left (side)*
šoob	*heat*
šooke šuwak	*fork*
šooraba	*soup*
ššaam (f)	*Damascus*
štaa' bištaa'	*long for*
štaġal bištġil	*work*
štara bištri	*buy*
šubbaak šababiik	*window*
šuġul 'ašġaal	*work, busniess*
šukran	*thank you*
šurub	*drinking*
šuu	*what*
šuu maalo ?	*what's wrong with him ?*
šuu maa (+ verb)	*whatever*
šwayy (f)	*a little bit*

šwayyit sukkar	*a little bit of sugar*
šwayy, šwayy	*slowly*

T

t'aaṣaṣ bit'aaṣaṣ	*be punished*
t'ammal bit'ammal	*hope*
t'assaf bit'assaf	*be sorry*
t'assas bit'assas	*be established, be founded*
t'axxar bit'axxar	*be late*
t'iil t'iile t'aal	*heavy*
ta'riiban	*approximately*
taab bituub	*repent*
taajir tujjaar	*merchant*
taalit taalte	*third*
taamin taamne	*eighth*
taani taanye	*second, other*
taariix tawaariix	*history ; date*
taasi9 taas9a	*ninth*
taḥriir	*editing*
taḥsiin	*improving*
taḥt	*under*
taḥtaani taḥtaaniyye	*under (adj.)*

talaa9ub	*being deceitful*
talabbuk	*being upset*
talabbuk mi9de	*upset stomach*
talfan bitalfin	*telephone*
talj	*ice*
tall tlaal	*hill*
tamaanye / taman / tamn	*eight*
taman tušhur	*eight months*
tamn sniin	*eight years*
tamaniin	*eighty*
taman ṭa9š / taman ṭa9šar	*eighteen*
taman ṭa9šar sane	*eighteen years*
tamm bitamm	*remain*
tammuuz	*July*
tanḍiif	*cleaning*
tannuura tananiir	*skirt*
tanẓiim	*organizing*
tarak bitrik *or* butruk	*leave*
tarbiye	*education*
tarjame tarjamaat	*translation*
tasjiil tasjiilaat	*recording*
taṣliiḥ	*arming*
tasliiḥ	*repairing*
taṭbii' taṭbii'aat	*application*
tawsii9	*expanding*
taxaṣṣuṣ	*specialty, specialization*

taxfiiḍ	*lowering*
taxt txuute	*bed*
tazwiid	*supplying*
ta9aal	*come !*
ta9diil ta9diilaat	*amendment, modification*
ta9liim ta9aaliim	*teaching*
ta9liimaat (pl)	*instructions*
tbaaḥas bitbaaḥas	*discuss*
tfaḍḍal bitfaḍḍal	*be kind enough to ...*
tfaḍḍal	*please (to a man, speaker offering something)*
tfaḍḍal striiḥ	*please sit down*
tfaḍḍal ma9i	*please come with me*
tfarraj bitfarraj	*look around*
tiin	*figs*
tijaari tijaariyye tijaariyyiin	*commercial*
tikram	*with pleasure, gladly*
tijaara	*commerce*
tilyaani tilyaaniyye tilyaan	*Italian*
tisi9 ṭa9š / tisi9 ta9šar	*nineteen*
tisi9 ta9šar sane	*nineteen years*
tis9a / tisi9 / tis9	*nine*
tisi9 tušhur	*nine months*
tis9 sniin	*nine years*
tis9iin	*ninety*

tišriin (l)'awwal	*October*
tišriin (t)taani	*November*
tizkaar tizkaaraat	*memorial, monument*
ti9ib bit9ab	*become tired*
tlaa'a bitlaa'a	*meet together*
tlaate / tlaat / tlat	*three*
tlaat wlaad	*three children*
tlat tiyyaam	*three days*
tlaatiin	*thirty*
tlaa9ab bitlaa9ab	*be deceitful*
tlat ṭa9š / tlat ṭa9šar	*thirteen*
tlat ṭa9šar sane	*thirteen years*
tnaawab bitnaawab	*take turns at*
tneen f. tinteen	*two*
tra"a bitra"a	*be promoted*
treen treenaat	*train*
tsaa9ad bitsaa9ad	*be helped*
tšarraf bitšarraf	*be honored*
tšarrafna	*how do you do ?*
ttafa' bittfi'	*agree*
ttaḥad bittḥid	*be united*
ttalaata	*Tuesday*
ttineen	*Monday*
tuffaaḥ	*apples*
tuffaaḥa tuffaaḥaat	*an apple*

tult tlaat	*third*
turkiyya	*Turkey*
tuum	*garlic*
tuut	*mulberries*
txarraj bitxarraj	*be graduated*
txaṣṣaṣ bitxaṣṣaṣ	*specialize*
t9ajjab bit9ajjab	*be astonished*
t9allam bit9allam	*learn, be taught*
t9arraf bit9arraf	*be introduced*
t9ašša bit9ašša	*dine*
t9azzab bit9azzab	*suffer*

Ț

ța'ș	*weather, climate*
țaab bițiib	*recover*
țaabi' țawaabi'	*floor, story*
țaabi9 țawaabi9	*stamp*
țaali9 țaal9a țaal9iin	*coming out*
țaawle țaawlaat	*table*
țaaẓa (invariable adj.)	*fresh*
țabba' bițabbi'	*apply, put into practice*
țalaa'	*divorce*
țțalaa' bittlaate	*triple divorce*

ṭalab ṭalabaat	*request*
ṭalab buṭlub	*request*
ṭall biṭull	*look*
ṭamman biṭammin	*keep (someone) informed*
ṭaraabluṣ (f)	*Tripoli*
ṭarii' ṭuru'	*road, way*
ṭayaraan	*aviation*
ṭayyaara ṭayyaaraat	*airplane*
ṭayyib ṭayybe ṭayybiin	*good, tasty*
ṭayyib	*all right*
ṭeer ṭyuur	*bird*
ṭibaa9a	*typing*
ṭibb	*medicine*
ṭifil 'aṭfaal	*child*
ṭiin	*clay*
ṭili9 biṭla9	*go up, come out, amount to*
ṭna9š / ṭna9šar	*twelve*
ṭna9šar sane	*twelve years*
ṭoor	*ox*
ṭuub	*bricks*
ṭuul	*length*
ṭuul ḥayaati	*all my life*
ṭuul lleel winnhaar	*all night and day*

W

w- / wi-	*and ; when, while*
w'iyye 'awaa'	*ukiyeh (200 grams)*
wa"af biwa"if	*stop*
wa't	*time*
wa't maa (+ verb)	*whenever*
waa'if waa'fe waa'fiin	*standing, stopping, stopped*
waajib waajbaat	*duty*
waaḥad f. waḥde	*one*
waaḥad, waaḥad	*one by one*
waalde waaldaat	*mother*
waalid waaldiin	*father*
wadda biwaddi	*lead*
wadda9 biwaddi9	*see (someone) off*
waja9 wjaa9	*pain, ache*
waja9 baṭin	*stomach ache*
waja9 dineen	*earache*
waja9 mi9de	*stomach ache*
waja9 raas	*headache*
waja9 snaan	*toothache*
wakaale wakaalaat	*agency*

wala	*at all (with negative)*
walad wlaad	*boy ; child*
walla biwalli	*appoint*
wal*l*a *or* wal*l*aahi	*by God*
war'a war'aat *or* wraa'	*sheet of paper*
wara'	*leaves, paper*
wara' 9inab	*vine leaves*
wara	*behind*
waṣṣal biwaṣṣil	*make (someone) arrive*
waṭan 'awṭaan	*homeland*
waṭani waṭaniyye	*national*
wazaara	*ministry, cabinet*
waziir wuzara	*minister of state*
waẓiife waẓaayif	*position, job*
wa9ad byuu9id	*promise*
ween	*where*
ween maa (+verb)	*wherever*
wilaade wilaadaat	*birth*
wilaaye wilaayaat	*state ; province*
lwilaayaat lmuttáḥide	*the United States*
willa	*or*
wiṣil byuuṣal	*arrive*
wizaara wizaaraat	*ministry, cabinet*
wuṣṭa	*central (f)*

X

xaab bixiib	*fail*
xaabar bixaabir	*communicate with*
xaadme xaadmaat	*maid*
xaaf bixaaf	*be afraid*
xaal xwaal	*uncle (mother's brother)*
xaale xaalaat	*aunt (mother's sister)*
xaamis xaamse	*fifth*
xaan bixuun	*betray*
xaarṭa xaraayiṭ	*map*
xaaṭir xawaaṭir	*wish, pleasure*
xaaṭrak	*good-by (to a man, said by person leaving)*
xabar 'axbaar	*news, message*
xabbar bixabbir	*inform*
xadd xduud	*cheek*
xaḍḍ bixuḍḍ	*shake*
xaffaf bixaffif	*lighten*
xafiif xafiife xfaaf	*light (of weight)*
xajjal bixajjil	*embarrass, put to shame*
xala' bixli'	*create*
xala9 bixla9	*overthrow*

xalla bixalli	*keep, allow*
xallaş bixalliş	*finish*
xamse/xamis/xams	*five*
xamis liiraat	*five pounds*
xams sniin	*five years*
xamsiin	*fifty*
xams ţa9š / xams ţa9šar	*fifteen*
xams ţa9šar sane	*fifteen years*
xanziir xanaziir	*pig*
xarbaan xarbaane xarbaaniin	*out of order*
xariif	*fall ; autumn*
xariiţa xaraayiţ	*map*
xarj	*expenditures*
xaruuf xirfaan	*lamb*
xass	*lettuce*
xaţab buxţub	*give a speech*
xaţţ xţuuţ	*line*
xayyaaţ xayyaaţiin	*tailor*
xeeme xeemaat *or* **xyaam**	*tent*
xeer	*good fortune, goodness*
xeer nšaa*lla*	*it's nothing serious, I hope.*
xeeţ xiiţaan	*thread*
xidme	*service*
xiffe	*lightness*

xiṭṭa xiṭaṭ	*plan*
xoox	*plums*
xsaara xasaa'ir	*loss*
xubz	*bread*
xuḍra	*vegetables*
xuṣuuṣi	*private*
xyaara xyaaraat	*cucumbers*
xyaara xyaaraat	*a cucumber*

Y

yaa	*particle of address and exclamation*
yaa siidna	*informal term of address (lit. our master)*
yaa xsaara	*what a shame !*
yaareet	*if only*
yamiiṇ	*right (side)*
yard yardaat	*yard*
ya9ni	*it means, that is, well..., more or less, for instance.*
yoom ('a)yyaam / tiyyaam	*day*
lyoom	*today*

tlat tiyyaam	*three days*
yuusif 'afandi	*tangerines*

Z

za"af biza"if	*clap the hands*
zaad biziid	*increase, exceed*
zaahir zaahre	*shining*
zaar bizuur	*visit*
zaat	*self, same*
zaayir zaayre zaayriin	*visiting*
zaayir zaayre zuwwar	*visitor*
zaka (m)	*intelligence*
zakar buzkur	*mention*
zamaan	*time*
zatt bizitt	*throw out*
zawwad bizawwid	*supply*
zawwar bizawwir	*have (someone) visit*
zbaale	*garbage*
zeet zyuut	*oil*
zeetuun	*olives*
zibde	*butter*
ziraa9a	*agriculture*

ziraa9i ziraa9iyye ziraa9iyyiin | *agricultural*
zirr zraar | *button*
ziyaara ziyaaraat | *visit*
zi9il biz9al | *be upset*
zooj zwaaj | *husband*
zooje zoojaat | *wife*
zyaade zyaadaat | *increase*
zyaara zyaaraat | *visit*

Ẓ

ẓaabiṭ ẓubbaaṭ | *officer*
ẓaahir ẓaahra ẓaahriin | *appearing*
ẓahar biẓhar | *seem, appear*
ẓann biẓunn | *suppose*
ẓġiir ẓġiire ẓġaar | *small ; young*
ẓulum | *injustice*

9

9aadatan	*usually*
9aadi 9aadiyye 9aadiyyiin	*regular, ordinary*
9aal (invariable adj.)	*fine*
9aalam	*world*
9aali 9aalye 9aalyiin	*high*
9aalim 9ulama	*learned man*
9aam 'a9waam	*year*
9aamil 9ummaal	*worker*
9aammi 9aammiyye	*general*
9aaraḍ bi9aariḍ	*oppose*
9aašir 9aašre	*tenth*
9abba bi9abbi	*fill out*
9adad 'a9daad	*number*
9add bi9idd	*count*
9afu	*fogiveness, pardon*
9afwan	*you're welcome (in reply to* šukran)
9ala / 9alee- / 9alay- / 9a-	*to ; on ; incumbent upon*
9ala yamiinak	*to your right*
9aleek	*on you*

9alayy	*on me*
9alyamiin	*to the right*
9abeeruut	*to Beirut*
9a(la) mahlak	*slow down*
9ala ḥaalo	*as he was*
9ala 9eeni	*with pleasure*
9ala raasi	*with pleasure*
9ala keefak	*as you wish*
9alaa'a 9alaa'aat	*relation*
9alam 'a9laam	*flag*
9alla' bi9alli'	*hang up*
9allam bi9allim	*teach*
9amal 'a9maal	*work*
9amali 9amaliyye 9amaliyyiin	*practical*
9amaliyye 9amaliyyat	*operation*
9amiid 9umada	*dean*
9amm 9maam	*uncle (father's brother)*
9ammaan (f)	*Amman*
9amme 9ammaat	*aunt (father's sister)*
9an / 9an- / 9ann-	*about*
9an 'iznak	*by your (m) leave*
9anhum	*about them*
9annak	*about you*
9an 'ariib	*shortly, soon*
9ara'	*arak (an alcoholic beverage)*

9arab (pl)	*Arabs*
'ibin 9arab	*Arab (m)*
bint 9arab	*Arab (f)*
9arabi 9arabiyye 9arab	*Arab, Arabic*
9araḍ bi9riḍ	*offer*
9arḍ	*width*
9arraf bi9arrif	*introduce*
9askari 9askariyye 9askariyyiin	*military*
9askari 9asaakir	*soldier*
9aṣa 9uṣi	*stick*
9aṣiir	*juice*
9aša (m)	*evening meal*
9ašiyye 9ašiyyaat *or* 9ašaaya	*evening*
9ašra / 9ašar / 9ašr	*ten*
9ašar tušhur	*ten months*
9ašr sniin	*nine years*
9azam bi9zim	*invite*
9aziime 9azaayim	*banquet*
9aẓiim 9aẓiime 9aẓiimiin	*great, magnificent*
9eele 9iyal	*family*
9een (f) 9yuun	*eye*
9iddit ...	*several*
9iddit marraat	*several times*
9iid ('a)9yaad	*feast day*
9iid miilaad	*birthday*

9iid lmiilaad	*Christmas*
9iid lfiṣiḥ	*Easter*
9iid listiqlaal	*Independence Day*
9iid raas ssane	*New Year's Day*
9iid lmawlid	*birthday of the Prophet*
9iid lfiṭir	*breaking of the fast of Ramadan*
9iid l'aḍḥa	*feast of the Sacrifice*
9ijil 9juul	*calf*
9ilm 9uluum	*knowledge, science*
9ilm lijtimaa9	*sociology*
9ilm nnafs	*psychology*
9uluum diiniyye	*religion, theology*
9uluum siyaasiyye	*political science*
9ilmi 9ilmiyye 9ilmiyyiin	*pertaining to knowledge*
9imil bi9mal	*do, make*
9imil 9amaliyye	*have an operation*
9inab	*grapes*
9ind / 9in-	*in the possession of, have*; *chez*
9indak	*you* (*m*) *have*
9inna	*we have*
9iraaqi 9iraaqiyye 9iraqiyyiin	*Iraqi*
9irif bi9raf	*know*
9išriin	*twenty*
9uḍu 'a9ḍaa'	*member*
9ulya	*higher ; highest*
9umur 'a9maar	*age, life*
9unwaan 9anawiin	*address*
9urs 'a9raas	*wedding*

VOCABULARY 2 • English-Arabic.

Certain kinds of expressions are omitted from this Vocabulary: many special combinations; most names of places; personal names; some number expressions; words with mainly a grammatical meaning.

A

able, be	**'idir bi'dar**
about	**9an**
about (approx.)	**ḥawaali**
above	**foo'**
absence	**ġeebe ġubaat**
absent, be	**ġaab biġiib**
accompany	**raafa' biraafi'**
account (bill)	**ḥsaab**
accountant	**mḥaasib mḥaasbiin**
accounting	**m(u)ḥaasabaat (pl)**

accounting	m(u)ḥaasabe
ache	waja9 wjaa9
across from	'baal
add	jama9 bijma9
address	9unwaan 9anaawiin
advance	'addam bi'addim
afraid, be	xaaf bixaaf
afternoon	ba9d ḍḍuhur
after	ba9id ; ba9id maa(+ verb)
again	min jdiid
age	9umur 'a9maar
agency	wakaale wakaalaat
ago	'abil
agree	ttafa' bittfi'
agriculture	ziraa9a
agricultural	ziraa9i ziraa9iyye ziraa9iyyiin
air (adj.)	jawwi jawwiyye jawwiyyiin
airline	širkit ṭayaraan
airmail	bariid jawwi
airplane	ṭayyaara ṭayyaaraat
airport	maṭaar maṭaaraat
alarm clock	saa9a mnabbih
alcoholic beverage	mašruub mašruubaat
Aleppo	ḥalab (f)
alive	ḥayy ḥayye 'aḥyaa'

all	**kull**
allow	**xalla bixalli**
all right	**ṭayyib**
also	**kamaan**
always	**daayman**
ambassador	**safiir sufara(a')**
amendment	**ta9diil ta9diilaat**
America	**'ameerka**
American	**'ameerkaani 'ameerkaaniyye**
	'ameerkaan
Amman	**9ammaan**
amount	**ṭili9 biṭla9**
annex	**'alḥaq bilḥiq**
annexed	**mulḥaq mulḥaqa mulḥaqiin**
annual	**sanawi sanawiyye**
answer	**jaawab bijaawib ; jaawab -aat**
	***or* 'ajwibe**
any	**'ayy**
anyone	**ḥad (a)**
appear	**ẓahar biẓhar**
appearing	**ẓaahir ẓaahra ẓaahriin**
apples	**tuffaaḥ**
application	**taṭbii' taṭbii'aat**
apply	**ṭabba' biṭabbi'**
appoint	**walla biwalli**

appointment	maw9id mawaa9iid
approximately	ta'riiban
apricots	mišmiš
April	niisaan
Arab, Arabic	9arabi 9arabiyye 9arab
arak (an alcoholic beverage)	9ara'
army	jeeš jyuuš
arming	tasliiḥ
arrange	dabbar bidabbir
arranged	mrattab mrattabe mrattabiin
arrive	wiṣil byuuṣal
arrive, make (someone)	waṣṣal biwaṣṣil
artichokes	'arḍi šooki
article	maqaale maqaalaat
as	mitil maa (+ verb)
as many as	'add maa (+ verb)
as much as	mitil maa (+verb) ; 'add maa (+ verb)
ask	sa'al bis'al
aspect	naaḥye nawaaḥi
assistant	msaa9id msaa9diin
astonished, be	t9ajjab bit9ajjab
attaché	mulḥaq mulḥaqiin
attention	baal
attributed to	mansuub mansuube mansuubiin

August	'aab
aunt (father's sister)	9amme 9ammaat
aunt (mother's sister)	xaale xaalaat
autumn	xariif
available, be	ṣaḥḥ biṣiḥḥ
aviation	ṭayaraan

B

bachelor	'a9zab 9izbaan
bad	baṭṭaal baṭṭaale baṭṭaaliin
Baghdad	baġdaad (f)
baklava	ba'laawe
bananas	mooz
bank	bank bnuuk
banquet	9aziime 9azaayim
barber	ḥallaa' ḥallaa'iin
basket	salle sallaat
bath (room)	ḥammaam ḥammaamaat
be	kaan bikuun
beans	luubya

beans, dried	faṣuulya
beans (Spanish)	fuul
beard	da'in d'uun; liḥye liḥa *or* liḥyaat
because	leeš ; li'anno
become	ṣaar biṣiir
bed	farše faršaat ; taxt txuute
beef	laḥim ba'ar
beer	biira
beets	šamandar
before	'abil ; 'abil maa (+ verb)
begin	bada bibda
beginning	'ibtidaa'
behind	wara
Beirut	beeruut (f)
believe	sadda' bisaddi'
belly	baṭin bṭuun
berry	ḥabbe ḥabbaat
best	'aḥsan
Bethlehem	beet laḥim (f)
betray	xaan bixuun
better, best	'aḥsan
between	been
big	kbiir kbiire kbaar
bigger, biggest	'akbar kubra (f)
bill	ḥsaab

bird	ţeer ţyuur
birth	wilaade wilaadaat
birthday	mawlid ; miilaad
black	'aswad sooda suud
black, become	swadd biswadd
bless	baarak bibaarik
blessed	mabruuk mabruuke mabruukiin ; mbaarak mbaarake mbaarakiin
blouse	bluuze bluuzaat
blow	habb bihibb
blue	'azra' zar'a zuru'
boat	baaboor bawabiir
book	ktaab kutub
bookstore	maktabe maktabaat
boiled	masluu' masluu'a masluu'iin
bother	ġallab biġallib ; ġalabe ġalabaat
bottle	'annine 'anaani
boundary	ḥadd ḥduud
boy	ṣabi ṣubyaan ; walad wlaad
box	sanduu' sanadii'
bread	xubz
breakfast	fţuur
breath	nafas

brethren	'ixwaan
bricks	ṭuub
briefcase	šanta šantaat
bring	jaab bijiib
broadcast	'azaa9 bizii9
broadcasting	'izaa9a
broiled	mašwi mašwiyye mašwiyyiin
brother	'ax ixwe
brown	binni binniyye binniyyiin
bruised	marḍuuḍ marḍuuḍa marḍuuḍiin
build	bana bibni
bulletin	našra našraat
business	šuġul 'ašġaal
busy	mašġuul mašġuule mašġuuliin
but	bass ; laakin
butter	zibde
button	zirr zraar
buy	štara bištri

C

cabbage	malfuuf
cabinet	wazaara wazaaraat ; wizaara wizaaraat
Cairo	lqaahira
calf	9ijil 9juul
call	naada binaadi
camel	jamal jmaal
car	sayyaara sayyaaraat
carrots	jazar
carry out (*fulfill*)	'ajra bijri
cauliflower	'arnabiiṭ
cause	qaḍiyye qaḍaaya
cemetery	ma'bara ma'aabir
central	'awṣaṭ wuṣṭa (f)
certainly	ma9luum
certificate	šhaade šhaadaat
cheek	xadd xduud
cigarette	siigaara siigaaraat *or* sagaayir
chair	kursi karaasi

cheese	jibne
cherries	karaz
chickens	jaaj
chickpeas	ḥummuṣ
child	ṭifil 'aṭfaal ; walad wlaad
chocolate (*hot*)	kakaaw (f)
choose	na"a bina"i
Christian	masiiḥi masiiḥiyye masiiḥiyyiin *or* masiiḥiyye
Christmas	9iid lmiilaad
church	kniise kanaayis
clap (*the hands*)	za"af biza"if
clay	ṭiin
clean	naḍḍaf binaḍḍif ; nḍiif nḍiife nḍaaf
cleaning	tanḍiif
clerk	kaatib kuttaab
climate	ṭa'ṣ
clock	saa9a saa9aat
close	sakkar bisakkir
closed	msakkar msakkara msakkariin
cloth	'maaš
cloud	ġeeme ġeemaat *or* ġyuum
coffee	'ahwe
coffee shop	'ahwe 'ahaawi

cola	**koola**
cold (illness)	**rašiḥ**
coldness	**bard**
collect	**jamma9 bijammi9**
college	**kulliyye kulliyyaat**
color	**loon 'alwaan**
come	**'aja biiji**
come!	**ta9aal**
come out	**ţili9 biţla9**
comb	**maššaţ bimaššiţ**
combat	**kaafaḥ bikaafiḥ**
combating	**mukaafaḥa**
coming, having come	**jaay jaaye jaayiin**
coming out	**ţaali9 ţaal9a ţaal9iin**
command	**'amar bu'mur ; 'amir 'awaamir**
commerce	**tijaara**
commercial	**tijaari tijaariyye tijaariyyiin**
communicate with	**xaabar bixaabir**
company	**širke širkaat**
compete	**naafas binaafis**
compose	**'allaf bi'allif**
compulsory	**'ijbaari 'ijbaariyye 'ijbaariyyiin**
concern	**'ahamm bihim ; 'ihtimaam**
concerned, be	**htamm bihtamm**

condition	ḥaal 'aḥwaal ; ḥaale ḥaalaat
confiscate	ṣaaḍar bişaaḍir
constructing	'inšaa'
consul	'unṣul 'anaaṣil
consulate	'unṣliyye 'unṣliyyaat
consult	stašaar bistašiir
contagious	saari saarye
contractor	mit9ahhid mit9ahhdiin
convenient, be	naasab binaasib
copy	nusxa nusax
correct	maẓbuuṭ maẓbuuṭa
	maẓbuuṭiin
correspond	kaatab bikaatib
corridor	mamša (m) mamaaši
cotton	'uṭun
cough	sa9al bus9ul
coughing	su9aal
counselor	mustašaar mustašaariin
count	9add bi9idd
counted, be	n9add bin9add
country, countries	blaad (f)
court	maḥkame maḥaakim
courteous, be	jaamal bijaamil
courtyard	saaḥa saaḥaat
cows	ba'ar

create	xala' bixl'i
cross roads	mafra' mafaari'
cucumbers	xyaar
cup	finjaan fanajiin
current	daarij daarje daarjiin
curse	sabb bisibb
customs	gumruk gamaarik
cut	'aṣṣ bi'aṣṣ
cut	'aṭa9 bi'ṭa9 ; ma'ṣuuṣ ma'ṣuuṣa ma'ṣuuṣiin
cut out (a garment)	faṣṣal bifaṣṣil
cutting	'aaṣiṣ 'aaṣṣa 'aaṣṣiin
cut to pieces	'aṭṭa9 bi'aṭṭi9

D

Damascene	šaami šaamiyye šwaam
Damascus	ššaam (f)
dancing	ra'ṣ
date	taariix tawaariix
daughter	bint (f) banaat
day	yoom (ti)yyaam

daytime	nhaar
dearer, dearest	'aḥabb
dean	9amiid 9umada
deceitful, be	tlaa9ab bitlaa9ab
deceitful, being	talaa9ub
December	kaanuun (l)'awwal
decide	batt bibitt
decrease	na'aṣ bun'uṣ
defend	raafa9 biraafi9
deficiency	nu'ṣaan
department	daa'ira dawaa'ir
deputy	naayib (*or* naa'ib) nuwwaab
delay	'axxar bi'axxir
delighted	masruur masruura masruuriin
demolish	hadd bihidd
deserve	staḥa" bistḥi"
destroy	hadam bihdim
Dhahran	ḍḍahraan (f)
dialect	lahje lahjaat
difference, make a	fara' bifri'
different	ġeer
difficulty	ṣ9uube ṣ9uubaat
digest	haḍam bihḍim
dine	t9ašša bit9ašša
diploma	šhaade šhaadaat

direct (manage)	'adaar bidiir
direct (point to)	dall bidill
director	mudiir mudara(a')
discuss	tbaaḥas bitbaaḥas
disease	maraḍ 'amraaḍ
dispute	jaadal bijaadil ; mujaadale mujaadalaat
disturb	'az9aj biz9ij
division	qisim 'aqsaam
divorce	ṭalaa'
do	9imil bi9mal
doctor	duktoor dakaatra
domestic	daaxli daaxliyye
donkey	ḥmaar ḥamiir
door	baab bwaab
dress	fusṭaan faṣaṭiin
drink	širib bišrab
drinking	šurub
dry	naašif naašfe naašfiin
ducks	baṭṭ
duty	waajib waajbaat
dwell	sakan buskun
dwelling	saakin saakne saakniin

E

ear	**daan dineen (*dual*)**
ear ache	**waja9 dineen**
early	**bakkiir**
east	**šarq**
Easter	**9iid lfiṣiḥ**
eat	**'akal byaakul**
eat, thing to	**ma'kuulaat (pl)**
economic	**'iqtiṣaaḍi 'iqtiṣaaḍiyye 'iqtiṣaaḍiyyiin**
economics	**'iqtiṣaaḍ**
edit	**ḥarrar biḥarrir**
editing	**taḥriir**
editor	**m(u)ḥarrir m(u)ḥarririin**
educate	**rabba birabbi**
educated	**mit9allim mit9allme mit9allmiin**
education	**tarbiye**
eggplants	**beetinjaan**
eggs	**beeḍ**

Egypt	maṣir (f)
eight	tamaanye
eighteen	taman ṭa9š
eighth	taamin taamne
eighty	tamaniin
elect	ntaxab bintxib
elected	muntaxab muntáxabe muntaxabiin
electing	'intixaab
elections	'intixaabaat (pl)
electricity	kahraba
eleven	ḥda9š
embassy	safaara safaaraat
embarrass	xajjal bixajjil
empty	faaḍi faaḍye faaḍyiin
engineer	m (u) handis -iin
engineering	handase handasaat
England	'ingiltra ; blaad lingliiz
English	'ingliizi 'ingliiziyye 'ingliiz
enlarge	kabbar bikabbir
enough, be	kaffa bikaffi
established, be	t'assas bit'assas
evening	masa ; 9aŝiyye 9aŝiyyaat *or* 9aŝaaya
evening (adj.)	massaa'i masaa'iyye

evening meal	**9aša (m)**
evening party	**sahra sahraat**
every	**kull**
example, for	**matalan**
exceed	**zaad biziid**
except	**'illa**
expanding	**tawsii9**
expenditures	**xarj**
exepensive	**ġaali ġaalye ġaalyiin**
expensive, be	**ġili biġla**
more expensive, most expensive	**'aġla**
explode	**nfajar binfjir**
exploding	**'infijaar**
explain	**fahham bifahhim ; šaraḥ bišraḥ**
export	**ṣaḍḍar biṣaḍḍir**
eye	**9een (f) 9yuun**

F

factory	**ma9mal ma9aamil**
fail	**xaab bixiib**
fall (autumn)	**xariif**

family	9eele 9iyal
family	'ahil (pl)
famous	mašhuur maṣhuura mašhuuriin
far	b9iid b9iide b9aad
farther, farthest	'ab9ad ; 'aqṣa
father	'ab 'abbayaat *or* 'aabaa'
father	waalid waaldiin
favor	faḍil 'afḍaal ; ma9ruuf
feast day	9iid 'a9yaad
February	šbaaṭ
festival	9iid 'a9yaad
fever	ḫaraara ; sxuune
fifteen	xams ṭa9š
fifth	xaamis xaamse
fifty	xamsiin
figs	tiin
fill out	9abba bi9abbi
filled out	m9abba (m) m9abbaay m9abbayiin
financial	maali maaliyye
find	laa'a bilaa'i
fine	kwayyis kwayyse kwayysiin
fine	9aal (invariable adj.)
finish	xallaṣ bixalliṣ

first	'awwal 'uula 'awaa'il
fish	samak
fitting	proova proovaat
five	xamse
flag	9alam 'a9laam
flirt	ġaazal biġaazil
floor	'arḍ (f)
floor (story)	ṭaabi' ṭawaabi'
flowing	jaari jaarye jaaryiin
folded, be	nṭawa binṭwi
food	'akil
forbid	ḥarram biḥarrim
forget	nisi binsa
forgiveness	9afu
fork	šooke šuwak
formal	rasmi rasmiyye rasmiyyiin
forty	'arb9iin
foundation	'asaas 'asaasaat
founded, be	t'assas bit'assas
fountain pen	'alam ḥibir
four	'arba9a
fourteen	'arba9 ṭa9š
fourth	raabi9 raab9a
France	fraansa
free	ḥurr ḥurra 'aḥraar

free (empty)	faaḍi faaḍye faaḍyiin
free, be	fiḍi bifḍa
French	fransaawi fransaawiyye fransaawiyyiin
fresh	ṭaaẓa (invariable adj.)
Friday	(yoom) ljum9a
fried	ma'li ma'liyye ma'liyyiin
friend	ṣaaḥib ('a)ṣḥaab
from	min
front of, in	'uddaam
fruit	fawaakih
fry	'ala bi'li
full	malyaan malyaane malyaaniin

G

garbage	zbaale
garden	bustaan basatiin
garlic	tuum
general	9aammi 9aammiyye
generous	kariim kariime kurama
German	'al*m*aani 'al*m*aaniyye 'al*m*aan

get up	**'aam bi'uum**
gift	**hadiyye hadaaya**
girl	**bint (f) banaat**
give	**'a9ṭa bya9ṭi**
glass	**kaas kaasaat**
go	**raaḥ biruuḥ**
go around	**daar biduur**
go around, have (someone)	**dawwar bidawwir**
God	**'a*ll*a**
going	**raayiḥ raayḥa raayḥiin**
good	**kwayyis kwayyse kwayysiin; mniiḥ mniiḥa mnaaḥ; ṭayyib ṭayybe ṭayybiin**
goodness	**xeer**
good time	**basṭ**
go up	**ṭili9 biṭla9**
government	**ḥukuume ḥukuumaat**
graduated, be	**txarraj bitxarraj**
grain	**ḥabbe ḥabbaat**
grandfather	**jidd jduud; siid syaad**
grandmother	**sitt sittaat**
grapes	**9inab**
grateful	**mamnuun mamnuune mamnuuniin**
gratitude	**mamnuuniyye**

grave	'abir 'buur
gray	ramaadi ramaadiyye ramaadiyyiin
green	'axḍar xaḍra xuḍur
greet	sallam bisallim
ground	'arḍ (f) 'araaḍi
guest	ḍeef ḍyuuf

H

hair	ša9ir
half	nuṣṣ nṣaaṣ
ham	jamboon
hand	'iid 'ayaadi
handkerchief	maḥrame maḥaarim
hang up	9alla' bi9alli'
happy	sa9iid sa9iide su9ada
happy, be	nbaṣaṭ binbṣiṭ
harbor	miina (m) mawaani
hat	burneeṭa baraniiṭ
he	huwwe
head	raas ruus

head (chief)	**ra'iis ru'asa(a')**
head man (village)	**muxtaar maxatiir**
health	**ṣiḥḥa**
healthy	**ṣiḥḥi ṣiḥḥiyye**
hear	**simi9 bisma9**
heard	**masmuu9 masmuu9a masmuu9iin**
hearing, having heard	**saami9 saam9a saam9iin**
heat	**šoob**
heavy	**t'iil t'iile t'aal**
hello	**marḥaba ; haloo (on telephone)**
help	**saa9ad bisaa9id**
helped, be	**tsaa9ad bitsaa9ad**
helping	**msaa9ade msaa9adaat**
here	**hoon**
here is, here are	**hayy**
high	**9aali 9aalye 9aalyiin**
higher, highest	**'a9la 9ulya**
hill	**tall tlaal**
hold	**misik bimsik**
homeland	**waṭan 'awṭaan**
honor	**šarraf bišarrif ; šaraf**
honored, be	**tšarraf bitšarraf**
hope	**t'ammal bit'ammal ; 'amal 'aamaal**

hors d'œuvres (with drinks)	maaza
hospital	mustašfa (m) mustašfayaat
hotel	'uteel 'uteelaat
hour	saa9a saa9aat
house	beet byuut
house	sakkan bisakkin
how	kiif
how many	kam
how much	'addeeš
hundred	miyye
hurried	musta9jal musta9jale musta9jaliin
hurry	sta9jal bista9jil
hurry, in a	mista9jil musta9*i*jle mista9*i*jliin
husband	zooj zwaaj; jooz jwaaz

I

I	'ana
ice	talj
ice cream	buuẓa

idea	fikra fikar
identity card	hawiyye hawiyyaat
if	'iza
if (contrary to fact)	law
if only	yaareet
important	muhimm muhimme muhimmiin
more important, most important	'ahamm
improving	taḥsiin
in	fii
inconvenience	'iz9aaj 'iz9aajaat
increase	zaad biziid ; zyaade zyaadaat
independence	'istiqlaal
independent, be	staqall bistqill
industrial	ṣinaa9i ṣinaa9iyye
industry	ṣinaa9a ṣinaa9aat
inexpensive	rxiiṣ rxiiṣa rxaaṣ
influenza	'influwenza
inform	xabbar bixabbir
information	ma9luumaat (pl)
informed, keep (someone)	ṭamman biṭammin
injustice	ẓulum
ink	ḥibir
in order to	(la)ḥatta
insist	'aṣarr biṣirr
instructions	ta9liimaat (pl)

intelligence	zaka (m)
intention	ġaaye ġaayaat
interest	maşlaḥa maşaaliḥ
internal	daaxli daaxliyye daaxliyyiin
introduce	9arraf bi9arrif
introduced, be	t9arraf bit9arraf
invite	9azam bi9zim
Iraq	l9iraaq
Iraqi	9iraaqi 9iraaqiyye 9iraaqiyyiin
iron	kawa bikwi; ḥadiid
ironed	makwi makwiyye makwiyyiin
ironing	kawi
irrigation	rayy
Italian	tilyaani tilyaaniyye tilyaan
Italy	'iiṭaalya

J

jacket	jakeet jake(e)taat
January	kaanuun (t)taani
Jerusalem	l'uds (f)

job	waẓiife waẓaayif
joke	nukte nukat
Jordan	l'urdun
Jordanian	'urduni 'urduniyye urduniyyiin *or* 'urduniyye
journalism	ṣaḥaafe
journalist	ṣuḥufi ṣuḥufiyyiin
journalistic	ṣaḥaafi ṣaḥaafiyye
journey	riḥle riḥlaat
judge	'aaḍi 'uḍa *or* 'uḍaa *or* quḍaat
juice	9aṣiir
July	tammuuz
June	ḥzeeraan

K

keep	ḥafaẓ biḥfaẓ ; xalla bixalli
keeper	ḥaafiẓ ḥaafẓa ḥaafẓiin
key	muftaaḥ mafatiiḥ
kind	jins jnaas
kind enough, be	tfaḍḍal bitfaḍḍal

kindness	faḍil 'afḍaal ; luṭuf 'alṭaaf
kitchen	maṭbax maṭaabix
knife	sikkiin sakakiin
know	9irif bi9raf
knowing	ma9rife
knowledge	9ilim 9uluum
Koran, The	lqur'aan

L

lamb	xaruuf xirfaan
lamb (meat)	laḥim xaruuf
land	'arḍ (f) 'araaḍi
language	luġa luġaat
late	mit'axxir mit'axxre mit'axxriin
late, be·	t'axxar bit'axxar
later on	ba9deen
laugh	ḍiḥik biḍḥak
laundry	ġasiil
law	ḥuquuq ; muḥaamaah (f) ; qaanuun qawaaniin

law (Islamic)	šarii9a
lawyer	muḥaami muḥaamiin
lead	wadda biwaddi
learn	t9allam bit9allam
learnèd man	9aalim 9ulama
leave	tarak bitrik *or* butruk
leave (permission)	'izin 'zuune *or* 'uzunaat
leaves	wara'
Lebanese	lubnaani lubnaaniyye lubnaaniyyiin
Lebanon	lubnaan
left (side)	šmaal
lemons	leemuun ḥaamiḍ
length	ṭuul
letter	maktuub makatiib
lettuce	xass
liar	kazzaab kazzaabiin
library	maktabe maktabaat
life	ḥayaah (f); 9umur 'a9maar
light	nuur 'anwaar
light (weight)	xafiif xafiife xfaaf
lighten	xaffaf bixaffif
lighter, (cigarette)	'addaaḥa 'addaaḥaat
lighter, lightest	'axaff
lightness	xiffe

like (similar)	mitil
like	ḥabb biḥibb
liked, be	nḥabb binḥabb
line	ṣaṭir 'aṣṭur *or* ṣṭuur ; xaṭṭ xṭuuṭ
linen	kittaan
literature	'adab 'aadaab
little bit, a	šwayy (f)
liver	kibde
loan	qirḍ quruuḍ
local	maḥalli maḥalliyye maḥalliyyiin
long for	štaa' bištaa'
longing	mištaa' mištaa'a mištaa'iin
look	šaaf bišuuf ; ṭall biṭull
look around	tfarraj bitfarraj
looking	šaayif šaayfe šaayfiin
look over	tfarraj bitfarraj
loss	xsaara xasaa'ir
lot	naṣiib
love	ḥabb biḥibb ; ḥubb

loved	maḥbuub maḥbuube maḥbuubiin
loved one	ḥabiib ḥabaayib
lowering	taxfiiḍ
luck	ḥaẓẓ ḥẓuuẓ

M

maestro	'ustaaz 'asaatze
magazine	majalle majallaat
magnificent	9aẓiim 9aẓiime 9aẓimiin
maid	ṣaan9a ṣaan9aat; xaadme xaadmaat
mail	bariid
maintain	ḥaafaẓ biḥaafiẓ
make	9imil bi9mal
man	rijjaal rjaal
manager	mudiir mudara(a')
major	'akbar kubra
map	xaarṭa (*or* xariiṭa) xaṛaayiṭ
March	'aaḍaar
market	suu' (f) swaa'

married	mijjawwiz mijjawwze mijjawwziin
married, be	djawwaz bidjawwaz
mason	banna (m) bannayiin
master	siid syaad
matches (box)	kibriite kibriitaat
matter	'amir 'umuur
May	'ayyaar
mayor	ra'iis baladiyye
meal (evening)	9aša (m)
meal (midday)	ġada (m)
measure	'aas bi'iis
measurement	'yaas 'yaasaat
meat	laḥim ; laḥme
medicine	dawa (m) 'adwiye ; ṭibb
meet	'aabal bi'aabil ; jtama9 bijtmi9 ; laa'a bilaa'i
meeting	'ijtimaa9 'ijtimaa9aat
meet together	tlaa'a bitlaa'a
member	9uḍu 'a9ḍaa'
memorial	tizkaar tizkaaraat
mention	zakar buzkur
menu	liista liistaat
merchant	taajir tujjaar
message	xabar 'axbaar

meter	mitir mtaar
middle	'awṣaṭ wuṣṭa ; nuṣṣ nṣaaṣ
Middle East, the	ššarq l'awṣaṭ
military	9askari 9askariyye 9askariyyiin
milk	ḥaliib
million	malyoon malayiin
minister (of state)	waziir wuzara
ministry	wazaara wazaaraat
minor	ṣuġra (f)
mint	na9na9
minus	'illa
minute	d'ii'a da'aayi'
mister	sayyid
mixed	maxluuṭ maxluuṭa maxluuṭiin
modification	ta9diil ta9diilaat
Monday	(yoom) ttineen
money	maṣaari
monk	raahib ruhbaan
month	šahir 'ašhur
monument	tizkaar tizkaaraat
more, most	'aktar
morning	ṣabaaḥ

morning (adj.)	**ṣaabaaḥi ṣabaaḥiyye**
morning, the	**ṣṣubuḥ**
Moslem	**mislim misilme misilmiin**
mosque	**jaami9 jawaami9**
most	**'aktar**
mother	**'imm (f) 'immayaat**
mother	**waạlde waaldaat**
move	**hazz bihizz**
movement	**ḥarake ḥarakaat**
movie	**sinama sinamaat**
moving	**hazz**
much	**ktiir ktiire ktaar**
mulberries	**tuut**
municipal	**baladi baladiyye**
municipality	**baladiyye baladiyyaat**
museum	**matḥaf mataaḥif**
music	**muusiiqa**
music (adj.)	**muusiiqi muusiiqiyye**

N

name	'isim 'asmaa'
napkin	fuuṭa fuwaṭ
nation	dawle duwal
national	waṭani waṭaniyye
nationality	jinsiyye jinsiyyaat
naval	baḥri baḥriyye baḥriyyiin
near	'adna ; 'ariib 'ariibe 'raab
Near East, the	ṣšarq l'adna
nearer, nearest	'a'rab
necessary	ḍaruuri ḍaruuriyye ḍaruuriyyiin ; laazim laazme laazmiin
necessary, be	lizim bilzam
necessity	ḍaruura ḍaruuraat
necktie	gravaat (f) gravattaat
need	ḥtaaj biḥtaaj
needle	'ibre 'ubar

neighbor	jaar jiiraan
new	jdiid jdiide jdaad
newer, newest	'ajadd
news	'anbaa' (pl) 'axbaar (pl)
news (adj.)	'ixbaari 'ixbaariyye 'ixbaariyyiin
newspaper	jariide jaraayid ; ṣaḥiife ṣuḥuf
New Year's	9iid raas ssane
next to	jamb ; janb
nice	ḥilu ḥilwe ḥilwiin
nice, consider	staḥla bistaḥli
nicer, nicest	'aḥla
night	leele layaali
nighttime	leel
nine	tis9a
nineteen	tisi9 ṭa9š
ninety	tis9iin
ninth	taasi9 taas9a
no	la' ; laa
noon	ḍuhur
not	laa ; maa ; miš
notebook	daftar dafaatir
November	tišriin (t)taani
now	halla
number	numra numar ; 9adad 'a9daad

O

observation	mušaahade mušaahadaat
object	ġaaye ġaayaat
October	tišriin (l)'awwal
office	maktab makaatib
offer	9araḍ bi9riḍ
officer	ẓaabiṭ ẓubbaaṭ
official	mwaẓẓaf mwaẓẓafiin
official (*adj.*)	rasmi rasmiyye rasmiyyiin
oil	zeet zyuut
okra	baamye
old	kbiir · kbiire kbaar
older, oldest	'akbar kubra
olives	zeetuun
on	9ala
one	waaḥad waḥde (f)
onions	baṣal
open	fataḥ biftaḥ
open	faatiḥ faatḥa faatḥiin

opened	maftuuḥ maftuuḥa maftuuḥiin
opened, be	nfataḥ binftiḥ
operation	9amaliyye 9amaliyyaat
opinion	ra'i 'aaraa'
opportunity	furṣa furaṣ
oppose	9aaraḍ bi9aariḍ
or	'aw ; willa
oranges	burd'aan
orchard	karm kruum
order	'amar bu'mur
ordinary	9aadi 9aadiyye 9aadiyyiin
organizing	tanẓiim
other than	ġeer
out of order	xarbaan xarbaane xarbaaniin
outside	barra
overcome	ġalab biġlib
overflow	faaḍ bifiiḍ
overthrow	xala9 bixla9
overwhelm	ġamar buġmur
owner	ṣaaḥib ('a)ṣḥaab
ox	ṭoor

P

pack	ḍabb biḍubb
packed	maḍbuub maḍbuube maḍbuubiin
pain	waja9 wjaa9
palace	'aṣir 'ṣuur
papa	*baaba* (m)
paper	wara'
pardon	9afu
parliament	barlamaan barlamaanaat
parliamentary	niyaabi niyaabiyye niyaabiyyiin
parsley	ba'duunis
part	qisim 'aqsaam
party	ḥafle ḥaflaat
pass	mara' bumru'
pass by	faat bifuut
past	maaḍi maaḍye
peace	salaam
peaches	durraa'

pears	njaaṣ
peas	bazeella
peasant	fallaaḥ fallaaḥiin
pen, pencil	'alam 'laam
people	naas ; ša9b
pepper	filfil
permission	'izin 'zuune *or* 'uzunaat
permit	samaḥ bismaḥ
person	šaxṣ 'ašxaaṣ
personal	šaxṣi šaxṣiyye
personality	šaxṣiyye šaxṣiyyaat
personally	šaxṣiyyan
phantom	šabaḥ 'ašbaaḥ
philosophy	falsafe falsafaat
piastre	'irš 'ruuš
piece	ša'fe šu'af
pig	xanziir xanaziir
pill	ḥabbe ḥbuub
pin	dabbuus dababiis
place	maḥall maḥallaat ; makaan 'amkine
placed	maḥṭuuṭ maḥṭuuṭa maḥṭuuṭiin
plain	saada (invariable adj.)
plan	xiṭṭa xiṭaṭ

plant	ma9mal ma9aamil
plate	ṣaḥin ṣḥuun
pleasant	laṭiif laṭiife laṭiifiin
	or luṭafa
please	'a9jab bi9jib
pleasure	suruur
pluck	nataf bintif
plums	xuux
pocket	jeeb jyaab
point out	'aššar bi'aššir
polish	lamma9 bilammi9
political	siyaasi siyaasiyye
political science	9uluum siyaasiyye
politics	siyaase
poor (without money)	fa'iir fa'iire fu'ara
poor (unfortunate)	maskiin maskiine masakiin
pork	laḥim xanziir
port	miina (m) mawaani
position	waẓiife waẓaayif
possible	mumkin
possible, be	'amkan bimkin
post office	boosṭa boosṭaat
potatoes	baṭaaṭa
pound (currency)	liira liiraat
pour	ṣabb bṣubb

practical	9amali 9amaliyye 9amaliyyiin
prefer	faḍḍal bifaḍḍil
prepare	ḥaḍḍar biḥaḍḍir
prepared	mḥaḍḍar mḥaḍḍara mḥaḍḍariin
present	ḥaaḍir ḥaaḍra ḥaaḍriin ; mawjuud mawjuude mawjuudiin
present	'addam bi'addim
presented	m'addam m'addame m'addamiin
presser	kawwa (m) kawwayiin
pressing	kawi
price	ḥa" ; si9ir 'as9aar
printed, be	nṭaba9 binṭbi9
private	xuṣuuṣi
problem	mas'ale masaa'il
proclaim	'a9lan bi9lin
products	mantuujaat (pl)
professional man	'ustaaz 'asaatze
program	barnaamij baraamij ; minhaaj manaahij
project	mašruu9 mašaarii9
promise	wa9ad byuu9id
promote	ra"a bira"i

promoted, be	tra"a bitra"a
prompt	musta9jal musta9jale musta9jaliin
proof	burhaan barahiin
propose	qtaraḥ biqtriḥ
prosperous	mwaffa' mwaffa'a mwaffa'iin
prove	barhan bibarhin
province	wilaaye wilaayaat
psychology	9ilm nnafs
pulling	saaḥib saaḥbe saaḥbiin
punish	'aaṣaṣ bi'aaṣiṣ
punished, be	t'aaṣaṣ bit'aaṣaṣ
punishment	'aṣaaṣ 'aṣaaṣaat
pure	fuṣḥa (f)
purpose	ġaraḍ 'aġraaḍ
put	ḥaṭṭ biḥuṭṭ
put in order	rattab birattib
put on (clothing)	libis bilbas
putting	ḥaaṭiṭ ḥaaṭṭa ḥaaṭṭiin

Q

quarter	**rubu9 rbaa9**
question	**su'aal- su'aalaat** *or* **'as'ile**

R

radio station	**'izaa9a 'izaa9aat**
radishes	**fijil**
rail	**sikke sikak**
railway	**sikkit ḥadiid**
read	**'iri bi'ra**
reading	**'raay(e)**
ready	**mist9idd mist9idde mist9iddiin ; ḥaaḍir ḥaaḍra ḥaaḍriin**
ready, get	**sta9add bist9idd**

reasonable	ma9'uul ma9'uule ma9'uuliin
reckon	ḥaasab biḥaasib
recording	tasjiil
recover	ṭaab biṭiib
red	'aḥmar ḥamra ḥumur
red, become	ḥmarr biḥmarr
redness	'iḥmiraar
reference	marja9 maraaji9
registered	msajjal msajjale msajjaliin ; msoogar msoogara msoogariin
rejected	marduud marduude marduudiin
relation	9alaa'a 9alaa'aat
relative	'ariib 'araayib ; nasiib nasaayib
religion	9uluum diiniyye
religious	diini diiniyye diiniyyiin
remain	bi'i bib'a ; tamm bitamm
remaining	baa'i baa'ye baa'yiin
remove	'aam bi'iim
renew	jaddad bijaddid
repair	ṣallaḥ biṣalliḥ

repairing	taṣliiḥ
repent	taab bituub
reply	jawaab jawa(a)baat *or* 'ajwibe
request	ṭalab buṭlub ; ṭalab ṭalabaat
resemblance	šabah
responsible	mas'uul mas'uule mas'uuliin
rest	staraaḥ bistriiḥ ; raaḥa
restaurant	maṭ9am maṭaa9im
return	radd birudd ; riji9 birja9
returning	raaji9 raaj9a raaj9iin
revive	'an9aš bin9iš
reviving	'in9aaš
rice	ruzz
rich	ġani ġaniyye 'aġniya
ride	rikib birkab
riding	raakib raakbe raakbiin
right	ḥa" ḥ'uu'
right (side)	yamiin
road	ṭarii' ṭuru'
roasted	mḥammar mḥammara mhammariin

roof	ṣaṭiḥ ṣṭuuḥ
room	'uuḍa 'uwaḍ ;
	ġurfe ġuraf
rooster	diik dyuuk
Russian	ruusi ruusiyye ruus

S

sacrifice	'aḍḥa (m)
safe, be	silim bislam
safe, keep	sallam bisallim
safety	salaame
said, be	n'aal bin'aal ;
	nḥaka binḥaka
sake of, for the	min šaan
salad	ṣalaṭa ṣalaṭaat
salary	ma9aaš ma9aašaat
salt	miliḥ
same	nafs ; zaat
sanctuary	ḥaram
Saturday	(yoom) ssabt
Saudi Arabia	ssu9uudiyye
savior	faadi

say	'aal bi'uul
scale	miizaan mayaziin
school	madrase madaaris
science	9ilim 9uluum
scissors	m'aṣṣ m'aṣṣaat
season	mawsim mawaasim
second	taani taanye
secretarial	kitaabi kitaabiyye
section	qisim 'aqsaam
see	šaaf bišuuf
seed	ḥabbe ḥabbaat
seeing	šaayif šaayfe šaayfiin
seem	ẓahar biẓhar
see (someone) off	wadda9 biwaddi9
seize	misik bimsik
self	nafs ; zaat
sell	baa9 bibii9
selling	baayi9 baay9a baay9iin
send	ba9at bib9at
send back	radd birudd
September	'ayluul
service	xidme
seven	sab9a
seventeen	saba9 ṭa9š
seventh	saabi9 saab9a

seventy	sab9iin
sever	ḥazz biḥizz
shake	hazz bihizz ; xaḍḍ bixuḍḍ
shaking, a	hazz
shame, put to	xajjal bixajjil
shave	ḥala' biḥli'
she	hiyye
sheet	šaršaf šaraašif
sheet (of paper)	war'a war'aat *or* wraa'
sheikh	šeex šyuux
shoes (pair)	kundara kanaadir
shortly	9an 'ariib
show	farja bifarji
shining	zaahir zaahre
shirt	'amiiṣ 'umṣaan
shrimp	'reedis
shrine	mazaar mazaaraat
sick	mariiḍ mariiḍa marḍa
side	janb jawaanib
side (aspect)	naaḥye nawaaḥi
silk	ḥariir
simple	baṣiiṭ baṣiiṭa baṣiiṭiin
sincere	muxliṣ mux*i*lṣa mux*i*lṣiin
singing	ġina (m)
sister	'uxt (f) xawaat

sit	**'a9ad bu'9ud**
situation	**ḥaale ḥaalaat**
six	**sitte**
sixteen	**sitt ṭa9š**
sixth	**saadis saadse**
sixty	**sittiin**
skirt	**tannuura tananiir**
sky	**sama**
sleep	**naam binaam**
slight	**'aliil 'aliile 'aliiliin**
slowness	**mahil**
small	**ẓġiir ẓġiire ẓġaar**
smaller, smallest	**'aẓġar**
snore	**šaxar bušxur**
so	**heek**
soap	**ṣaabuun**
sociology	**9ilm lijtimaa9**
socks	**kalsaat (pl)**
sold	**mabyuu9 mabyuu9a mabyuu9iin**
soldier	**9askari 9asaakir**
some	**kam**
something	**šii 'ašya(a')**
son	**'ibin wlaad ; ṣabi ṣubyaan**
soon	**9an 'ariib**

sorry	mit'assif mit'assfe
	mit'assfiin
sorry, be	t'assaf bit'assaf
sort	jins jnaas ; noo9 'anwaa9
so that	(la)ḥatta
soul	nafs
soup	šooraba
sour	ḥaamiḍ ḥaamḍa ḥaamḍiin
source (of income)	daxil
Spanish	s*b*anyooli s*b*anyooliyye
	s*b*anyool
speak	ḥaka biḥki
specialize	txaṣṣaṣ bitxaṣṣaṣ
specialty	taxaṣṣuṣ
speech, give a	xaṭab buxṭub
spend (time)	'aḍa bi'ḍi
spin	ġazal biġzil
spinach	sabaanix
spirit	ruuḥ 'arwaaḥ
spoon	ma9la'a ma9aali'
spring (season)	rabii9
squash	kuusa (m)
stamp	ṭaabi9 ṭawaabi9
standing	waa'if waa'fe
	waa'fiin
star	najme njuum

state	dawle duwal ; wilaaye wilaayaat
station	mḥaṭṭa mḥaṭṭaat
stay	bi'i bib'a; ḍall biḍall
staying	naazil naazle naazliin
steamship	baaxira bawaaxir
stepfather	jooz 'imm
stepmother	mart 'ab
stick	9aṣa 9uṣi
stimulus	ḥaafiz ḥawaafiz
stomach	mi9de mi9daat *or* mi9ad
stomach ache	waja9 baṭin ; waja9 mi9de
stop	wa"af biwa"if
stopped	waa'if waa'fe waa'fiin
stopping place	maw'if mawaa'if
story (floor)	ṭaabi' ṭawaabi'
straight ahead	duġri
strawberries	freez
street	šaari9 šawaari9
strike	ḍarab buḍrab
studio	stuudyo stuudyowaat
study	daras budrus
stuff	ḥaša biḥši

stuffed	maḥši maḥšiyye maḥšiyyiin
stuffed vegetable	maḥši maḥaaši
succeed	najaḥ binjaḥ
succeed, make	najjaḥ binajjiḥ
successful	mwaffa' mwaffa'a mwaffa'iin
suffer	t9azzab bit9azzab
sugar	sukkar
suit	badle badlaat
suit case	šanta šantaat
sultan	ṣulṭaan ṣalaṭiin
summer	ṣeef
summer (adj)	ṣeefi ṣeefiyye
summertime	ṣeefiyye ṣeefiyyaat
Sunday	(yoom) l'aḥad
supply	zawwad bizawwid
supplying	tazwiid
support	'ayyad bi'ayyid
suppose	ẓann biẓunn
supreme	'a9la 9ulya (f)
suspended	manṣuub manṣuube manṣuubiin
swallow	bala9 bibla9
sweep	kannas bikannis

sweet	ḥilu ḥilwe ḥilwiin
sword	seef syuuf
Syria	suuriyya

T

table	ṭaawle ṭaawlaat
tail	danab dnaab
tailor	xayyaaṭ xayyaaṭiin
take	'axad byaaxud
take place	ṣaar biṣiir
talk	kalaam
talk to	ḥaaka biḥaaki
tangarine	(yuusif) 'afandi
tastier, tastiest	'aṭyab
tasty	ṭayyib ṭayybe ṭayybiin
taught, be	t9allam bit9allam
tax	ḍariibe ḍaraa'ib
tea	šaay
teach	9allam bi9allim
teacher	'ustaaz 'asaatze ; m9allim m9allmiin

teaching	ta9liim
telephone	talfan bitalfin
tell	'aal bi'uul
ten	9ašra
tent	xeeme xeemaat *or* xyaam
tenth	9aašir 9aašre
testimony	šhaade šhaadaat
thank	šakar buškur
thankful	mamnuun mamnuune mamnuuniin
thank you	šukran
then (in that case)	'izan
theology	9uluum diiniyye
there	hunaak
there is, there are	fii
thermometer	miizaan ḥaraara
these	hadool (pl)
they	humme
thread	xeeṭ xiiṭaan
three	tlaate
throw down	baṭaḥ bibṭaḥ
throw out	zatt bizitt
thimble	kuštbaan kašaatbiin
thing	šii 'ašya(a')

think	ftakar biftkir
thinking	miftkir miftikre miftikriin
third	taalit taalte ; tult tlaat
thirteen	tlat ṭa9š
thirty	tlaatiin
this	haada (m); haadi (f)
thousand	'alf 'aalaaf
Thursday	(yoom) lxamiis
thus	heek
time	marra marraat ; wa't ; zamaan
tired, become	ti9ib bit9ab
to	9ala
today	lyoom
together	sawa
toilet	beet *mayy*
tomatoes	bandoora
tomb	'abir 'buur
tomorrow	bukra
tonight	lleele
too	kamaan
tooth	sinn snaan
tooth ache	waja9 snaan

total	majmuu9 majmuu9aat
tourism	siyaaḥa
tower	burj 'abraaj
town	balad (f) blaad
train	treen treenaat
transfer	ḥawwal biḥawwil
translation	tarjame
translator	mtarjim mtarijmiin
travel	safar
travel	saafar bisaafir
traveling	msaafir msaafre msaafriin
treat (medically)	daawa bidaawi
trees	šajar
trip	safra safraat
Tripoli	ṭaraablus̩ (f)
trouble	ġalabe ġalabaat
truth	ḥa'ii'a ḥa'aayi'
try	jarrab bijarrib
Tuesday	(yoom) ttalaata
turkey	diik ḥabaš
Turkey	turkiyya
turn	daar bidiir
turn around	daar biduur
turnips	lift

turns, take	tnaawab bitnaawab
twelve	ṭna9š
twenty	9išriin
two	tneen tinteen (f)
typing	ṭibaa9a

U

uncle (father's brother)	9amm 9maam
uncle (mother's brother)	xaal xwaal
under	taḥt
under (adj.)	taḥtaani taḥtaaniyye
undershorts	kalsoon kalsoonaat
understand	fihim bifham
unfortunate	maskiin maskiine masakiin
united	muttaḥid muttáḥide muttaḥidiin
united, be	ttaḥad bittḥid
United States, The	lwilaayaat lmuttáḥide
university	jaam(i)9a jaam(i)9aat
upset, be	zi9il biz9al

upset being	**talabbuk**
upset stomach	**talabbuk mi9de**
up to now	**ba9d ; lissa**
use	**sta9mal bista9mil**
useful, be	**'afaad bifiid**
usually	**9aadatan**

V

vacant, be	**fiḍi bifḍa**
vacation	**furṣa furaṣ**
varied	**mnawwa9 mnawwa9a mnawwa9iin**
veal	**laḥim 9ijil**
vegetables	**xuḍra**
very	**jiddan ; ktiir**
vice consul	**naa'ib 'unṣul ; naayib 'unṣul**
village	**'arye qura**
vineyard	**karm kruum**
visit	**zaar bizuur ; z(i)yaara z(i)yaaraat**

visited, be	nzaar binzaar
visit, have (someone)	zawwar bizawwir
visiting	zaayir zaayre zaayriin
visitor	zaayir zuwwaar
voice	ṣooṭ ('a)ṣwaaṭ

W

wages	ma9aaš ma9aašaat
wait	stanna bistanna
wake (someone)	fayya' bifayyi'
wake up	faa' bifii'
walk	maša bimši
walking	maaši maašye maašyiin
wall	ḥeet ḥiiṭaan
want	raad biriid
wash	ġassal biġassil; ġasiil
wash down	šaṭaf bušṭuf
watch	saa9a saa9aat
watchmaker	saa9aati saa9aatiyye
water	*mayy* (f)
watermelon	baṭṭiix

way	ṭarii' ṭuru'
we	niḥna
weather	ṭa'ṣ
wedding	9urs 'a9raas
Wednesday	(yoom) l'arba9a
week	'usbuu9 'asabii9 ;
	jum9a juma9
what (adj.)	'ayy
what (pron.)	'eeš ; šuu
whatever	'add maa (+ verb)
when	'eemta (n) ; lamma(n)
whenever	'eemta maa (+ verb)
where	feen ; ween
wherever	feen maa/ween maa
	(+ verb)
which (adj.)	'ayy
white	'abyaḍ beeḍa biiḍ
white, become	byaḍḍ bibyaḍḍ
who, whom, whose	miin
why	leeš
width	9arḍ
wife	zooje zoojaat ;
	mara niswaan
window	šubbaak šababiik
wine	nbiid

winter	šita
winter (adj.)	šatawi šatawiyye šatawiyyiin
winter resort	mašta (m) mašaati
wintertime	šatawiyye šatawiyyaat
wipe off	masaḥ bimsaḥ
wish	keef
with	ma9
without	bala
woman	mara niswaan
wool	ṣuuf
word	kilme kilmaat
work	štaġal bištġil ; 9amal 'a9maal
worker	9aamil 9ummaal
workshop	mašġal mašaaġil
world	dinya ; 9aalam
wrestle	baaṭaḥ bibaaṭiḥ
write	katab buktub
writer	kaatib kuttaab
writing	ktaabe
writing (adj.)	kaatib kaatbe kaatbiin
wrong	ġalaṭ (invariable adj.) ; maġluuṭ maġluuṭa maġluuṭiin

Y

yard (measure)	**yard yardaat**
year	**sane sniin ; 9aam 'a9waam**
yellow	**'aṣfar ṣafra ṣufur**
yes	**'aywa ; na9am**
yesterday	**mbaariḥ**
you	**inte (m) ; inti (f.) ; 'intu (pl)**
young	**ẓġiir ẓġiire ẓġaar**
younger, youngest	**'aẓġar**

Z

zero	**sifir ṣfaar**